THE OTHER AMERICAN DILEMMA

THE OTHER AMERICAN DILEMMA

Schools, Mexicans, and the
Nature of Jim Crow, 1912–1953

RUBÉN DONATO AND JARROD HANSON

SUNY PRESS

Cover photo of the *Ted Hendrix Grocery* (Arkansas); courtesy of Archivo Histórico Genaro Estrada. Acervo Histórico Diplomático. Secretaria de Relaciones Exteriores. Mexico City.

Published by State University of New York Press, Albany

For information, contact State University of New York Press, Albany, NY
www.sunypress.edu

Library of Congress Cataloging-in-Publication Data

Names: Donato, Rubén, author | Hanson, Jarrod, author.
Title: The other American dilemma : schools, Mexicans, and the nature of Jim Crow,
    1912–1953 / Rubén Donato and Jarrod Hanson.
Description: Albany : State University of New York Press, [2021] | Includes
    bibliographical references and index.
Identifiers: ISBN 9781438484532 (hardcover : alk. paper) | ISBN 9781438484525
    (pbk. : alk. paper) | ISBN 9781438484549 (ebook)
Further information is available at the Library of Congress.

10 9 8 7 6 5 4 3 2 1

To the memory of my father, Juan M. Donato, 1923–2016
To my always supportive wife, Amy, and family

Contents

Illustrations

Acknowledgments

We want to express our gratitude to a number of individuals who assisted us in the preparation of this book. As we put this project together, we thank the anonymous reviewers who provided feedback on the articles that form the foundation of this book. We received excellent suggestions and criticism. With permission, we used revised versions of "*Francisco Maestas et al. v. George H. Shone et al.*: Mexican American Resistance to School Segregation in the Hispano Homeland, 1912–1914," *Journal of Latinos and Education*; "Porque tenían sangre de 'NEGROS': The Exclusion of Mexican Children from a Louisiana School, 1915–1916," *Association of Mexican American Educators Journal*; " 'In These Towns, Mexicans Are Classified as Negroes': The Politics of Unofficial Segregation in the Kansas Public Schools, 1915–1935," *American Educational Research Journal*; and "Legally White, Socially 'Mexican': Mexican Americans and the Politics of De Jure and De Facto Segregation in the American Southwest," *Harvard Educational Review*. We also want to thank Gonzalo Guzmán for his keen sense of historical inquiry in chapter 1, "*Francisco Maestas et al. v. George Shone et al.*" This chapter would not have been possible without him. Finally, we thank the anonymous reviewers who read our book manuscript in its entirety. They provided invaluable insights, asked important questions, provided us with additional sources, and they offered ways to make the book have a better flow.

We collected data from different states in the US and from Mexico City. With this in mind, we thank the individuals who helped us access information in school district offices, town libraries, museums, and historical societies in Colorado, Kansas, Louisiana, and Texas. We thank them for their patience in addressing all the requests we made. We are especially indebted to Jorge Fuentes Hernandez, director of the Archivo Histórico

Genaro Estrada, Secretaría de Relaciones Exteriores, in Mexico City. After two visits at the Archivo in Mexico City, Jorge contacted us almost two years later and asked us to return. He had found information we could not locate during our visits. We returned to the Archivo Genaro Estrada in Mexico City for the third time. Given our travels to multiple locations, we are most grateful to the Spencer Foundation for funding this project. If it were not for the Spencer Foundation, this study could not have been achievable. We also received a small grant from the University of Colorado, School of Education, *Woman Investing in the School of Education* (WISE). The WISE grant allowed us to return to Mexico City for the third time to collect information that was central to our book.

Finally, I (Rubén Donato) want to thank my friend Lin Petzinger. I thank Lin for the many times she listened to me read this manuscript orally. She was patient, critical, and offered insightful feedback to my ideas, research questions, and writing. I (Jarrod Hanson) thank my wife, Amy, for her patience and support through the writing process.

Introduction

In 1928, University of Texas at Austin professor Max Sylvius Handman delivered a paper in Chicago to the American Sociological Society. To provide context to this group of scholars interested in rural sociology, he informed them that European nations with higher standards of living recruited people from neighboring countries to fulfill their labor demands. He used Europe to describe the intricacies of immigrant labor, how such arrangements were formulated, and how agreements were undertaken over space and time. His audience, however, did not attend his session to learn about European labor. They attended because they wanted to know about Mexican immigrant workers who were coming to the United States. Handman contended that immigration from Europe to America had come to a virtual standstill, that African Americans were moving from rural areas to urban centers, and that the Mexican Revolution of 1910 had pushed thousands of Mexicans to the United States. Given these events, Handman declared that Mexicans had become the chief source of agricultural and railroad labor in the United States.[1]

While the geographic proximity of Mexico to the United States simplified labor recruitment, Handman claimed that US farmers and the railroad industry preferred Mexicans over other groups because they worked harder, for lower wages, and because they tolerated living in conditions others would not accept.[2] Handman believed these two industries were ruining the United States because Mexicans were establishing permanent roots in the United States and, as a by-product of their settlements, they were creating "slum conditions" and causing problems in locations where their numbers had "reached a certain height."[3] Handman deemed Mexicans to be so inferior that "[e]ven the Negro has managed to climb higher in the general raising of the average standard of living."[4] Given

1

these circumstances, Handman predicted that Mexicans would one day become the group in the United States that would symbolize "how the other half lives."[5]

Toward the end of his presentation, Handman asserted that the United States faced an uncertain future because Americans did not have a "social technique for handling partly colored races." He explained that the United States had "a place for the Negro and a place for the white man," but that "the Mexican is not a Negro, and the white man refuses him an equal status."[6] Handman essentially informed his audience that Mexicans were neither Black nor White. He saw them as a partly colored race, declared they were unwanted in the United States, and believed they needed to be controlled. Handman, however, did not explain what it meant for communities to have "a place" for Blacks and Whites, did not offer examples how Whites refused to see Mexicans as their equals, and did not describe what social techniques were needed to control them. By having a "place for the Negro and a place for the white man," we assume he was referring to the 1896 *Plessy v. Ferguson* decision, the US Supreme Court ruling that upheld racial segregation under the doctrine of "separate but equal."[7] He must have also recognized *Plessy* and the segregation resulting from Jim Crow laws as some of the "social techniques" that empowered Whites and marginalized African Americans. Given the social, political, and economic disposition of his paper, Handman appeared to be nervous that what was legally "in place" to control African Americans did not include Mexicans, a partly colored race.

It is difficult to understand why Handman did not say more about the conditions Mexicans faced in the United States. As a professor of economics at the University of Texas from 1926 to 1931,[8] Handman knew most Mexicans were relegated to segregated *colonias* and knew they were exploited in the labor market.[9] However, he was reticent to discuss how other forms of segregation often applied to Mexicans, how Jim Crow–like conditions also applied to them, how their children were generally placed in separate classrooms or separate schools, and the brutal conditions some endured in the United States.[10] Put another way, Handman did not acknowledge the fine line that existed between the legal segregation intended for African Americans and the "unofficial" social techniques that were used to segregate, relegate, and control Mexicans.[11]

About ten years after Handman delivered his paper in Chicago, Gunnar Myrdal, the Swedish sociologist/economist, was funded by the Carnegie Corporation to study race relations in the United States. By 1944, Myrdal published the highly acclaimed book, *An American Dilemma: The Negro Problem and Modern Democracy*. Myrdal argued that the United States faced a moral dilemma, one that conflicted with the "American Creed."[12] The American Creed was a set of values and principles related to liberty, equality, individualism and values that, in the abstract, all Americans were supposed to enjoy.[13] Throughout the book, however, Myrdal explained how values in the American Creed were not extended to African Americans as they were denied social, political, and civil rights. Myrdal's book, said historian Walter A. Jackson, was "one of the most influential works of social science ever written in America."[14]

We partly draw from Myrdal's *American Dilemma* to make sense of the Mexican-origin experience in American society. While Myrdal was commissioned by the Carnegie Corporation to study the African American experience, he acknowledged the lives of Mexicans in America. Myrdal described how in "many parts of the country Mexicans are kept in a status similar to the Negro's or only a step above,"[15] that "Mexicans . . . have as much segregation as Negroes,"[16] and that "Mexicans, have not been allowed to assimilate as have European immigrants."[17] Myrdal's observations were compelling. He identified how the social status of Mexicans was similar to that of African Americans, how both groups were almost equally segregated, and how Mexicans were not permitted to assimilate into the American mainstream as other European immigrants were allowed to do.

This book is about the experiences of Mexican immigrants, Mexican Americans, and Hispanos in their schools and communities between 1912 and 1953. We examine specific communities during particular years in Arkansas, California, Colorado, Kansas, Louisiana, and Texas. Our goal is to add to the existing literature that chiefly focuses on the Southwest by exploring other regions of the nation and by drawing from archival sources that have rarely been used.[18] This regional exploration is important as it highlights the existence of the "social techniques" that Handman was concerned about and how they appeared throughout the country as the populations of people of Mexican origin increased above the "certain height." While each of our chapters in this book has specific arguments, our overall contention is that the experiences of the Mexican-origin population in the United States were similar to that of African Americans in important ways in that there were social techniques being used to segregate and otherwise marginalize Mexicans throughout the United States. Whether Mexicans were recent immigrants, longtime residents, or Hispanos with deep roots in the United States, they were forced to live in segregated neighborhoods,

Jim Crow laws crafted for African Americans were unofficially aimed at them, their children were placed in separate classes or separate schools, were not expected to melt into the American mainstream, and were seen as a "mongrel" race.[19] But, unlike the experiences of African Americans in their schools and communities, the segregation of the Mexican-origin population in the United States was different because it evolved in a way where laws did not have to be ratified in order to foster their separation. We also examine how communities engaged in attempts to "race" the Mexican population in various ways to maintain social control. From declaring them Caucasian in Colorado, to disagreements and confusion over how to classify Mexicans in Louisiana, to the creation of a triracial school system in Kansas, City, Kansas, this book seeks to identify how the racialization of Mexicans was used as a technique of social control across communities.

As we explore intersections between the Mexican-origin population with that of African Americans, we recognize that African Americans came out of slavery, an experience no other group in America can claim. Comparisons have also been made between Mexicans and southern and eastern European immigrant groups.[20] We maintain, however, that the experiences of the Mexican-origin population were different from those immigrant groups. David Tyack reminds us in *The One Best System* that Stanford University professor Ellwood P. Cubberley in 1909 viewed Southern and Eastern European immigrants as "illiterate, docile, often lacking initiative, and almost wholly without the Anglo-Saxon conceptions of righteousness, liberty, law, order, public decency, and government."[21] These Southern and Eastern European immigrants were seen as inferior and were discriminated against on many fronts. Tyack also informs us how these groups came to the United States with distinctive skills and experiences, how some acquiesced to, or contested, Americanization,[22] and "why certain immigrant groups prospered academically while others did not."[23] We claim that while Southern and Eastern European groups were seen as inferior and had different experiences in the United States, they assimilated into the American mainstream.[24] Whereas these immigrant groups were eventually embraced by the American Creed, Mexicans, Mexican Americans and Hispanos/as were rejected.

We highlight Max Handman as the paragon of the "inferior" Eastern European immigrant who became an American and how he succeeded in a short period of time. Handman was born in Romania in 1885, immigrated to the United States in 1903 at the age of eighteen, earned his bachelor's degree in 1907 from the University of Oregon, became a US citizen in 1915 at the age of thirty, and received his PhD in 1917 from the University of Chicago.[25] As we saw, Handman became a professor of sociology and economics and spent part of his career studying Mexican immigrants. He must have been socially and politically aware during his lifetime as both a college student and academic that Southern and Eastern Europeans were seen as inferior in the United States. As an Eastern European immigrant who became a prominent scholar, he focused on Mexicans, saw them as a threat to the United States, believed White communities needed to create "social techniques" to control them, claimed they were inferior, and identified them as a "partly colored race."[26]

The Politics of Mexican Consuls in the United States

In addition to primary and secondary sources collected in the United States, we also draw from the National Archives in Mexico City. The Archivo Histórico Genaro Estrada, Secretaría de Relaciones Exteriores stores Mexican consul archival records, including numerous complaints filed by Mexicans who were living in the United States during our period of analysis. Records from the Archivo Histórico in Mexico City led us to particular states, specific communities, and individual school districts in the United States. As we use these archival sources, one needs to understand the evolution of Mexican consuls, why they were established, and the role they played in the United States. In brief, the United States recognized Mexico as a nation after it won its independence from Spain in 1821. Mexican envoys were subsequently established in the United States. Mexican diplomats were supposed to protect the interests of Mexico and its citizens living in the United States. During and after the United States–Mexican War of 1846–1848, however, relations were fractured and national boundaries were redrawn. After Mexico lost what is now the American Southwest, relations were eventually restored and Mexican diplomats returned to the United States. But it was not until 1899 that a Mexican Embassy was established in Washington, DC.[27] Mexican consul offices were opened in selected locations and by the mid-1930s approximately fifty-two were functioning across the United States.[28] Similar to other nations from around the world that had consul offices in the United States, they all had similar responsibilities—to maintain diplomatic relations with the United States. A particularly important objective for Mexican

consuls in the United States, said Lareen Laglargaron, was to "protect
its citizens . . . from discrimination and exploitation."[29] Finally, Mexican
consuls located in various cities communicated with the Mexican Embassy
in Washington, DC. The Mexican Ambassador reviewed complaints, communicated with the Secretaría in Mexico City, and grievances were sent
to the US Department of State.

As we use Mexican consul archival records, we acknowledge that
some historians have examined Mexican consuls and the degree to which
they provided adequate or inadequate support to Mexican nationals in
the United States.[30] In *Mexican Consuls and Labor Organizing*, Gilbert
Gonzalez draws from labor historians to look deeper into their activities.[31]
It was clear that Mexican nationals had different experiences with Mexican consuls. Gonzalez used four variants to explain how consuls were
perceived by Mexican nationals. In short, the first variant saw Mexican
consuls in a positive light, as Mexican workers felt protected. The second
perceived them as providing minimal protection and felt subordinated
to the Mexican government and American employers. The third took a
middle-ground position; it felt Mexican consul involvement was depen-
dent on specific interests and only intervened when it benefited them.
The fourth viewed consuls to be either minor players or that they were
omitted in most affairs. As we look at these experiences, some Mexican
workers valued their services, others felt subordinated, there were those
who believed they responded to specific interests, and there were those
who believed they were inconsequential.[32]

The work of Mexican consuls was politically sensitive. They had no
authority in the United States and relied on diplomacy to resolve Mexican
national complaints. It is also worth noting that Mexican consuls sometimes blurred the line as to whom they were supposed to serve in the
United States. That is, they occasionally assisted Mexican Americans. On
this point, Francisco Balderrama discusses how US government officials
treated Mexican nationals and Mexican Americans in Los Angeles during
the Depression era of the 1930s, a period when most Americans were
experiencing hard times. "Mexican nationals," said Balderrama, "were
categorically denied assistance because of a 'citizen only' policy." Denying
assistance to non-US citizens was not surprising and politically expected.
However, said Balderrama, "Mexican Americans were also frequently
refused help by public officials . . . [because they] . . . did not recognize
their citizenship."[33] In other words, Mexican Americans were often treated
as non-US citizens. Because some Mexican Americans had maintained

close ties with Mexico, they sought assistance from Mexican consuls and sometimes received their support.[34]

As we examine these issues, we want to make an important observation. Records accessed in Mexico City allowed us to better understand what highly trained Mexican government officials were thinking about the treatment of Mexicans in their schools and communities. They were witnessing social and educational structures being created by White Americans to segregate and disenfranchise Mexicans. We were given insights as to how high-ranking Mexican consuls were challenging school segregation and Jim Crow in different parts of the nation. In California, for example, the Mexican consul in San Francisco, California, wrote to the Mexican Ambassador in Washington, DC, to inform him that "El Mexicano, en vista de que sus condiciones economicas son muy parecidas a las del negro, es clasificado como este y recibe el mismo tratamiento" (The Mexican, after looking as his economic conditions, they are similar to that of African Americans, are classified as such, and receive the same treatment).[35] In the South, Mexican consuls also learned how local authorities became perplexed with Mexicans and did not know how to treat them in their racial hierarchy because race was understood within a Black–White context. In Kansas, White parents and civic organizations saw Mexican children as neither Black nor White, but they were visible enough as mestizos that they pressured school officials to establish separate classrooms or separate schools in many school districts across the state. Mexican children were so distinguishable to White parents in Kansas that they demanded immediate separation. In the Southwest, school authorities were more familiar with Mexicans. They also did not recognize them as White citizens but were at times cautious not to segregate them exclusively on race. They instead used language and culture as pretexts to keep them apart from White children. We will incorporate multiple voices and cases to understand what various groups in the nation believed the Mexican-origin population deserved in American schools and communities.

We are mindful of Gonzalez's variants about Mexican consul activities in Mexican labor disputes. Our focus, however, is on how Mexican consuls were addressing Mexican community complaints about unequal education and segregated schools—indeed, how some Mexican communities received assistance from Mexican consuls and others did not. In the Hispano homeland (southern Colorado), for example, we will demonstrate how Mexican Americans challenged segregated education without the assistance of Mexican consuls. As US citizens who were deeply rooted in

America, Hispanos used novel arguments to challenge the segregation of their children. In the rest of our book, we will show how Mexican consuls challenged the ways school officials were creating physical divisions between Mexican and White children, how they confronted those in power who were excluding Mexican children from public schools,[36] and how they challenged local officials who were turning a blind eye to business practices that were refusing to serve Mexicans in restaurants, barbershops, theaters, hotels, and other public places.[37]

The Racialization of the Mexican Population

The Mexican consul also provides insight into the issue of how Mexicans were seen in terms of race in the United States. Mexican consuls were cognizant that Mexicans were legally White according to American laws and treaties,[38] and saw how inconsequential that racial classification was in the United States. Some scholars, in fact, believed the White category given to Mexicans was disingenuous. Economics professor Glenn E. Hoover at Mills College in California, for example, observed in the 1920s that "all natives of Mexico are listed as white in our official census and immigration reports, a practice which also is followed by the various states of the Union." Professor Hoover, however, also made clear that "there is a tacit but universal understanding among government officials that the biological characteristics of the Mexican people shall be assumed to be what they are not in fact." In other words, Hoover pointed out that even though Mexicans were listed as White in official census records, government officials knew that "the population south of the Rio Grande is predominantly Indian."[39]

Indeed, Mexicans were not seen as White in America. In 1911, for example, Mexicans in Garden City, Kansas, were banned from all public places. Mexicans came together in the community and wrote a letter to the Mexican consul to explain the severity of their segregation. They were so segregated in Garden City, the group described, that "no quieren que nos aserquemos a ellos" (they don't want us to get near them).[40] In 1920, Mexicans in Lyons, Kansas, filed a complaint with the Mexican consul, explaining how they numbered approximately 150 in the community and describing how they were told by White residents they would not be served in their establishments because they were "GENTE DE COLOR."[41] In the same year in the town of Salina, Kansas, Mexicans made similar complaints. It was not clear why the chief of police responded to the Mexican consul rather than the town mayor, the official who would be in a position to respond to the complaint. Nevertheless, the chief of police acknowledged that Mexicans were in fact barred from restaurants and barbershops and explained how some African American businesses were serving Mexicans. He also offered some solutions to the complaint. For example, rather than challenging Jim Crow conditions for Mexicans in the community, the chief of police asked the Mexican consul to send a Mexican barber to Salina. He believed the service was needed and was certain the business would thrive in the community.[42] Written communication between the Mexican consul and the Salina chief of police verified that Jim Crow targeted Mexicans, African Americans were serving Mexicans, and Mexicans were encouraged to open businesses of their own.[43]

Methods

We used historical methods to understand the schooling experiences of Mexicans in Colorado, Kansas, Louisiana, Texas, and Arkansas, relying on primary and secondary sources. We traveled to and accessed Mexican consul records from the Archivo Histórico Genaro Estrada, Acervo Histórico Diplomático, Secretaría de Relaciones Exteriores in Mexico City. These data were digitally photographed and organized according to file number, date, theme, and name of complaint. After analyzing files to identify themes and relevant geographical areas, we also traveled to and accessed material from libraries in Kansas, Louisiana, Texas, and Colorado. We also photographed, organized, and analyzed public records such as school board minutes from the following school districts: Kansas City, Hutchinson, Salina, Lyons, and Emporia, Kansas; Alexandria, Louisiana; Mission, Texas; and Alamosa, Colorado. We collected additional information in these communities from local libraries, museums, state archives, and newspapers. Finally, secondary sources, including books, journal articles, dissertations, master's theses, online sources, and other material, enriched our study. We compared archival information with other primary sources and contrasted that data with secondary sources to substantiate claims.

Book Outline

We include revised versions of previously published works. Chapter 1, "*Francisco Maestas et al. v. George H. Shone et al.*: Mexican American Resistance to Segregation in the Hispano Homeland, 1912–1914," was published in the *Journal of Latinos and Education* (2017). Chapter 2, "Porque tenían sangre de 'NEGROS': The Exclusion of Mexican Children from a Louisiana School, 1915–1916" appeared in the *Association of Mexican American Educators Journal* (2017). Chapter 3, " 'In These Towns, Mexicans Are Classified as Negroes': The Politics of Unofficial Segregation in the Kansas Public Schools, 1915–1935," was part of the Centennial Issue in the *American Educational Research Journal* (2017). Finally, chapter 5 "Legally White, Socially 'Mexican': Mexican Americans and the Politics of De Jure and De Facto Segregation in the American Southwest" was published in *Harvard Educational Review* (2012).[44]

We bring these articles together because it allows us to tell a wider, longer, and deeper narrative about the Mexican American experience across time, space, and location in American schools and society. It provides a more coherent, complicated, and connected story than individual articles can tell on their own. Moreover, our data let us cover a time frame that spanned from 1912 to 1953. We begin at a time when large numbers of people were fleeing Mexico because of the Mexican Revolution of 1910. It was a period when Mexicans were seeking refuge, when Americans were recruiting them for their labor, and when they simply wanted to improve their lives in the United States. We conclude in 1953, the year before *Brown v. Board of Education* was decided. Our goal is to capture the schooling experiences of Mexicans, Mexican Americans, and Hispanos during the pre-*Brown* era, a time when racial segregation for African Americans was legal in a number of states in America. During this time the Mexican-origin population used novel strategies to contest social and school segregation. In their quest for racial justice and equal education, some had the support of the Mexican government. Others did not. They took it upon themselves, organized, and challenged those in power. They challenged school segregation and Jim Crow, wanted simple justice, wanted to live with dignity, and displayed agency across space, time, and location in the United States.

In our first chapter, *Francisco Maestas et al. v. George H. Shone et al.* (1914), we provide an account about one of the earliest known Mexican American challenges to school segregation in the United States. Unidentified for over a century, the lawsuit took place in southern Colorado, a region of the nation where Mexican Americans (i.e., Hispanos/as) have deep historical roots. This case was unique because the racial background and linguistic needs of Mexican American children were contested. First, plaintiffs argued that Mexican American children were racially distinct and used the Colorado Constitution to challenge segregation in their community because the state prohibited public schools from classifying and distinguishing children based on color and race. Defendants—school board members and the superintendent—countered that Mexican American children were Caucasian and claimed that they were no different from other White children in the school district. Second, school district officials maintained that non-English-speaking Mexican American children were being served in a separate "Mexican" school in order to serve their linguistic needs. To the extent that many Mexican American children were English speaking, the district court judge ruled in favor of Francisco Maestas on the grounds that school board members and the superintendent could not prevent English-speaking Mexican American children from attending schools of their choice and schools that were closer to their homes. This early case illustrates how in the Hispano homeland, where Mexicans had deep roots, the social techniques used by those in power focused on language and a fluid racialization of the students, based on the needs of those who wanted to segregate the students.

During the same time period (1915), Mexican Americans had a much different experience in the deep South, where their history and societal positioning was markedly different. In chapter 2, "Porque tenían sangre de 'NEGROS,' 1915–1916" we examine the exclusion of Mexican children from a White Louisiana public school. About the same time the *Maestas* case was decided, a school board trustee in the town of Cheneyville threw Mexican children out of the White school because he believed they were racially mixed and had "negro blood." Although school officials did not see Mexican children as Black or White, their mestizo appearance became a racial marker to exclude them from a White school. Given this time and location—where legal segregation was understood in Black-and-White terms—Mexicans posed a dilemma because they did not fit into the South's binary racial system. This chapter extends the conversation about the treatment and racialization of Mexicans in public schools outside the Southwest by highlighting the complexities of race and segregation in the deep South, and how Whites struggled to identify the appropriate tools of social control for the Mexicans who did not fit within the racial binary that was deeply ingrained in their society. Placing these two chapters together allows us to illustrate how Mexicans were raced in Louisiana and Colorado and why the Mexican government became involved in one location and not in the other.

As we move to chapter 3, "In These Towns Mexicans Are Classified as Negroes, 1915–1935," we explain why a critical mass of Mexicans settled outside of the Southwest, what drew them to Kansas, and how their experiences were different from those in Louisiana and Colorado. We examine why Mexicans were not treated as Black or White. We tell a story that shows how a triracial school system in Kansas City was established by 1925. We note that Kansas was the state that gave rise to *Brown v. Board of Education* in 1954. Even though Mexicans were not referenced in Kansas's school segregation laws, they were seen and treated as a racially distinct group. White parents and civic organizations pushed school officials to establish separate facilities for Mexican children. In the Kansas City, Kansas, school system, a triracial school system was created. There was legal separation between African American and White children, and Mexican youth were unofficially placed in separate classrooms, school annexes, and some attended a separate Mexican school in the city. We maintain in this chapter that the contradictory and enigmatic responses to school segregation from high-ranking United States and Mexican government officials pointed to a degree of uncertainty about whether Mexican children could be segregated. That ambiguity, however, did not prevent local school officials from segregating Mexican children.

Chapter 4, "Diplomatic Relations to School Segregation and Jim Crow" is heavily based on archival sources from the Archivo Histórico Genaro Estrada in Mexico City. This chapter examines communication between Mexican consuls, Mexican Ambassadors, educational professionals, and high-ranking American government officials. We show how Mexican government officials learned that Mexican children were unwanted in White schools, how Jim Crow laws were unofficially aimed at Mexican communities, and how Mexicans were not perceived as "immigrants" but regarded as a group similar to African Americans. This chapter provides vignettes, evocative descriptions, and other accounts that reveal how Mexican and American government officials discussed, and responded to, school segregation and Jim Crow in the United States.

Chapter 5, "Legally White, Socially 'Mexican,' 1930–1947," brings multiple lawsuits together to show how the history of Mexican American school segregation is complex, often misunderstood, and unresolved. The literature suggests that Mexican Americans experienced de facto segregation because it was local custom and never sanctioned at the state level in the United States. However, the same literature suggests that Mexicans experienced de jure segregation because school officials implemented various policies intended to segregate Mexican Americans. We show in this chapter that although Mexicans were legally categorized as "White," we show the complexity of that category and how Mexicans were treated as socially "colored" in their schools and communities.

As we juxtapose Max Handman's assertion that there were "no social techniques" in place to control Mexicans—or partly colored races—against Gunner Myrdal's findings that conditions for Mexicans were similar to those of African Americans, there seemed to be serious discrepancies about what life was like for Mexicans in their schools and communities during the pre-*Brown* era. While important historical studies have recently been written and have advanced our understanding about the Mexican, Mexican American, and Hispano/a quest for equal education, more needs to be known about their struggles in different regions of the nation, in different time periods, and the influence of Mexican consuls.

Chapter 1

Francisco Maestas et al. v.
George H. Shone et al., 1912–1914

(WITH GONZALO GUZMÁN)

We begin by chronicling a school desegregation lawsuit, *Francisco Maestas et al. v. George H. Shone et al.* (1914), filed by Mexican Americans in Alamosa, Colorado, against the Alamosa School District Superintendent and Board of Education in 1913.[1] The *Maestas* lawsuit provides a portrait of a community organizing to advocate for the education of their children. This case is important because it precedes other challenges to the segregation of Mexican children in public schools. The *Maestas* case was tried over ten years before *Romo v Laird* (Arizona, 1925), sixteen years before *Del Rio ISD v. Salvatierra* (Texas, 1930) and seventeen years before *Alvarez v. Lemon Grove* (California, 1931). These cases became visible in the history of education literature, and *Alvarez* became known as the first successful Mexican American school desegregation case in the United States.[2] The *Maestas* case, however, is different from the more well-known cases of *Salvatierra* and *Alvarez* in three fundamental ways that are important to highlight prior to describing the case.

First, unlike *Salvatierra*, in Del Rio, Texas, and *Alvarez*, in Lemon Grove, California—communities that were located along, or close to, the US-Mexican border—the *Maestas* lawsuit was filed in Alamosa. Located in Colorado's San Luis Valley, this is part of the country that historian Richard Nostrand calls the "Hispano homeland." Nostrand maintains that southern Colorado (and northern New Mexico) is a location where people

15

of Mexican descent were isolated and culturally removed from Mexico. It was a place where unique "Mexican" identities (i.e., Spanish Americans or Hispanos Americanos) evolved over time.[3]

Second, how race was used to challenge school segregation in the *Maestas* lawsuit differed from *Salvatierra* and *Alvarez*. In *Salvatierra*, the Mexican plaintiffs argued that Mexicans were part of the "other white race" and were exempt from legal segregation under the laws of Texas.[4] Similarly, plaintiffs in *Alvarez* argued that California did not have a law that allowed for the segregation of Mexican children, as there were laws that explicitly permitted the segregation of other named races but not Mexicans.[5] In *Maestas*, Mexican American plaintiffs asserted that race was a driving force for the school officials' actions to segregate their children, and it was the defendants who responded that Mexican American students were Caucasian and therefore race could not have motivated their decisions.

Third, Mexican American plaintiffs in Alamosa did not receive legal assistance from the Mexican government. They were historically removed from Mexico and had deep roots in northern New Mexico and southern Colorado.[6] Because of the long-standing roots of many Mexicans in the San Luis Valley and the plaintiffs' status as American citizens, the Mexican consulate was not used as a resource either politically or legally in the community's fight against segregation. In a way, the "citizenship sacrifice," as coined by historian Carlos Kevin Blanton, impacted the ways in which the Mexican Americans in Alamosa challenged racial segregation in schools by limiting any possible aid the Mexican government could have given.[7]

With the *Maestas* case, we begin our challenge of Handman's claim, made in the introduction, that no techniques of social control were being used against the Mexican American population. Although this school district was unsuccessful in fully segregating the Mexican students in the younger grades, it provides insight into a technique that was not uncommon at the time to separate White from Mexican students. We also see how the definition of race begins to be used as a technique of control, even while the judge in the case skirts the issue and does not definitively make a determination about the students' race.

We argue that the *Maestas* lawsuit is one of the earliest Mexican American–led school desegregation lawsuits in the United States. In fact, the *Denver Catholic Register* noted in 1914 that the lawsuit "was the first time in the history of America that a court fight was made over an attempt to segregate Mexicans in school."[8] We further argue that this lawsuit was unique not only because of its geographical location and because Mexican Americans did not have support from the Mexican government, but—most importantly—because a novel strategy was used at the time to challenge the segregation of their children. Mexican Americans rejected their legal White status, claimed they were racially distinct, and used the Colorado Constitution to challenge segregation because it was illegal for schools to distinguish and classify children in public schools according to color or race.[9]

The Emergence of a Lawsuit

The *Maestas* lawsuit was triggered when the school board and superintendent established a policy to send *all* Mexican children to the district's newly constructed Mexican School in 1912.[10] The school was built in 1909, when the Alamosa School Board of Education purchased a piece of property on the "Mexican side" of town, with the intent to build a school to serve non-English-speaking Mexican American children.[11] When the school was constructed, it was a modest building with four classrooms, was staffed by three teachers, and served approximately 140 Mexican American children (see figure 1.1).[12] Once completed, the school attracted much local interest

SPANISH SCHOOL FOR SPANISH-SPEAKING CHILDREN

Figure 1.1. "Spanish School for Spanish-Speaking Children," Alamosa, Colorado.

with one newspaper editor from Creede, Colorado, reporting, "back east and south they build separate schools for negro children. At Alamosa they have just built one exclusively for Spanish children."[13]

In 1912, not long after the school opened, a local newspaper reported that a group of Mexican Americans filed a complaint "to see if the school board has any authority to compel Mexican children to attend any particular school building when another one is more convenient."[14] Mexican American parents viewed the policy change as a matter of racial discrimination. A visiting Jesuit priest during the same year reflected on the social environment, stating that "the Americans in that community had built a school where the Mexicans alone came together so that the American boys would not have to mingle with the Mexicans." The social conditions were so disconcerting that "Americans treated those poor Mexicans as the black sons of Africa."[15] Another year and a half passed before the *Rocky Mountain News* in Denver reported that Mexican Americans in Alamosa had complained to the Colorado State superintendent of instruction, Mary C. C. Bradford, to see if school officials in Alamosa had the authority to segregate their children in one school. The story described how Mexican children in the district were forced to attend one school in the community. State Superintendent Bradford told the press that she was going to ask the Colorado attorney general for an opinion about the complaint.[16]

The *Denver Catholic Register* further added that racial tension in Alamosa was escalating because Mexican American families believed school officials were segregating their children unjustly.[17] Two days later, the *Denver Times* reported that the "State Board Cannot Stop Segregation of Mexicans" and that Mexican children in Alamosa "must continue to attend a school in which they are segregated from whites and blacks." The story was clear that after an investigation into its powers, the "state board of education can do nothing in the matter."[18] Similarly, the *Alamosa Independent Journal* reported the same outcome and added that "Mexican children of Alamosa must continue to attend a special school in which they are segregated from whites and blacks [or] appeal to the county school board or take the case into the courts."[19]

Seeing that the Alamosa School Board of Education, the School District superintendent, the Colorado State Board of Education, and the Colorado State attorney general were unable or unwilling to address their complaint, Mexican Americans organized, pulled their children out of the Mexican School, staged a boycott, and filed a lawsuit in the District Court.[20] As these actions unfolded, the *Denver Catholic Register* explained that Mexican American parents challenged school officials' assertion that their children were being segregated because they lacked English language skills. Mexican American parents believed language was being used as an excuse to segregate their children when race was the real issue behind school board and superintendent actions.[21] As a result, Mexican American parents staged a walkout in the fall of 1913 and refused to send their children to the Mexican School. The *Denver Post* reported that a "school strike, engineered by the Mexicans of Alamosa against the public school of the city, reached such a serious state yesterday that a court fight became the only solution."[22] The *Denver Catholic Register* also noted that "rather than retract from its stand," school officials "let the children go without education."[23]

Grassroots Activism

The lawsuit was a significant undertaking for the Mexican American community. Unlike later lawsuits challenging the segregation of Mexican children, the Mexican American community in Alamosa did not have the assistance of the Mexican consulate as the plaintiffs were United States citizens. In this section, we investigate the organizing that led to the lawsuit, who the leaders were, how they acquired legal counsel, and how the lawsuit was funded.

In 1962, Luther Bean, Nancy Denious, and Elinor Kingery interviewed a former teacher and activist who was involved with the case. J. R. C. Ruybal was not only an activist in the community but was one of the first teachers to teach at the Mexican School.[24] Ruybal, born in 1879, was eighty-three years old at the time of the interview and was thirty-three years old in 1913, the time when the lawsuit was being filed. In 1962, the time of the interview, forty-eight years had passed since the *Maestas* decision was handed down. In the interview, Ruybal explained that many "Spanish Americans" had moved to Alamosa from New Mexico to work on the railroads. As the Spanish American population began to grow in Alamosa, their children started to attend school. Teachers, he said, had problems in mixed classes. Ruybal explained that the Alamosa School Board and Superintendent Kendall decided to construct a Mexican School to serve non-English-speaking Mexican American children. At the time, Ruybal explained, he supported the Mexican School which, he said, was a place where Mexican American children were taught in English but concepts were explained in Spanish.[25]

The problem started, according to Ruybal, when the School Board and new School District superintendent, George Thompson, established a policy to segregate all Spanish American students in the school district. "On February 5, 1912," said Ruybal, "the school board made all Mexican children go to the Mexican School." This was a problem, Ruybal clarified, because half of the Spanish American children in the district were able to speak English. After school officials began to force all Mexican American children into the Mexican School, Mexican Americans started to inquire about the policy. A group was subsequently formed—the Spanish American Union. The group met, discussed the issue, drafted a resolution, and met with the Alamosa School Board of Education. "We presented those resolutions to the board," said Ruybal, "protesting the segregation. They did not pay attention to us."[26] Ruybal and the Spanish American Union were disappointed that their concerns about the segregation of their children fell on deaf ears.

Because the School Board and superintendent would not listen to their concerns, the Spanish American Union tried something else. They went to the *Alamosa Journal* with the intent to publish their resolution, but the editor of the newspaper, Ruybal remarked, refused to publish the document. At this time, Ruybal was still employed at the Mexican School, but his tenure at the school did not last long. Ruybal explained that the school board would not communicate with him. However, the board asked Mr. French, another teacher at the Mexican School, to speak to him. Mr. French asked Ruybal, "how long are you going to stay with these people?" Ruybal responded that he was going to "stay with them to the last." Ruybal said that "[Mr. French told me that I would] 'not last very long.' It was true. They refused me a position." Based on the interview, Ruybal suggested that he was fired because he was part of a group that was challenging the segregation of all Mexican children in the Mexican School.

After Ruybal was dismissed from the Mexican School, he purchased an interest in a Spanish American newspaper in Antonito, a small town south of Alamosa. Ruybal used the newspaper as a means to challenge the Alamosa schools. When Ruybal joined the newspaper, he began to write about various issues in the area. At first, he said, he was not writing about the Alamosa schools. But that quickly changed. He started to write about the Alamosa schools because a Mr. Gallegos tried to enroll his children at a White school in Alamosa that was closer to his home. His children were denied admission to the school. Mr. Gallegos wanted to challenge the school board and even thought about filing a lawsuit, but after Gallegos spoke with an attorney, he was discouraged from going forward. He was told it was expensive, and that he had "no chance to win. So he stopped."[27]

Soon after, a Mr. Quintana contacted Ruybal and encouraged him to write about the segregation of Mexican American children in the Alamosa schools. But Quintana asked Ruybal to do more. He encouraged him to appeal to "Spanish Americans to raise money to fight the matter in court." Ruybal began to reach out to the Spanish American communities in the San Luis Valley, pleaded for their support, and asked them to contribute to a fund to begin a lawsuit. "Raising money to go to court," said Ruybal, "started to come in from the Spanish settlements." Many Spanish Americans were supportive of the lawsuit and they contributed what they could.[28] Once money was raised, a committee was formed. It had ten members and Ruybal was part of the group. Among the members, said Ruybal, was "Father Montell, a Catholic priest." As the committee started to strategize about how they were going to challenge the Alamosa School District, they knew it would be difficult to acquire legal counsel and that it would be expensive. But in one meeting, as Ruybal explained, "Father Montell said 'I know a young man. He is a very bright man. I believe I can get him for a reasonable price.' We told him to go ahead." Father E. J. Montell went to Denver, spoke with an attorney named Raymond Sullivan, and an agreement was made. Sullivan agreed to represent Mexican Americans in Alamosa, charged the group $200 plus expenses, Francisco Maestas was named plaintiff, and the lawsuit began.[29]

A Lawsuit Is Filed

In his petition to the District Court, Raymond Sullivan described the Alamosa context and the school board's actions from the Mexican American parents' perspective. At the time, there were approximately 800 Mexicans in the city and 150 of them were between 6 and 21 years old. The district had three schools: The North Side School or high school (it also included a primary or grammar school), in Ward One at Bell Avenue and Main Street; the South Side School, situated in Ward Four at Eleventh Street and Hunt Avenue; and a third, "known as the Mexican school, in Ward Three at Ninth Street and Ross."[30] Sullivan averred that "all the Mexican children or children of Mexican descent are and have been for more than two years last past, obligated by order of said Board of Education to attend said Mexican School up to the fifth grade thereof, where other children were and are permitted to attend the schools most convenient to their residence." Sullivan pointed out that some schools were "convenient to the residence of the Mexican children and from which they are excluded on account of their race."[31]

Sullivan explained that the "plaintiff who is himself of the Mexican race" went to see School District superintendent, George O. Thompson, to enroll his eleven-year-old son, Miguel, in a school that was more convenient to his home. But on September 2, 1913, Superintendent Thompson "refused to admit said child as a pupil and directed him to attend the Mexican School."[32] Sullivan added that on August 25, 1913, a group of Mexican American parents contacted the Alamosa School Board of Education for permission to enroll their children at the North Side School, because it was more convenient to their homes. School board officials informed Mexican American parents that "their children and all children of Mexican descent would be confined to the Mexican school up to the fifth grade."[33] Sullivan explained that Francisco Maestas's son was "forced to cross and re-cross said tracks in his travel to and from the said Mexican School to his great danger and to plaintiff's distress of mind."[34]

Sullivan maintained that by denying the Maestas children access to the closest school and thereby forcing them to attend the Mexican School, school officials were making a "distinction and classification of pupils in the public schools on account of race or color contrary to the Constitution of the laws of the State of Colorado." Article 9, Section 8 of the Colorado Constitution stated that "no sectarian tenants or doctrines shall ever be taught in the public schools, nor shall any distinction or classification of pupils be made on account of race or color."[35]

Sullivan asked for an alternative writ of mandamus to be issued by the court directing the school board and superintendent to "admit the said child of plaintiff to the North Side School or the most convenient of the public schools of said city to which he has the right of admission without any distinction or classification on account of his race or color, and pay the costs of this action, or to show cause why they should not do so."[36]

As the news media covered the case, the *Alamosa Independent Journal* reported that the decisions to segregate Mexican American children was "adopted several years ago by the directors, and it has been proven that it was the best system ever inaugurated in any school district" and that the "percentage of those Spanish American children who advance beyond the fourth grade has steadily increased." The paper also reported that "last year's advancement of scholars increased over 400 per cent over the number of those advanced before the system was inaugurated five years ago, with practically the same attendance."[37] The *Alamosa Independent Journal* clearly supported the School Board of Education and School District Superintendent. The paper claimed that school officials were "giving the children of the Spanish American families of this city advantages they have never enjoyed elsewhere," and also cautioned that "if the board is wrong, they will simply have to go back to the old and far inferior system of educating the children of these citizens."[38]

In the complaint and the media coverage, the tools of social control that were being used against the Spanish American families of Alamosa were highlighted. The school board chose to use language as a means of segregating and controlling the students. In the process, the media lauded the segregation of these students as being to their advantage, and, as the Board's response reveals, to the advantage of all students in the district.

In response to the Mexican Americans' complaint, District Court Judge Charles Holbrook determined that the Maestas petition had made a sufficient case for admittance of the students that he issued an order to the school board and superintendent to either admit the children to the most convenient public school or file an answer arguing why they should not.[39]

The Answer

John T. Adams responded to Raymond Sullivan's petition on behalf of the School Board. In his answer, Adams specified what the Alamosa School Board of Education and the School District Superintendent admitted and what they denied. Among other things, they admitted that Francisco Maestas was a US Citizen and a tax-paying resident of Alamosa. The Answer also admitted that Francisco Maestas tried to enroll his son, Miguel (aka Mike), at North Side High School on September 2, 1913, and that Superintendent Thompson refused to admit Miguel into the North Side School and ordered him to attend the preparatory school.[40]

Adams, however, challenged Sullivan on several counts. Adams denied that school officials ordered all Mexican children to attend the preparatory school, denied that the school board and school district superintendent had distinguished or classified Mexican children based on color or race, and denied that Mexican children were excluded from any school that was convenient to their residence because of their race.[41]

Adams argued that Miguel Maestas and other Mexican American children were not segregated on account of race, because the Mexican American children were, in fact, "Caucasian." He argued that "all of the children of said school district are of the same race and color, to-wit, white children of the Caucasian race, with the exception of a few negroes."[42] Adams was trying to make the case that school officials were not segregating Mexican children based on race because Mexican children were Caucasian.[43]

Rather, he argued, Miguel Maestas (see figure 1.2) was denied admission to the North Side School because he lacked English skills and was academically unprepared. He pointed out that Miguel had failed an English exam and that he was "behind in all of his classes and studies, and . . . unable to carry on the work thereof." Miguel was also behind academically, said Adams, because his parents had "permitted" him to stay out of school for three months (due to the walkout).[44] Adams then maintained that Miguel was required to attend the preparatory school, "where special facilities were and are provided for the use of all children who are deficient in a working knowledge of the English language."[45]

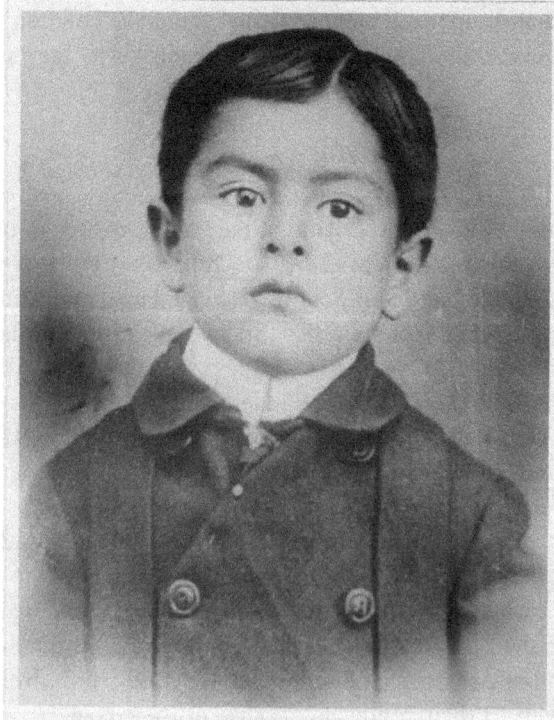

Figure 1.2. Miguel Maestas, Alamosa, Colorado. Courtesy of Tony Sandoval and Ronald W. Maestas.

Building on the argument that language was the key issue, Adams argued that the school had employed teachers with special skills at the school and that it offered the "best and most efficient system of teaching pupils unfamiliar with English language and where a new language must be taught and learned." Adams also argued that Mexican children received "more individual attention from the teachers in the use of English language; and the course of general (manual training) is the same for the children attending the school."[46]

Perhaps in a nod to *Plessy v. Ferguson*, Adams also made a case for the quality (and equality) of the facilities at the Mexican School. Adams argued that the school building was one of the best in the city, that it was sanitary, and that the "equipment is equal to, if not superior to any other school building." Children at the school, Adams claimed, "receive equal educational advantages with all the children in the said city."[47]

Adams also challenged the idea that distance and safety were serious issues. He averred that the preparatory school was not far from the Maestas home and argued that it was not a perilous walk to the preparatory school and that, given the seven-block distance, it was "within reasonable walking distance from plaintiff's place of residence." He also claimed that his walk to the school was not dangerous because of passing trains as railroad companies were required to protect pedestrians by using warning signs and signals and that walking across the tracks was no more dangerous than crossing any street in the city.[48]

Finally, Adams argued that segregation was important for the education of all students in Alamosa. He claimed that it was "impossible to efficiently teach the non-English speaking children in said school district, in English grammar, or any other subject, without seriously retarding and impairing the educational advancement and development of the school children of said city."[49] Adams cautioned the court about allowing non-English-speaking Mexican American children to attend one of the other schools in the district where teachers did not understand Spanish and warned the court that "the graded system of schools in said city would be seriously injured and impaired if not altogether destroyed, and the advancement of educational development of the pupils of the said city would be thereby retarded, including not only those speaking the Spanish language but also those speaking only the English language." Adams asserted that it was impossible "to provide for adequate teaching facilities for said pupils in more than one of the buildings in said city." To "change the present system of instruction in said school district," he concluded, "would result in great and irreparable injury and loss to said school district and tax payers thereof."[50]

Adams ended by putting forth the Board's perspective about who was behind the lawsuit. He said defendants believed the lawsuit was instigated by individuals who did not have children in the school district, individuals who did not pay taxes in the district, individuals who were of Mexican birth, and individuals who wanted to destroy and discredit the school and school officials for personal reasons. He said, in short, that it was individuals who wanted to embarrass and handicap the "principal and instructors in said schools, and the defendant directors of said School District."[51]

The Board's response illustrates how those in charge attempted to use race as a means of social control. In this instance, the Board asserted that the students were Causasian so that they could claim that their act of segregating the students did not violate the Colorado Constitution. However, we will see throughout the book how the racing of students becomes an important tool, and how the use of race by those in power changes depending on their need to control the population.

In the Court

There is no transcript from the trial, but there are some court records and newspaper accounts. In the trial, race became an issue because it was key to the plaintiffs' argument that Mexican Americans be understood as racially distinct. The *Alamosa Independent Journal*, however, reported how plaintiffs wanted to raise questions of race but that the "issue fell flat." It did so, the story noted, because the "general impression among our citizens seems to be that the Spanish Americans . . . are having their children take advantage of a system that is for the best interest of all concerned." It also pointed out that "these Spanish American parents, of which there are several hundred families represented in this city, appear to sincerely believe that they are not being treated justly."[52]

For their part, the school district subpoenaed a professor from the Greeley Normal School to testify on their behalf. Professor W. B. Mooney praised the school board and superintendent for the "good work done in the Alamosa schools through the segregation of the Spanish American scholars and the competent teachers for their instruction, who understood the custom and language of these children." Mooney opined that school officials were segregating Mexican children because it was pedagogically sound and praised them for hiring teachers with special skills at the school. The press described Professor Mooney as someone who was rational and that he was "very convincing to an unprejudiced mind."[53]

But the coverage by the *Alamosa Independent Journal* was limited. The *Denver Catholic Register* had more to report. It provided brief accounts of testimony from school board members, the superintendent, a principal, two teachers, several parents, a number of schoolchildren, and other community members. School District Superintendent George O. Thompson testified that Mexican American children were "put in a school by themselves because of their deficiency in the English language." He also told the court that no "American" children attended the school. When board member J. H. Darling took the stand, Sullivan asked him if he thought there was race prejudice toward Mexicans in Alamosa and if he believed "public sentiment had not been in favor of segregating their children in the public schools." Darling told Sullivan that he "would rather not answer the question."[54] Darling, however, not only admitted that he "would never permit his children to attend school with the Mexicans," but affirmed that "he was still of that mind." In addition, he also told the court that "the school set aside for the Mexican children was at all times designated the Mexican School in the official records of the board."[55]

George Shone, president of the school board, told the court that they acted in the best interest of all children. In his testimony, C. L. Lahrmann, treasurer of the school board and baker by trade, suggested he was responsible for conceptualizing the establishment of the Mexican School. But when he was asked if "certain American persons had not called upon him and asserted that if the Mexican children were allowed to attend the American schools they would withdraw their children," Lahrmann told the court that he "could not remember—that he was not positive."[56]

Francisco Maestas and his son, Miguel, were also put on the stand. The *Register* however, focused on Miguel. It reported how he "was timid and abashed by reason of the crowded court room." However, Miguel "understood and answered the questions put him by counsel in English." When defendants asked Miguel questions through an interpreter, "he responded in English before the interpreter could finish the questions." Miguel told the court that he was "often made late for school by reason of waiting for trains to pass." Other children were "put on the stand and answered readily in English the questions put to them by counsel."[57]

Other Mexican American parents and their children were put on the stand. Parent after parent testified that "their children knew English." One parent, Victor Gallegos, told the court that two of his children of school age "had been refused admission to the American school and that he had, rather than send them to the Mexican school, placed them in a convent in Denver." He said that he and his wife had spoken English to them since they were born and were well acquainted with the English language. Another Mexican American parent, Efren Quintana, claimed the "majority of the children in the Mexican school spoke English as well as his children and that he could see no reason except that of race prejudice as to why they were segregated." He maintained that the "great majority of the Mexican people wished to have their children attend the schools nearest to them without discrimination." Quintana also told the court that he had "never been in favor of a separate school" and that he had been a "member of a committee of Mexicans who appeared before the school board with a petition signed by 180 Mexican heads of families asking for their 'constitutional rights' in the schools." Quintana unabashedly told the court that the committee of Mexicans were "informed by Director Lahrmann that they had no rights."[58]

The principal of the South Side School in the District, Miss Carrie Body, testified, telling the court that she was ordered "to send all Mexican children to the Mexican School." Teachers from the Mexican School also testified. Miss Mary Lister asserted that "most of the children in her grades had a sufficient knowledge of the English to carry on the work in those grades." The other teacher at the Mexican School, Miss Loretta McGraw, stated that they spoke with "the children mostly in English and found that [was] the best way to teach them." But she told the court that they were "required by the board to use Spanish in teaching them." Miss McGraw concluded that "she was acquainted with all of the children in the school and that most of them spoke English."[59] Overwhelming evidence seemed to suggest that Mexican American children at the Mexican School were able to speak and understand English.

The Ruling

District Court Judge Charles Holbrook ruled in favor of Francisco Maestas and other Mexican American children in the Alamosa school district in March of 1914. Judge Holbrook was convinced that school officials had used the English language deficiency and the academic unpreparedness of some Mexican American children as a rationale to send all Mexican American children to the Mexican School up to the fifth grade.[60] He explained that English-speaking Mexican American children had the right to attend public schools near their homes, or schools of their choice, in the Alamosa school district. In his decision, Holbrook ordered the school district to "admit Miguel Maestas, plaintiff's son, and the children of other Mexican people to attend the school or school nearest them respectively."[61]

In his decision, Judge Holbrook showed that he understood the school board's arguments about the educational purposes of the school. He noted that the "school was built for their [the Mexican students'] benefit, and supplied with teachers especially selected, because of their ability to speak both English and Spanish." Judge Holbrook believed that the Mexican School served a valuable service, because "children sitting in a room wherein the instruction given is in a language which they do not understand, however bright the children may be, cannot make progress, and must necessarily fall behind their classes."[62]

However, he ultimately rejected those arguments and decided in favor of Maestas. He noted that some of the Mexican American children "in the lower grades may be able, and doubtless are able, to speak English."[63] He also understood why "Spanish speaking people believe that their children are excluded from the two English speaking schools, upon account of race." Rejecting the school board's argument, he believed that this "feeling must be eradicated before the school can reach its greatest efficiency." He did not think it was just to send English-speaking Mexican children to the Mexican School because he saw "evidence [that showed there were] children in different grades in the Mexican Primary School, who know enough English to understand instruction in the same grades in the other schools." Thus, Holbrook stated that "in the opinion of the court . . . the only way to destroy this feeling of discontent and bitterness which has recently grown up, is to allow all children so prepared, to attend the school nearest them."[64]

Holbrook explained that "Miguel Maestas convinced the court that he is entitled to the privilege of attending the school nearest his home: and, the court is of the opinion that others in the primary school should be allowed to attend the schools nearest their respective places of residence." Holbrook, however, stipulated that if there were any errors about the English-language proficiency of children, the children themselves would know and would "soon ask to be returned to the primary school." In other words, Holbrook's ruling also meant school officials were able to keep the non-English-speaking students at the Mexican School.[65]

The Media Reports the Decision

When Judge Holbrook delivered his decision in March of 1914, a number of newspapers in Colorado and from neighboring states reported the outcome of the case. *The Rocky Mountain News* described how school officials in Alamosa had to admit "Mexican children as pupils and must give them the same instruction as is given the American children of the city." The press reported that school board members had "arbitrarily fixed a rule that Spanish-speaking pupils could not enter any of the other schools until after having completed the fourth grade in the Mexican school."[66]

On the following day, the *Denver Post* reported how "Mexican children have the same rights in the public schools in the state and cannot be lawfully segregated." The story explained that Judge Holbrook understood that the school in Alamosa was built for the benefit of children who could not speak English. But it was clear to Holbrook that Mexican American parents believed their children were "excluded from the two English-Speaking schools on account of race." The press also explained that Holbrook understood that "the only way to destroy this feeling of discontent and bitterness that has grown up is to allow all the children so prepared to attend the schools nearest them."[67]

The *Denver Catholic Register* not only reported that the school segregation of Mexican American children had to stop in Alamosa, but that the lawsuit was historic. That it "was the first time in the history of America that a court fight was made over an attempt to segregate Mexicans in school."[68] The front page of the *Alamosa Courier* read that Mexican Americans had won the court decision. The paper published Holbrook's entire decision and explained that the segregation was not because the Mexican child could not speak English "but because of race prejudice the school board and the city superintendent held against his people."[69]

In Akron, Colorado, a small community located in the northeastern part of the state, its newspaper reported that school officials in Alamosa had to admit Mexican children into their schools and "give them the same instruction as is given the American children of the city." The story in Akron reported that the school was built to serve non-English-speaking Mexican American children but that the "board arbitrarily fixed a rule that Spanish-Speaking pupils could not enter any of the other schools until after having completed the fourth grade in the Mexican school."[70]

Because the lawsuit was tried in the Hispano homeland, a Spanish-language newspaper, *La Revista de Taos* from Taos, New Mexico—a community located about ninety miles south of Alamosa—reported that Hispanos in Alamosa were victorious, that school officials in Alamosa had to admit Mexican American children into White schools, and that they had to provide them with the same instruction as American youth. In Spanish, the editor of *La Revista* told its readers, "congratulamos a los hispanos americanos residentes de Alamosa, estado de Colorado, por su valor y firmeza en defender sus garantias civicas como ciudadanos Americanos . . ." Translated to English, it congratulated the Hispanos Americanos of Alamosa for their courage and for defending their rights as American citizens.[71]

Legal Loose Ends

Although Holbrook's decision was public and many newspapers had reported his ruling, the lawsuit was not entirely over. John Adams filed a motion to vacate judgment and to dismiss the action.[72] Judge Holbrook denied the motion to vacate on April 17, 1914. Adams filed a notice that the school board planned to appeal to the State Supreme Court; however, we could not find evidence of an appeal being filed at or heard by the Colorado Supreme Court.[73]

Shortly after the trial, there is a handwritten order from Judge Holbrook regarding whether two additional students in the preparatory school could select another school in the district. It appears that Judge Holbrook examined the students' English abilities and determined that Juan Ortega was "qualified to receive instruction in English without retarding the class," and Judge Holbrook ordered that he be allowed to attend the school nearest his residence. However, he also determined that "Juan Maestas should acquire a little better knowledge of the English language, both for his own good and for the progress of the class to which he would be assigned" and ordered that he not be transferred until he was "able to pass a better examination in English."[74] This highlights the challenges of the Mexican American community faced after the decision. Judge Holbrook made the determination about the language abilities of these two additional students, but the prospect of appealing the school district's determination about the language abilities of each Mexican student was impractical.

Discussion

The *Maestas v. Shone* case needs to be understood as one of the earliest Mexican American challenges to school segregation in the United States. The decision meant that the Alamosa School District was required to admit English-speaking Mexican American children in White schools near their homes, but those who did not have a command of English were kept at the Mexican School. It is instructive to read how different newspapers interpreted the outcome of the case. The editor of the *Alamosa Leader*, for example, was partially correct. He reported that "the decision, in effect, is that the Mexican children can go to any school in Alamosa, nearest their homes, provided they are proficient to do so by having a knowledge of the English language." He also believed "the decision was very fair." However, unlike other newspaper accounts, the editor distorted the recent past and discounted why Mexican Americans filed the lawsuit in the first place. He claimed the "Alamosa school board never contended that the Mexican children in this district should be barred from the north side school."[75] The *Leader* was incorrect. Other newspapers were accurate about how the lawsuit came about. As the *Hooper-Mosca Tribune* noted, it was not about Miguel Maestas's inability to understand English but "because of race prejudice the school board and city superintendent held against his people."[76]

What also became clear in this case was how Judge Holbrook showed confidence in his decision when he discussed the language deficiency of Mexican children. As we saw, he argued in his ruling that it made pedagogical sense to provide non-English-speaking children with teachers who understood their language. He believed bright Mexican American children were unable to learn in an environment where they did not understand the language. At the same time, Judge Holbrook appeared ambiguous, hesitant, and uncomfortable when race was concerned. Given Holbrook's hesitation on race, his ruling needs to be understood within that space and time. Racial politics in America were intense. It had only been eighteen years since the 1896 *Plessy v. Ferguson* landmark US Supreme Court decision upheld the constitutionality of state laws allowing racial segregation in public facilities under the "separate but equal" doctrine.[77] Moreover, the Colorado State Constitution prohibited schools from classifying and distinguishing children based on color or race.[78]

Judge Holbrook was astute. He most likely developed certain sensibilities about race because he was raised in the South. He was born in

Virginia 1848, was a former schoolteacher in Kentucky, was admitted to the Kentucky Bar in 1876, came to Colorado in 1877, and was elected as district attorney in District 12 in Colorado in 1881. Holbrook was so well regarded as a magistrate in Alamosa that he was put on the primary ballot to run for the Colorado State Supreme Court before he died in August of 1914. As a judge, he was described as ruling on decisions "always as near fair as he could possibly render them, and he made it a rule to give no attorney the best or the worst of it."[79] Given Holbrook's ruling, school officials did not pursue an appeal and it did not go to the Colorado Supreme Court.[80]

To the extent that Judge Holbrook was from the South, it was not certain how much he knew about the legal construction of race as it applied to Mexican Americans. The racial category of Mexican Americans had a complicated history. It was complicated because the federal government made the decision to grant American citizenship to Mexicans living in the newly ceded territory after the US-Mexican War in 1848, an area that included Alamosa. The "Treaty of Guadalupe Hidalgo," said K. L. Bowman, "stipulated that former Mexican citizens were to be given 'all the rights of citizens of the United States.' "[81] Because people of color were ineligible for US citizenship during the mid-nineteenth century, the federal government categorized Mexicans as White.[82] Classifying Mexicans as White became a political act because most were racially mixed. Most were mestizos, a combination of Spanish and Indian.[83] But because the federal government was forced to make a decision about how to incorporate Mexicans into the newly ceded territory, the treaty, said George Martinez, turned Mexicans "into whites."[84]

Classifying Mexicans as White during the mid-nineteenth century was not a simple narrative where Mexicans became White US citizens who were accepted in American society. Laura Gomez argues that for "many Americans, it was the fact of Mexicans' 'mongrel' status that most strongly signaled their racial inferiority." And because naturalization was restricted to White persons, Gomez maintained that the "Mexicans' collective naturalization in 1848 prompted a *legal* definition of Mexicans as 'White.' "[85] Legal scholar Ariela Gross argued that "while a small elite of Mexican-American landholders who could prove that they were 'Spanish' maintained white status, the majority of 'Mexicans' were viewed and treated by Anglos as a separate race."[86] This case supports what these scholars had to say. Throughout the reporting of the case and in the testimony given in the case itself, the Mexican Americans of Alamosa could be called just

Mexican or Mexican American or Hispano, but never just American. This is true even as the school argued that the Mexican American students were Caucasian. Mexicans were viewed in social terms as a separate race.

It was not surprising, then, that Judge Holbrook did not know how to respond to Raymond Sullivan's claim that Mexican children were racially distinct or John Adam's position that Mexican Americans were Caucasian and no different than other White children in the school district. Judge Holbrook did not respond to these issues in his decision. Given that Mexican Americans were legally White in the United States, Holbrook could have, in principle, agreed with Adams and ruled Mexican American children were White and were thus not being segregated in the Mexican School.[87] But he did not. Holbrook did not seem to be convinced that Mexican American children were White, but he was also careful not to state that they were racially distinct.[88]

In his ruling, Holbrook suggested that school board members and the previous superintendent were well intentioned and that they constructed the school to serve the non-English-speaking children. But he also believed the School Board and Superintendent had strayed from the original goal and implemented a policy that forced all Mexican American children to the Mexican School. Without officially stating that school board members had established a policy that was based on race, Holbrook forced school officials to admit English-speaking Mexican children in White schools near their homes.

After the decision was delivered, Raymond Sullivan was interviewed by the *Denver Catholic Register* and was asked to respond to the ruling. Sullivan told the *Denver Catholic Register* that the peremptory writ of mandamus granted by Judge Holbrook forced school board members to permit all children who understood English in schools near their homes. Sullivan was lukewarm about the decision but was satisfied because, he said, "the decree applies to practically all the Mexican children in Alamosa, as nearly all have the knowledge indicated." In other words, Sullivan seemed content with the ruling because very few Mexican American children were going to be relegated to the Mexican School. Nevertheless, he was bothered with the idea of segregated schooling based on language. In fact, he told the *Denver Catholic Register*, "it is still our contention that even though totally deficient in a knowledge of the English language, children cannot be placed in a separate race school in Colorado on that ground."[89] Sullivan understood the importance of local control and that school districts were given power to operate and govern their schools. But he told the *Denver*

Catholic Register that "nowhere in the statutes of Colorado are school boards authorized to segregate school children on account of language." He argued that when one segregates based on language, "you are getting perilously close to separation on account of race." Sullivan hypothesized that under "this theory you have to have separate schools for Germans, French, Italians, Greeks, Bulgarians and so on until every race is isolated and reared in a separate school." This separation, said Sullivan, was counterproductive to the spirit of the Colorado Constitution and it went against the American ideal of being a nation "composed of many races and many peoples." Sullivan believed that racial diversity made America a "strong and united commonwealth." Separate schooling, he believed, "would tend toward race consciousness, dissolution and disintegration."[90]

Despite this victory, we are not suggesting that race relations in Alamosa were ameliorated. They were not. The Mexican American struggle for racial justice was far from over. Two years after the *Maestas* ruling, Raymond Sullivan returned to Alamosa. This time he came to assist the district attorney on a lawsuit brought on by a Mexican American against the owners of a bowling alley. The suit was filed under the Civil Rights Act of Colorado, which prohibited "the exclusion of any person from a public place of amusement on account of race or color." The owners of the bowling alley posted signs that read: "Mexican trade not wanted." In this case, the jury found overwhelming evidence that Mexican Americans were being barred from that establishment. One of the owners was found guilty and the other was acquitted.[91] Our point here is that even though Mexican Americans were allowed to attend schools of their choice with White children after 1914, and whereas the district attorney forced some business owners to take Jim Crow signs down in 1916, racial discrimination continued for decades.[92] Like other Mexican American communities in the United States, Hispanos in Alamosa understood they lived on the margins of American life, but they slowly started to move from the margins to the center of the struggle for racial equality.

Chapter 2

"Porque tenían sangre de 'NEGROS,'"[1] 1915–1916

Approximately one year after the *Maestas v. Shone* lawsuit was decided in Alamosa, Colorado, another racial incident affecting Mexican children in public schools took place. This case, however, was very different from the *Maestas* lawsuit. It was different because it took place in the deep South, because the case did not go to court, and even though the Mexican government and the US Department of State became involved, the complaint did not receive media attention. We begin this chapter with an excerpt written by Eliseo Arredondo, Mexican ambassador to the United States, to Robert Lansing of the US Department of State on February 21, 1916, explaining what had occurred in a small Louisiana town.

> I have the honor to bring to Your Excellency's attention a complaint I have received from the Mexican Consul at New Orleans, Louisiana, relative to the attitude assumed by a Mr. Ford, a member of the Local Board of Education, of Cheneyville, La., who has forcibly prevented several Mexican children from attending school, on the plea that they are mixed blood and ought not to be allowed to attend the school where American children are receiving their education. I am informed that Mr. Ford has carried his determination to keep the above-mentioned children out of school to the extent of menacing them and their parents with violent personal injury if they insisted in entering the school building, and to this end, he stationed

himself at the door entrance and actually forced the children
to return to their homes.[2]

Mexican ambassador Arredondo complained to US Secretary of State
Lansing that a school trustee had thrown Mexican children out of a White
school and threatened their parents, and that school officials refused to
readmit them because they were racially mixed. Arredondo called on
Lansing to help "prevent this unjust discrimination."[3]

It is important to understand the period when this complaint was
filed to the US Department of State. It was 1915–1916. Public schools in
the South were segregated under the "separate but equal" doctrine sanctioned by the 1896 Supreme Court decision *Plessy v. Ferguson*.[4] Indeed,
Mexican families and their children were entering a region of the nation
where very little was known about them, where their numbers were small,
where their racial/ethnic status was ambiguous to White Southerners, and
where rigid boundaries were drawn between Black and White communities
in all avenues of American life. This was also an era when the Mexican
Revolution was raging, when World War I was starting to intensify, when
diplomatic relations between Mexico and the United States became tense,
and when D. W. Griffith's film *Birth of a Nation* was released.[5] In short,
the Mexican Revolution (1910–1920) was pushing thousands of Mexicans
to the United States to seek refuge and employment. In addition, relations
between Mexico and the United States were strained because of a political
incident that took place in Mexico in 1914. The United States military
forces landed at Veracruz, Mexico, and occupied that port city for more
than six months. The occupation was, in short, over the treatment of
American nationals in Mexico.[6] Finally, race relations in the United States
intensified during this period. *Birth of a Nation*, the silent film directed
by D. W. Griffith, was released in 1915. The film chronicled two families
after the Civil War and during Reconstruction. More than anything else,
the film portrayed Black men (White actors in Black faces) as unintelligent
and sexually aggressive toward White women, and the Ku Klux Klan was
cast as heroic.[7]

This was also an era when Mexican consulates in the Southwest were
beginning to receive complaints about how Mexican children were being
mistreated, segregated, and excluded from public schools.[8] As we mentioned in our introduction, the Mexican consulate was a resource Mexicans
could draw on for redress of their complaints. In certain Southwestern
communities, Mexicans were starting to organize for their own advocacy

and in some instances found liberal allies to pursue redress for the mistreatment of Mexican children. Mexican consulates, however, were also registering complaints about Mexicans in their schools and communities from locations outside of the Southwest. In the South, there were fewer sources of social power for Mexican immigrants, and the Mexican consulate served as an important resource to draw attention to the struggles of Mexican residents.

We seek to understand the experiences of Mexican children in the Jim Crow South in a Louisiana community in 1915–1916 to drive further the conversation about their racialization and its impact on their experiences in public schools. It helps to illustrate how the racialization that was used as a tool of social control in Alamosa (discussed in chapter 1) was different in the South, where race was predominately experienced through a Black/White binary. This chapter documents the exclusion of Mexican children from a White school by a local school trustee, because he perceived them as racially mixed. We examine how school officials in the parish responded to their removal, what the Mexican consulate in New Orleans found and reported, and how the Mexican Ambassador to the United States and the US Department of State responded, respectively, to the incident. This story, however, is incomplete. We do not know if this case was ever resolved. That is, we were unable to uncover or infer whether the Mexican children involved in this case were placed in White schools, Black schools, or whether they were allowed to attend school at all.[9]

To complicate the story further, available school board minutes provide no record of discussion of the incident by school trustees, and the incident was not reported in the local newspaper, the *Alexandria (LA) Daily Town Talk*. Finally, although the US Department of State ordered the Louisiana governor to investigate the incident, and that order was passed on to the State superintendent of Instruction, there is no record of an investigation.[10]

Even though the story is incomplete, we have data that illuminate the context of the incident. Specifically, we know that orders were given by the county superintendent to permit the children to attend school, how his orders were received by multiple actors in the parish, and what the Mexican consulate in New Orleans found. This information is not inconsequential, as it reveals potential differences in the roles school officials played in the education of Mexican students in the South compared to cases in the Southwest. While we chiefly want to know how school leaders in this Louisiana community responded to the school trustee's actions to keep

Mexican children out of a White school, we are also interested in understanding how Mexican children were perceived in a place and time where legal segregation was understood in exclusively Black and White terms.

We argue in this chapter that while Mexican children in this Louisiana parish were most likely not seen as Black or White, their mestizo appearance became the racial marker that kept them out of a White school. Given this time and location in the deep South, where a dual system of education existed between Whites and Blacks, school authorities were uncertain about the racial classification of Mexican children. To the extent that Mexicans were legally White in the United States, the category in this location was either unrecognized or rejected. In the excerpt Ambassador Arredondo sent to US Secretary of State Lansing, we saw that a school trustee forced the Mexican children out of the school because he saw them as non-White, as racially mixed and, in order to keep them out of the White school, he claimed they had "Sangre de Negros," or Black blood. We hypothesize that the school trustee used a "Black blood" argument to "legally" justify keeping Mexican children out of the White school. We also believe the school trustee did not see the Mexican children as similar to European immigrants, but as a "colored" group that was similar to African Americans.

Historical Context

Very few studies have documented Mexican American challenges to unequal education during this time period. Other than the *Maestas* case we discussed in chapter 1, historian Arnoldo De Leon chronicles a 1910 school boycott by Mexican Americans who sought to overturn racial segregation in schools in West Texas.[11] De Leon argues in part of his book that Whites in the school district believed "Mexicans had no right to complain as long as they were given equal school facilities with the Whites, and in order to gain entrance into the White schools the Mexicans would have to prove that they were deprived of equal treatment."[12] This argument was similar to that of *Plessey*, which ruled "separate but equal" facilities for African Americans satisfied the requirements of the Equal Protection Clause. De Leon concluded that, at that time, no government agency was able to enforce desegregation, safeguards for quality education were not available, and the promises made in the Treaty of Guadalupe Hidalgo for Mexicans in the United States were not upheld.[13]

Rather than a community struggle that played out in the school boycott in West Texas or the *Maestas* lawsuit in Colorado, this incident took place in plantation country, a location with few Mexicans and without the benefits of an organized Mexican community. In Cheneyville, White Southerners knew very little about Mexicans. Thus, this case was not about segregating Mexican children. It was about denying them access to the school. In addition, the racial classifications of Mexicans as legally White were far away from the minds of the members of this southern community, whose understandings of race were marked by the Black/White racial binary. It is against the backdrop of this time and location that we want to understand how school officials responded to the exclusion of Mexican children in the deep South.

Race, Segregation, and the Deep South

The history of Mexicans and Mexican Americans in the South is beginning to emerge. Historian Julie Weise found that Mexicans arriving in Louisiana and Mississippi during the early twentieth century had varied experiences that depended on social class, skin color, and where they lived and worked.[14] Indeed, life was different for Mexicans who lived in the Mississippi Delta compared to those who settled in New Orleans. New Orleans was racially diverse, urban, and cosmopolitan. It also had historical connections to Latin America. Mexican immigrants coming to New Orleans were from diverse social classes, and their immigration more closely resembled that of European immigrants as they arrived by boat rather than crossing the border in the American Southwest.[15] New Orleans was also unique in that it had a variety of ethnic communities that were pursuing social mobility in the context of Jim Crow.

These communities provided a variety of models for addressing racialization and its consequences.[16] As middle-class Mexicans moved into New Orleans, Weise notes that some were able to obtain the social benefits of Whiteness. This, however, did not mean skin color was unimportant for Mexicans. Weise, in fact, describes Armando Amador, the vice consul of Mexico in New Orleans during the late 1920s, as being highly educated, multilingual, and a journalist, novelist, and poet before and after he worked as consul for the Mexican government. To the extent that Amador was a mestizo, Weise recognized that in "Louisiana his racial descriptors might have earned him a spot in the back train car along side another mixed-race intellectual, Homer Plessy."[17] However, Amador remained silent about his race. Mexicans like Amador with social status could rely on class and culture to mitigate the effects of Jim Crow. Others, however, had to remain mindful of the color line in New Orleans.

Weise, however, found that within 100 miles of New Orleans, where sugar-producing areas of the state recruited Mexicans for low-wage agricultural work that was performed by black laborers, "Mexicans were definitely not considered to be white."[18] Mexicans in the Mississippi Delta had a much different experience. To the extent that Mexicans went to the Delta to pick cotton and to work as wage laborers, they faced significant barriers and they were unable to achieve social mobility.[19] Conditions were harsh, they were unwanted, and Jim Crow applied to them.[20] From the moment recruiters' trucks delivered them to their new work sites in Mississippi, Weise argued, Mexicans "tasted the brutality and exclusion that the region's white planters had used to segregate, terrorize and control African Americans."[21] The abuse they experienced "would have been intimately familiar to the African Americans picking cotton a few rows away in the same fields and plantations."[22] Moreover, the residential segregation that was a feature of cities and towns in the South also existed in the back roads of plantations. "Mexicanos lived among black and white sharecroppers, though most often among blacks."[23]

Though occurring several years later, it is important to acknowledge that the 1927 US Supreme Court case, *Gong Lum v. Rice*, arose in the deep South. The case allowed the exclusion of a Chinese child from a Mississippi high school and the court ruled that such exclusion did not violate the Fourteenth Amendment to the US Constitution.[24] We underscore this case because it highlights the social climate of the South where "undesirable immigrants" were unwanted. Weise notes that around the time *Gong Lum* was decided, a significant number of Mexican workers came into the state and, as a response to their presence, "the Bolivar County School Board of Trustees voted to prohibit Mexicans from attending the Gunnison Consolidated School with white children."[25] While some Mexican children were able to attend White schools, said Weise, they received strong messages in the South that they were "not welcome in white society."[26]

These experiences, however, were not limited to the Mississippi Delta or other rural areas outside of New Orleans. Mexicans were rejected in many Southern and border-state communities. In 1911, for example, Juan Almazán filed a complaint with the Mexican consulate in Washington, DC, about his experience in St. Louis, Missouri, a border state between north and south.[27] In his handwritten letter to the Mexican consulate, Almazán described how he was invited by his White supervisors to have a beer at a local tavern. When they arrived at the establishment, Almazán was denied entry and was not served. He was denied service not because he was seen as Black, but because he was *"Indio."* In his letter, Almazán conveyed the message to the consulate that he was aware of his racial identity and that *"aun lo seré [Indio] . . . soy ciudadano Mexicano"* (even though I am Indian . . . I am a Mexican Citizen). Almazán understood his racial identity and knew he was an indigenous Mexican. But, he said, he was a Mexican citizen. He wanted to make a point to the Mexican consulate that his Mexican citizenship in America was meaningless.

In 1918, Luis Rincón also filed a complaint with the Mexican consulate in Washington, DC. He informed the consulate that he had been barred from restaurants, the theater, hotels, and other public establishments in Maryville, Tennessee.[28] Rincón was denied service in Maryville's establishments because he was "Mexican." That same year, the Mexican consulate in Washington, DC, received another complaint; Mexicans were being denied admission to public parks in Oklahoma City.[29]

It is safe to say that the racialization of Mexicans in the South was complicated and it depended on context. In New Orleans, middle- and upper-class Mexicans may have had access to White privilege but they appeared to be careful about claiming biological Whiteness because of their mestizo roots and national politics in Mexico. They pursued "Whiteness" in New Orleans not on legal or biological grounds, but based on culture and class.[30] In the Mississippi Delta and other parts of the South, the Mexican experience was similar to that of Blacks. They were rejected, exploited, and Jim Crow also applied to them. It is in the rural South where this case study emerges.

CHENEYVILLE

Located approximately 25 miles south of Alexandria, Louisiana, and the county seat of Rapides Parish, Cheneyville was settled in 1811 by Protestant immigrants from South Carolina. The town was named after William Fendan Cheney, a merchant who settled on the banks of the Bayou Boeuf Country. Cheneyville and its surrounding communities, said Jimmie Charlene Hammond, became known for its plantations. It was also "one of the finest agricultural areas in the state."[31] The town's economy prospered not only because of its cotton and sugar cane industry, which were supported by sharecropping, but also because of its proximity to the Red River, a tributary to the Mississippi River. Its location allowed growers to ship cotton "down the bayou and on to New Orleans."[32]

Similar to other locations in the Deep South, the population in Rapides Parish was divided between Black and White. Other racial minority groups were relatively small. Between 1910 and 1920, the population in Rapides Parish grew from 44,545 to 59,444. Ward 3 (the Cheneyville area) grew from 5,918 to 5,957, and the village of Cheneyville grew from 498 to 678. During these years, the White population in Rapides Parish grew from 20,968 to 33,250; foreign Whites dropped from 1,389 to 1,170; Blacks grew from 21,445 to 24,992; Native Americans dropped from 102 to 14; and Chinese grew from 7 to 8. The Mexican-born population in the state of Louisiana grew from 1,641 to 2,399, from 275 to 1,242 in New Orleans, and from 22 to 112 in Rapides Parish. There were about eleven Mexican-born residents in Cheneyville in 1920.[33] Rapides Parish was operating a dual system of education, where Black and White children attended separate schools. As the school board minutes noted, there were "white schools" and "colored schools." In 1914–1915, there were 240 White and 174 Black children attending schools.[34] The demographic profile of Rapides Parish and the community of Cheneyville was largely Black and White. Mexicans in the state, in the parish, and in Cheneyville were very small in numbers.

THE CHENEYVILLE INCIDENT

The incident in Cheneyville began with the exclusion of four Mexican children from a White school by a local school trustee. It is important to understand who the school trustee, Walter P. Ford, was in the community and why he was so adamant about keeping Mexican children out of the school. Born in 1848, Ford was a boy during Antebellum America and the Civil War, a young man during Reconstruction, and a planter, businessman, Baptist deacon, and school trustee during his adult years.[35] Ford became an influential citizen and a person with relative wealth. His roots ran deep in the community, as he was the son of William P. Ford, the Louisiana planter who purchased Solomon Northup, the free Black man from New York who was abducted in Washington, DC, in 1841, the Black man who was sold into slavery, and the Black man who spent *Twelve Years a Slave* in the Red River region of Louisiana.[36] Raised on a plantation, Walter P. Ford had steadfast beliefs about race and segregation. After he learned that Mexican children were attending the White school in Cheneyville in the fall of 1915, he forced them out because he saw them as racially mixed.

After Ford pushed the Mexican children out of the White school, written communication began to flow in the Parish between the County Superintendent, D. B. Showalter, the school principal, J. M. Johnson, a school trustee, W. H. Orr, and a local resident, Ivey Cannon. Our data show that Orr and Cannon both wrote to County Superintendent Showalter on the same day. School trustee Orr informed Showalter that a "few Mexican children have been for a few days to our school and lately they have been objected to and sent home."[37] Orr did not mention who had thrown the Mexican children out of the school, but he was clear that they were forced out because they were racially "mixed." Orr also distanced himself from these actions, stating that he and some of the teachers were not involved in the exclusion of these children. Orr requested that the County Superintendent come to Cheneyville to have the issue resolved.[38]

But it was not as simple as it appeared. Trustee Orr did not seem to tell the entire story. On the same day Orr sent his letter, Ivey Cannon, a young woman who lived near Cheneyville, also wrote to Showalter. Cannon knew the Mexican children who were denied entrance to the school. In fact, the Mexican children and their parents were living and working on her father's property. Records show that Ivey Cannon had previously spoken with Showalter over the phone and followed up with a letter. In her letter to Showalter, Cannon claimed that after they had spoken, "I sent the Mexican children to the school."[39] However, counter to the letter that school trustee Orr had written to Showalter that suggested he and the teachers at the school were not involved, Cannon claimed that "the teachers refused to give them [Mexican children] seats."[40] It appeared that some teachers at the school were refusing to seat Mexican children in class. Cannon continued to explain that Mr. Ford and Mr. Johns, two of the three school trustees, were refusing to admit Mexican children into the school because they had "negro blood."[41] Cannon retorted that the Mexican children did not have Black blood.[42] While it was not clear what role trustee Orr and the teachers were playing in keeping Mexican children out of the school, it was Ford and Johns, said Cannon, who forced Mexican children out of the school and were refusing to readmit them. Cannon told Showalter, "Ford stood at the gate this morning and sent the children home."[43]

Showalter immediately wrote a letter to the Cheneyville principal, J. M. Johnson, to inform him that he knew "some Mexican children, attending your school, have been excluded."[44] Showalter explained that he had consulted with the District Attorney and found that there was "no law that would exclude from the White schools Mexican children." Acting under legal advice, Showalter wrote to the principal "to request that you admit said children."[45] In response to Showalter, Principal Johnson claimed he "had nothing to do in keeping the Mexican children out of school." In fact, said Johnson, he informed "those people we could not keep them out and that I would not attempt it."[46]

THE NEW ORLEANS MEXICAN CONSULATE'S REPORT

It is not clear who contacted Francisco Villavicencio, the Mexican consulate in New Orleans, about the exclusion of Mexican children in Cheneyville, but it became evident that he quickly became involved. Seeking assistance from the Mexican consulate was not unusual. When Mexicans in the Mississippi Delta faced problems in their communities during the 1920s and 1930s, said Weise, they "turned to the Mexican consulate in New Orleans."[47] Thus, Head Consul Villavicencio in New Orleans directed special agent Salvador Lozano to conduct an investigation of the incident and to report back to him. In his report, Lozano informed Villavicencio that the case would be resolved in a manner that would be acceptable to Mexico, given the assistance he had received from various individuals in the community.[48] Given Lozano's findings, it appeared that the issue was not resolved.

The report, written in Spanish, read as though Lozano began the investigation with phone calls, but he ultimately traveled to Rapides Parish to interview individuals who were involved in the case. Lozano reported that in October of 1915, four Mexican children were removed from the Cheneyville School under the leadership of Principal J. M. Johnson.[49] Lozano had spoken with Ivey Cannon. Cannon informed Lozano that when she found out that the Mexican children were thrown out of the school, she confronted the principal.[50]

The principal told Cannon that it was W. P. Ford and U. H. Johns who had thrown the Mexican children out of the school because they were racially mixed and refused to have them interact with White children because they had "*sangre de 'NEGROS.'*"[51] Lozano claimed that although Principal Johnson had disagreed with Ford and Johns, they continued to ban Mexican children from the White school.[52] In fact, Lozano reported that Ford came to the school, positioned himself in front of the door, threatened the children, and told them to go home. In addition, Ford told Mexican children that he would physically harm them if they attempted to return to the school. Lozano also found that Ford had threatened the Mexican parents. As Lozano learned about Walter P. Ford, he characterized him as arrogant and despotic.

Given Ford's actions, Cannon contacted Showalter to inform him what Ford had done.[53] To the extent that Showalter subsequently ordered Principal Johnson to reinstate Mexican children into the school, Lozano discovered that Ford continued to impose himself and prohibited Mexican children from attending the school.[54] Lozano made clear in his report that most of his information was orally communicated and most of it was coming from Ivey Cannon and her father. At first, said Lozano, the Cannons were unwilling to put anything in writing because they feared Walter P. Ford. They feared the financial repercussions they could suffer and the power and influence he possessed in the community. But Ivey Cannon ultimately made a formal complaint (the letter she had written) because of the harm Ford was imposing on Mexican children and their parents. The Cannons, the report noted, were willing to assist the Mexican Consulate in any way they could.

Up to this point, Lozano had been unable to obtain sufficient proof of Ford's actions because the incident had been orally communicated.[55] He went to Alexandria to gather information that would be the hard evidence he needed. He interviewed Jonas Rosenthal and R. S. Cummins, school board president of Rapides Parish and the principal of the grammar school at Alexandria. The essence of the interview was that Rosenthal and Cummins were more than willing to help resolve the case. Rosenthal, however, wanted to resolve the case internally and did not want the complaint to go to Washington, DC. Lozano reported that Rosenthal had also heard that Ford was trying to exclude the Mexican children as a private citizen.[56] In other words, he was not acting in his role as a local school trustee but as an ordinary citizen when he blocked the Mexican children from entering the school. Rosenthal told Lozano that he supported the Mexican consulate and was in favor of having the Mexican children reinstated into the White school and hoped justice would prevail on the side of the Mexican government.

Lozano was finally able to acquire information about Ford's actions in writing.[57] County Superintendent Showalter shared the letters with Lozano to show how the district was responding. This was the hard evidence Lozano needed to go forward with the case. Indeed, Showalter wanted to demonstrate that the exclusion of Mexican children in the Cheneyville School did not come from him, but from Walter P. Ford. He presented evidence that he had contacted the district attorney, received legal advice, and ordered Principal Johnson to allow the Mexican children back to the school. The letters also disclosed that Ford was recalcitrant, uncooperative, and that his reason for removing Mexican children out of the White schools was based on race.[58]

To the extent that the issue had not been resolved, New Orleans Consul Francisco Villavicencio contacted the Mexican Ambassador in Washington, DC. In his letter to the Mexican Ambassador, Villavicencio (1916) informed him of Lozano's investigation and forwarded all the information.[59] After Mexican Ambassador Arredondo received the information, he contacted the US Department of State. The Mexican Ambassador provided the Department of State evidence that Walter P. Ford had removed and was keeping Mexican children out of a White school because they were racially mixed. The Third Assistant Secretary of State responded and confirmed that they had received the information about Walter P. Ford and how he was "preventing certain Mexican children from attending schools for white children at that place."[60] It was understood that Mexican Ambassador Arredondo wanted the Department of State to act and to "exert its good offices to prevent this discrimination."[61]

The Department of State confirmed that it would send the Mexican ambassador's complaint to the Louisiana governor with the request to investigate the case. The Department of State conveyed to Arredondo that they did "not doubt that the Governor will take steps to obtain for these Mexican children such educational facilities as the laws of Louisiana may seem to entitle them to."[62]

The Mexican Ambassador received another letter from the Department of State in March of 1916 to inform him that they were aware of the "the alleged refusal of the authorities of Rapides Parish of Louisiana, to permit certain Mexican children to attend schools at Cheneyville."[63] This letter, moreover, displayed that the governor of Louisiana had ordered the state superintendent of instruction to investigate the case. Also, once the governor received a report from the state superintendent of instruction, the Department of State would then respond.[64] However, there is no record that the Mexican Ambassador received a report from the Department of State.

Discussion

The complaint about the exclusion of Mexican children in this Louisiana town reached Washington, DC in 1916, but it was not clear why school officials did not record the issue in their school board meetings, why the case was not reported in the local press, and why the Department of State did not receive a report from the Louisiana governor. We hypothesize that a number of events made it difficult to bring closure to this case. First, Walter P. Ford and D. B. Showalter died when the case was pending. Because two major players in the case passed, the complaint may have been dropped. Walter P. Ford was no longer around to be charged for his actions and there was little reason to see if D. B. Showalter had mishandled the case. Second, Ford's social and economic standing in the community as a businessperson and planter may have influenced the local press not to cover the story. This was not unusual in the parish. In fact, Louisiana historian Sue Eakin argued that after the *Plessy* decision in 1896, planter action in Rapides Parish was clear and vocal since they were the government.[65] They also owned the newspapers. "So great was their confidence," said Eakin, "that movements of great importance simmering beneath the surface of society received little, if any, notice. Or, if noticed, they were ridiculed."[66]

In other words, residents with social, political, and economic stature in Rapides Parish were not going to challenge Walter P. Ford. Finally, when the Department of State ordered Louisiana governor Luther E. Hall to investigate the issue in March of 1916, his term ended two months later. Ruffin G. Pleasant then took office. Because the governorship in Louisiana was in transition, correspondence could have been lost or ignored, especially if the Department of State did not press the case.

It is unsettling that we do not know what happened to the Lopez and Perez children and their families after the incident. The records of the parish do not list names of individual students, and other available information does not indicate whether they attended school that year, whether "White" or "colored." Their families also do not appear in the 1920 Census records as residents of the Cheneyville area. Their lives remain largely invisible in the public records.

In spite of what cannot be known, there is much to learn from this case study. It supports some things already known about the racialization of Mexicans in the Southwest. Mexicans were generally not viewed as White in their schools in their communities. But the case raises new questions about Mexicans in the South. In the Black/White racial world of Central Louisiana, there was no consensus on how people like Mexicans, who did not fit into the binary system, should be classified. School officials and community members were divided on how Mexicans should be "raced." Indeed, there were disagreements about whether Mexican children had "Negro blood." Ford claimed the Mexican children had Black blood while Ivey Cannon disagreed. But no one in this case claimed Mexican children were White, the legal classification that was given to them by the American government at that time.[67]

As we think about the disagreement that took place about the racial category of the Lopez and Perez children, they positively did not "pass" as White in the Cheneyville school. They were also not of a social or economic standing that could have provided additional leverage to challenge their exclusion from school. Indeed, they were excluded because they were viewed as racially mixed. This attests to the importance of continuing the work on the experiences of Mexicans in the South. We need to better understand the social construct of race as it was applied to Mexican mestizos in Southern schools.

This incident also raises new questions about the interaction between race, education, and the local political economy. As we saw, the Lopez and Perez students were attempting to enroll in the White school in late October. According to school records, the White schools would have been in session for well over a month and the "colored schools" would just be starting so that the Black students could work through the harvest. In instances in the Southwest, school administrators often used this late enrollment and the work life of Mexican families as a technique of social control and to provide cover for segregating Mexican students. The claim was that their different schedule would be disruptive to White students and that entering a White school at a later date would put Mexican students at a disadvantage. That excuse for enrolling the Mexican students into the "colored schools" would have been readily available for school officials in Cheneyville, but no school official made this argument to justify keeping the Mexican children out of the White school. In fact, there were no attempts or discussions about enrolling Mexican children in a "colored school." The incident was about keeping "racially mixed" Mexican children out of the White school.

The controversy, it seemed to us, was about Mexican children's access to public education in the community. This case points to a difference in how race was perceived and acted on in this place and time. The social context of this community was different from that of other cases in the Southwest because school officials did not try to mask the exclusion of Mexican children. They excluded Mexican children from a White school on the grounds that they were racially "mixed" or that they had "Black blood." There is more work to be done to determine the extent to which the mestizo backgrounds of Mexican children factored in decisions to exclude or segregate them in Southern schools. What we found in this case was that Mexican children in Cheneyville, Louisiana, were excluded from a White public school because of how their race was understood.

This incident also shows the crucial role the Mexican consulate played at the time the case was occurring and in recounting the incident today. At the time of the incident, the Mexican consulate provided support to Ivey Cannon and the school officials who were willing to admit the Mexican students into the White school. Several months had passed between the initial complaint by Ivey Cannon and Lozano's report, and the Mexican students were still excluded from the school. Although we have no evidence of a positive outcome for the Mexican students, it is likely that the situation would not have changed for them without the consulate's involvement.

The importance of Mexican consulates becomes more apparent because it provided additional perspectives.[68] In this case, the report from the Mexican consulate provided a point of view that would otherwise have been unavailable in the public records of the time. For example, we gain information about the social context of the incident through reports that Ivey Cannon and her father feared Walter P. Ford. They feared him because of the financial and political power he held in the community. Moreover, we gain further understanding of why incidents involving race are often hidden from the public record. School board president Jonas Rosenthal expressed to investigator Lozano that he did not want the complaint to go to Washington, DC, implying that he would have been pleased to keep other public records devoid of the incident. It seems that Rosenthal received his wish. It is difficult to identify the extent to which school officials in the parish and those in power in the community went to make certain this incident would not receive attention in Cheneyville and Alexandria. They must have wanted this story to be lost, buried, or untold. In the end, it is the involvement of the Mexican consulate and the records kept in the Mexico City Archives that preserves what we know about the exclusion of Mexican children from a Louisiana public school. It was the Mexican consulate that pushed for written evidence that was needed to move the complaint forward. If the records in this incident were limited to those of the dominant groups in Cheneyville, Alexandria (i.e., the local press), and the Rapides Parish (i.e., school board minutes), this story would have been lost and certainly could not have been told.

Chapter 3

"In These Towns Mexicans Are Classified
as Negroes," 1915–1935

As we think about the previous two chapters, it is important to recognize that the history of Mexican American education is evolving and is being continually uncovered. What occurred in Alamosa and Cheneyville had either been suppressed, lost, or forgotten for over 100 years. It is not clear why the *Maestas* case went unrecognized for so long, because it was covered by multiple newspapers at the time.[1] The Cheneyville case seemed to be intentionally concealed, as it was neither recorded in the Rapides Parish School Board Minutes nor reported in the local press. It was only through the Mexico City archives that we learned about the case. As we continue our quest to understand how Mexican children were treated in public schools in different parts of the nation during the pre-*Brown* era, we shift to Kansas. This account is different from our previous two chapters in that a number of scholars have written about the schooling experiences of Mexican children in the state. Nevertheless, those experiences in Kansas are not part of the dominant historical discourse, because the literature has focused on the Southwest in general and California and Texas in particular.

In this chapter we examine the emergence of Mexican American school segregation from 1915 to 1935 in Kansas, the state that gave rise to *Brown v. Board of Education* in 1954. Even though Mexicans were not referenced in Kansas's school segregation laws, they were seen and treated as a racially distinct group. Kansas was fascinating because it did not have the legacy of being a slave state and, unlike most of the American Southwest, it did not have a long history of interaction between Whites and

Mexicans. This story, then, is about the emergence of Mexican American school segregation in an environment where it was not legally permitted, yet Mexican and White children were generally kept apart. We begin in Hutchinson, Kansas, where the following petition was presented to the school board on May 5, 1930:

> WE, THE UNDERSIGNED, are either residents, property owners, or parents of the children going to school, in the Lincoln School District located in the City of Hutchinson, County of Reno, State of Kansas. We hereby support . . . taking the Mexicans out of our school, and . . . putting them into a school to themselves.[2]

White residents wanted Mexican children out of their school and for school officials to construct a separate school for the Mexicans. Two additional petitions were circulated as more White residents, who had not been able to sign the first petition, sought to join this cause.[3] In total, residents gathered 590 signatures supporting a separate Mexican school.

This incident is compelling because the Mexican population at the time was small, comprising only 1.9 percent of the district's enrollment, and because this occurred outside the Southwest. Educational historians have generally focused on Mexican experiences in California, Texas, Arizona, and Colorado.[4] This is understandable given the numbers of Mexicans arriving in these states from 1910 to 1930. They were fleeing the Mexican Revolution of 1910, were recruited for labor during the 1920s, and became visible and permanent in the Southwest by 1930. Mexicans were also moving to other parts of the United States, including Kansas, to work in agriculture, the packing industry, and for the railroads.[5] What is noteworthy about Mexican population trends in Kansas is that their numbers were consistently small. Unlike the Southwest, their numbers in Kansas increased between 1900 and 1930, but decreased in the years preceding World War II.[6]

We argue in this chapter that even though Mexicans were not referenced in the state's school segregation laws, they were seen and treated as a racially distinct group. White parents and civic organizations pushed school officials to establish separate facilities for Mexican children. The strong parental and community involvement sheds light on the explicitly racial nature of segregation that was often obscured by pedagogical arguments made to justify the isolation of Mexican children. Within this context, Kansas City schools established a dual system of education for White and Black children.[7] By 1924, the school district developed an unofficial triracial system serving White, Black, and Mexican children.[8] In this system, the line between official and unofficial segregation for Mexicans was often blurred. We maintain that the contradictory and enigmatic responses to school segregation from both the Kansas attorneys general and Mexican consuls pointed to a degree of uncertainty about whether Mexican children could be segregated, but that ambiguity did not prevent their placement in separate facilities.

Legal Framework for School Segregation in Kansas

The legal framework surrounding school segregation in Kansas has a complex history rooted in African American struggles for educational equality after the Civil War.[9] During the years of interest here, the power of school boards to create segregated schools remained stable. Each city had a school board; the powers of those boards to create segregated schools depended on the city's population. Statutes authorized school boards in cities of the first class, with populations greater than 15,000, to "organize and maintain separate schools for the education of white and colored children, including the high schools in Kansas City, Kan."[10] The law also provided that in cities of the first class, "no discrimination on account of color shall be made, except as provided herein."[11] The law permitted school boards to create separate elementary schools based on race but did not permit segregated high schools except in Kansas City.

In cities of the second class, with populations from 2,000 to 15,000, and cities of the third class, with populations of less than 2,000, the statutes did not give school boards the authority to create separate schools for "white" and "colored" children. The statutes simply authorized those boards to "organize and maintain a system of graded schools."[12] The Kansas courts determined that the legislature did not intend to give school boards in cities of the second class the authority to establish separate schools for "white" and "colored" children.[13] Educational policies in Kansas were not as legally defined and rigid as they were in the South, where Jim Crow applied to African Americans in all avenues of life. In Kansas, however, legal segregation of African Americans was permitted in elementary schools if it was a city of the first class and was permitted at the high school level only in Kansas City.

Against this backdrop, the complexity of the segregation of Mexican children in Kansas emerges. Unlike Black students, statues did not mention Mexicans. But as they arrived in schools, White parents began to demand segregation. Their segregation appeared to depend on the power of parents and civic organizations and how school officials were able to manipulate the law. One explanation for why segregation statutes did not include Mexicans may have been their federal classification as White. The federal government granted citizenship to Mexicans living in the newly ceded territory after the 1948 US-Mexican War. "The Treaty of Guadalupe Hidalgo," said K. L. Bowman, "stipulated that former Mexican citizens were to be given 'all the rights of citizens of the United States.'"[14] Because people of color were ineligible for US citizenship during the mid-nineteenth century, the federal government categorized Mexicans as White—a political act, because most were mestizos, a combination of Spanish and Indian.[15] Because the federal government was forced to make a decision about how to incorporate Mexicans into the newly ceded territory, the treaty, said legal scholar George Martinez, turned Mexicans "into whites."[16]

The legal White category had little meaning for Mexicans in the Southwest.[17] In Kansas as elsewhere, Mexicans were not recognized as White.[18] Their experiences, in fact, were similar to those of Blacks. One characteristic that differentiated Mexicans' experiences from Blacks was access to Mexican consuls. Mexican citizens living in Kansas registered various complaints with Mexican consuls about discrimination.[19] In 1911, for example, Mexicans in Garden City were banned from all public places, and they wrote to the Mexican consul that "*no quieren que nos aserquemos a ellos*" (they don't want us to get near them).[20] In Herington, conditions were so harsh in 1915 that the Mexican consul insisted the Kansas governor intervene. Police officers broke into Mexican homes in the middle of the night searching for "Mexican offenders."[21] In 1920, Mexicans in Lyons informed the Mexican consul that they were not served in public establishments because they were seen as "GENTE DE COLOR" (PEOPLE OF COLOR).[22] In the same year, the chief of police in Salina told the Mexican consul that Mexicans were barred from White establishments.[23] The chief further informed the Mexican consul that Black establishments served Mexicans and encouraged Mexicans to open their own businesses.[24]

During this period, social conditions for Mexicans in Kansas were tense. Their White legal categorization was inconsequential; they were seen as folk of color and were unwanted in their towns.[25] Given the complaints Mexican consuls received, it was clear that Mexicans in Kansas were not seen as immigrants, akin to other European immigrant groups, but similar to Blacks.[26] With this in mind, we turn to their experiences in public schools.

The Making of a Triracial School System

KANSAS CITY

Kansas City was the center of Kansas economically and demographically, if not geographically. It grew from 82,331 in 1910 to 131,857 in 1930. It also had the largest Mexican population in the state, growing from 506 in 1915 to 2,911 in 1930. In 1930, Mexicans comprised 2.2 percent of the city's population. Their numbers in public schools were smaller because some attended parochial schools.[27] With its power to segregate Black youth at all grade levels, Kansas City was the only school district in Kansas that had an official dual education system.

The segregation of Mexican students was complicated, controversial, and paradoxical. The narrative about Mexicans in Kansas City and the Argentine neighborhood has been well explained by Judith Laird, and the school segregation of Mexican children has been closely analyzed by Robert Cleary.[28] Laird argued that from 1909 to 1924, Mexican children attended school with White children. After their numbers began to increase, "school and civil officials sought to prevent the entry of additional Mexican children in the public school system."[29] By 1924, school board officials, civic organizations, and parent-teacher groups created a triracial school system.[30] Cleary maintained that Kansas City welcomed various immigrant groups during the early twentieth century and that schools Americanized and taught them English. But when "faced with the same obligations for the children of Mexicans," Cleary explained, "race became a great concern"; Whites could not envision Mexicans as their equals and "took the same steps to exclude them as they had with African Americans."[31]

White parents noted increasing Mexican enrollments in 1918, and by 1922, school officials discussed the establishment of separate classrooms and a separate school for the Argentine and Armourdale districts within the city. White parents did not want their children sharing rooms with Mexican children, and they objected "to their children mixing with the Mexicans on the playground."[32]

A newspaper story claimed that the parent-teacher association, led by Dr. K. C. Haas, "waited upon Miguel Angel Rico, Mexican consulate in Kansas City, Mo., today and obtained his sanction to the plan of putting all Mexican children in school by themselves."[33] It was reported that about "100 Mexican children were attending Emerson school and parents wanted to take steps to reduce overcrowding and put Mexican children in a different school."[34] These complaints led school officials to move forward with establishing a Mexican school. One story suggested that school officials were as concerned about establishing a Mexican school as they were about filling it. To settle this issue, Superintendent M. E. Pearson announced that if "the Santa Fe [Railroad Company] intends making the employment of Mexican labor in the Argentine district a fixed policy, the board will order the erection of a new school."[35] Thus, if Mexican workers were going to keep their jobs, the school district would go forward and establish a Mexican school.

Consequently, it was announced that "Mexican children of all grades in the Argentine district will attend the new Mexican school at Twenty-fourth and Cheyenne."[36] School officials assured the public that the Mexican school was built "with no expense to the taxpayers," with the $7,000 expense coming from "savings in the department of buildings and grounds."[37] The "Mexican school" in the Argentine neighborhood was renamed the Clara Barton School.[38]

City planner Daniel Serda maintains that "Clara Barton originally contained three classrooms that housed approximately 125 students"—that the school averaged a forty to one student-teacher ratio and soon became overcrowded. Two additional classrooms were later added to the building in order to accommodate more Mexican children.[39]

This appears to be the first instance in a major city outside the Southwest where school officials publicly informed residents that it was establishing a separate Mexican school. Unlike most school districts across the Southwest where Mexican children were being segregated based on pedagogical and linguistic rationales, Cleary argued that there was little concern about the English proficiency of these children. School officials assumed all Mexican children were deficient in English because "no attempt to test these children in English was mentioned."[40] For Cleary, the segregation of Mexican children was based on race rather than linguistic or cultural differences.

The lack of controversy about the construction of the Clara Barton School is a mystery. Statutes permitted Kansas City to operate a dual Black/

White system of education, but because Mexicans were not mentioned in state segregation statutes, it was not clear why the Mexican school was permitted. The narrative indicated that White parents and civic organizations wanted the separate school, school district officials moved forward with the plan, the Mexican consul sanctioned it, and paradoxically, the attorney general did not intervene.

Although there was little controversy about Clara Barton, there was uproar about the exclusion of Mexicans from other schools. Two cases received much attention within one year of each other. The first case occurred in 1924, when four Mexican students were excluded from a newly constructed elementary school. The second case occurred in 1925, when a different set of four Mexican students were prohibited from attending a high school. In both instances, the actions of White parents forced Mexican youth out of the schools. In the first case, the new Major Hudson Elementary School was constructed for White students, and the old Major Hudson Annex became designated for Mexican children.[41] Mexican Consul Romulo Vargas became aware of this and contacted Kansas Governor Jonathan Davis to ask why "Mexican children who have been attending the Major Hudson School District are going to be segregated from the American children."[42] Vargas asserted that the plan would intensify segregation.

Governor Davis told Consul Vargas he would look into his complaint and wrote to State Superintendent of Public Instruction J. W. Miley about "the segregation of Mexican school children in Kansas City, Kansas."[43] Miley immediately responded that, "I fail to see where there are any evidences of oppression existing."[44] In fact, continued Miley, "it seems to me that the United States is providing better schools for Mexicans than the Mexicans provide for their own children."[45] Miley told the governor that Consul Vargas was uninformed, and he would not act on this until he heard from the superintendent of the Kansas City Schools. Miley saw "no great injustice . . . being done to the Mexican children."[46] But in a follow-up letter, Mexican Consul Benigno Cantu told the governor that these children were being segregated "chiefly for being of Mexican nationality."[47]

With the construction of the new Major Hudson School, the press reported that the district solved a "racial problem": White students would not have to attend school with the Mexican children. In fact, the press noted, the "school board proposes to keep exclusively [the old Major Hudson] for people of that race."[48] This story also reported that when four Mexican children arrived at the new Major Hudson School, "a miniature race riot broke out among the white patrons of the school, who objected to their attending at that place."[49] The issue was "cleared up when the school board assured the objectors that separate educational facilities would be provided."[50]

The press, however, did not tell the entire story. It was not just a "miniature race riot." It was a vicious protest. White protesters were so hostile that the Mexican consul contacted the governor to inform him that parents and students threatened the Mexican boys and that one of the teachers "had to call the police to protect the Mexican boys against the infuriated mob which numbered close to two hundred."[51] In September, the Mexican boys were taken out of the school. In February, the judge, citing compulsory attendance laws, ordered them to return to "either to the old Major Hudson building, which is maintained for Mexicans alone, or to the John J. Ingalls," a school with Mexican classrooms.[52]

One newspaper story described a seven-year history "of agitation against the presence of Mexican children in K.C. schools."[53] White parents at the Emerson school had "objected to the presence of Mexican children" since 1918 and, as a result, Mexican children in the Emerson School were placed in separate rooms.[54] It was ironic that while Mexican Consul Manuel Tellez noted that "Mexican children were receiving 'disparaging segregation,'" an agreement was later reached to allow the segregation of Mexican children in the early and middle grades.[55] Mexican Consul Tellez accused school officials of refusing admission to Mexican children after the fourth grade. School officials denied the allegation. However, an agreement was made that school officials could place Mexican children below the fifth grade in "rooms devoted exclusively to Mexican pupils" on the rationale that "both they and the native children progress faster when not hampered by the former's deficient knowledge of English."[56]

The story further explained where Mexican children attended school. Of the 364 Mexican children, 15 were enrolled at Cooper, 8 at Morse, 7 at Riverview, 98 at the Clara Barton "Mexican school," 31 at the old Major Hudson, and 142 at the John J. Ingalls Mexican rooms. It was not known where the remaining 63 Mexican students attended school. These figures suggest that segregation of Mexicans in the Kansas City schools was pervasive but not complete.

Nothing was said about where Mexicans attended high school, and with this as context, the second controversy emerged. Cleary maintains that the fate of the Mexican children at the new Major Hudson was "soon eclipsed by the Alvarado case."[57] Known as the "Saturnino Alvarado case,"

White parents in 1925 protested the attendance of four Mexican graduates of Clara Barton Mexican School at Argentine High School.[58] Under Kansas City's official dual system of education, Black youth attended Sumner High School, but Mexican students had nowhere to go.[59] Unlike Clara Barton and other schools that placed Mexican children in segregated classrooms, annexes, or basement floors, there were no such arrangements at the high school level. Cleary notes that the Alvarado case became complicated because school officials were unable to use "arguments of linguistic deficiency to justify segregation" and there were "no overt arguments for segregation based on race."[60]

Yet it *was* about race. When White parents protested the admission of four Mexican youth at Argentine High, school officials, purporting to support integration, mediated. School officials "authorized a separate room and teacher for the four students" and approved the cost of tuition and carfare to send the Mexican students to a nearby high school in Missouri.[61] Mexican parents refused both offers. The Alvarado case became important, Cleary states, because it was one of the first cases where a group of "dark-skinned Mexican-American students in Argentine . . . had pursued education beyond the eighth grade," and it was an "example of successful early resistance to discrimination in a relatively young Mexican American community in Argentine."[62]

As questions of segregation emerged, local newspaper stories described how the county attorney, attorney general, governor, Mexican Embassy in Washington, DC, and the US Department of State became involved and that the incident caused international conflict, a treaty between Mexico and the United States may have been violated, and a lawsuit was imminent.[63] In the end, little changed for Mexican youth. There was no international conflict, the allegation of a treaty violation was dropped, and the Alvarado "case did not proceed as a suit against the Kansas City Kansas Schools."[64]

Although the Alvarado case never went to court, it is significant because of how race and nationality were treated in public discourse. While this case was clearly about rejecting Mexican youth from a public high school, the strategy relied on the idea that "Mexican immigrants could not be legally segregated based on their racial status as Mexicans."[65] It was never mentioned that Mexicans were legally White. The argument was that Mexicans were not covered in the state's segregation laws. In the end, said Cleary, the case was "resolved" by local authorities because they realized "segregation beyond the eighth grade was hard to justify, except for racist reasons."[66] The result was that Mexicans in Kansas City were able to attend Argentine High School.

In the final analysis, school officials, White parents, and civic organizations succeeded in keeping non–high school Mexican children in separate and inferior school facilities for years to come. When health inspectors studied the conditions of the district's schools in 1939, they found that the Clara Barton Mexican School and the Major Hudson School Annex had "toilet facilities of the poorest and worst type."[67] It was not until 1949 that the city installed sanitary facilities similar to other district schools.

In short, school officials in Kansas City limited Mexican students' admission to White schools.[68] As a Kansas City superintendent told a Mexican Methodist minister in 1938: "Mexicans have no business moving or living away from the Mexican school. We would rather pay their transportation to the Mexican school than let them attend any other school in the city."[69] Given the indistinguishable line between official and unofficial school segregation, Kansas City residents must have been under the impression that its public schools had an official triracial system of education, separating White, Black, and Mexican children. Indeed, said Serda, the establishment of the "Mexican annex" at Major Hudson and the Clara Barton School "was consistent with *Plessy v. Ferguson*,"[70] the "separate but equal" doctrine aimed at African Americans. Serda seemed to suggest that *Plessy* was unofficially used to guide segregation of Mexican children in Kansas City.

BEYOND KANSAS CITY

Outside Kansas City, school districts struggled with both Mexican and Black children. The segregation of Black children depended on the size of cities and was only permitted in elementary schools. School officials in Salina, a city of the first class after 1920, had the power to construct an elementary school for "colored" children. The push to establish a Black elementary school began when the secretary of the chamber of commerce contacted Salina Superintendent W. S. Heusner about the "proposition of separate schools for white and colored children."[71] The chamber adopted a resolution recommending that the board of education establish "separate schools for white and colored children in the city of Salina."[72]

The Black community challenged the separate school, but receiving formal support from the chamber of commerce and the Rotary Club, the school board unanimously supported the resolution that "public schools of Salina should be segregated and that steps be taken looking toward a bond issue for the erection of a suitable school building for colored school children."[73] School Board President O. D. Walker explained that supporting a bond revealed an overall sentiment about the "question of the separation of colored children for school purposes."[74] The bond passed, and the school opened in 1924.

A year before the Black school opened, school officials were also interested in the "establishment of a separate school for Mexican children."[75] A Mexican school never came to fruition, but separate "Mexican Rooms" were created. Mexican children were sent to Longfellow Elementary School where they were placed in separate classrooms to teach them English and Americanize them.[76]

How Mexicans were understood racially is evident in the way school officials in Salina tracked race over time, identifying students as "white," "colored," and "Mexican." In 1933, the district reported 4,832 "white," 103 "colored," and 104 "Mexican" students.[77] By 1935, the district no longer differentiated between "colored" and "Mexican" children. The district counted "white males," "white females," and "Colored & Mexican" students. Black and Mexican children were tallied as a single group.[78]

Emporia is near Salina and was a city of the second class with few Mexicans. Carman and Associates and Ricart found there were no Mexicans in Emporia in 1900 but that the population increased to 125 in 1915, and 449 in 1930.[79] By the early 1920s, "a delegation of parents from Central Avenue district called on the board and presented a petition requesting that the Mexican children be segregated from the American children and placed in a separate building."[80] White parents asked school officials to place Mexicans in a separate school. The school board instructed Emporia's attorney to contact the attorney general to find out if the district could assign Mexican children to a separate building. Board President Peach and Board Clerk Wood received information from the attorney general that school boards of education in second class cities had "no authority to segregate children on account of race or color or condition."[81]

Because Emporia was a city of the second class, Peach and Wood told school officials and petitioning parents on January 8, 1923, that it had been clear all along that the district "had no authority to exclude from school, or segregate and place in another school, the children of any Mexican, or other foreigners."[82] Peach and Wood asserted that Mexican children needed to go to school, "learn the English language, and be Americanized as rapidly as possible."[83] Because conditions for Mexicans in the community were so poor, they told parents that "it would seem now that our only recourse is to take steps as a community to see that these Mexicans are better housed, and that sanitary conditions about their homes are improved."[84] Peach and Wood knew White parents were dissatisfied with their responses, but the attorney general clearly communicated that they could not build a separate Mexican school.

Horton sits seventy-four miles from Kansas City and was also a city of the second class. Rider Stockdale, Horton's school superintendent, wrote to the attorney general to tell him that his town had approximately 400 Mexicans and that 100 or so were attending school.[85] Stockdale believed the Mexican population was large enough to warrant a separate school. He asked if it was "possible for me to organize a ward school for Mexican children?"[86] Stockdale also wanted to know if "some of them demanded the right to attend the other ward schools, would the school district be compelled to accept them?"; and because Horton had a small Black population, he also asked if he could create "a separate school . . . for colored children."[87] The attorney general responded that as a city of the second class, Horton "has no authority to establish separate schools for either Mexican or Negro Children."[88] Similar to other school districts in the state, separate classrooms were most likely created in its schools.

Located in central Kansas, Hutchinson was a city of the first class with a population of 27,085 in 1930.[89] The Mexican community grew from 168 in 1915, to 473 by 1930.[90] In 1925, there were 5,987 "white," 245 "Black," and 159 "Mexican" students enrolled in the district.[91] By 1931, the number of "white" students increased to 6,792, "colored" enrollment dropped to 243, and "Mexican" children were at 145.[92]

Most Mexican students attended the Avenue A and Lincoln schools where they comprised one-fourth to one-third of the schools' enrollments. White parents circulated three petitions demanding the school board create a school for Mexican children. The parents, led by J. H. Dawson, a local accountant, "handed to the board members petitions signed by 390 voters in the Avenue A school district and 200 in the Lincoln district asking for a separate building."[93] Dawson asserted that Mexican children were creating problems, entering school without understanding English, and holding White children back. "[I]t takes too much of the teacher's time to get them ready for lessons, to the detriment of our children's school work," Dawson said.[94] Dawson also claimed that White parents were uncomfortable with the "environment of the foreign element in the school life."[95] He claimed that some of the Mexican children in the "lower rooms were much older than the Americans and this is another bad element, we feel. We hope," continued Dawson, "that some action can be taken by the board before another school year starts."[96] The school board agreed to meet with the parent-teacher association, and Superintendent Gowans vowed to look into a separate school for Mexican children.

Board of Education Clerk J. E. Geyer informed Kansas Attorney General W. A. Smith that they had "been requested by the White citizens of one section of Hutchinson to establish and maintain a separate school for the Mexican children."[97] He told the attorney general that the board was willing to build a separate school and thought it would help all students, but that they were not sure it was legal to do so.[98] Attorney General Smith's response was short and to the point: The "Board of Education of the City of Hutchinson has no authority to establish and maintain a separate school for Mexican children."[99]

At the June school board meeting, Superintendent Gowans reported the attorney general's response.[100] He discussed a plan that would circumvent the prohibition on building a separate school by dividing the kindergarten room into two classrooms at the Avenue A School to house Mexican children from kindergarten through third grade. Segregation of Mexican children within the school became an accepted solution by White parents and the parent-teacher association.

Mexican parents in Hutchinson filed a complaint with the Mexican consul, informing him of the school board's plan.[101] Mexican Consul Alfredo Vasquez told Hutchinson School Board President C. D. Jennings that Mexican children had "as much right to get an education as any other children in any part of the world" and demanded to know the "reason or reasons why the Board of Education wants the Mexican children separated from the American children in their studies."[102] Board President Jennings responded that Mexicans were segregated because Avenue A was their designated neighborhood school. Moreover, he explained that the school was crowded and while some White parents did not want their children to interact with Mexicans, the

> Board of Education wishes to do every thing that it can to give all children the very best of opportunities [and] felt that by giving an additional room to the school as a whole and placing the Mexican children of the kindergarten, first, second, and third grades in rooms by themselves they would receive more personal instruction than they could in the large groups.[103]

He also told the consul that the "rooms occupied by the Mexican children are newer than those housing the rest of the children of the school."[104]

This incident showed that even though Hutchinson was a city of the first class, the attorney general was clear that school officials could not construct a separate Mexican school. Yet school officials succeeded in remodeling the school to separate Mexican children—a historical moment Mexican children never forgot. Kathie Hinnen interviewed Vera Hernandez, a student who had attended the Avenue A School. She did not remark on the physical condition of the school but recalled that "they didn't want us to mix with the whites."[105]

Discussion

Local control has always been a central feature of US public schools, giving school boards and superintendents power to manage their schools. But where racial segregation is concerned, state statutes were important, and they differed across the nation. Unlike the South where a dual system of education existed, Kansas was distinctive.[106] It shared features with both Northern and Southern states. It was legal to segregate Black children in elementary schools in cities of the first class and in high schools only in Kansas City. The segregation of Mexicans in Kansas was complicated. While not mentioned in state statutes, they were seen as socially "colored," and their segregation seemed to depend on the power of White parents, civic organizations, and school officials' ability to manipulate state law.

Most Mexican parents did not have the political power to push back against White parents. They did, however, have access to the Mexican consul, who possessed limited power and was unable to prevent school segregation. Our research did not uncover underlying reasons for the varied responses of the Mexican consul to segregation, but it does reveal the significant role they played in highlighting their treatment. The mixed messages from high-ranking US and Mexican government officials adds to the complexity of this case. It is difficult to explain why the attorney general would send strong messages to school boards and superintendents that they lacked the power to construct separate Mexican schools yet failed to challenge the Clara Barton Mexican school in Kansas City. Moreover, why Mexican Consul Miguel Angel Rico acquiesced to the construction of Clara Barton remains unresolved. It is also unclear why Mexican consuls permitted segregated classrooms for pedagogical purposes. Such decisions went against the intents of Mexican consuls because they were challenging school segregation across the nation.

In Hutchinson, for example, it is not clear why Mexican Consul Vasquez would challenge school officials for creating separate Mexican classrooms and at the same time report to his superiors in New Orleans about a visit he made to a Mexican school in Kansas City. Vasquez did not name the Mexican school but indicated that it was located in the Kansas City *colonia*, that it served sixty-five Mexican students, had a principal and two teachers, teachers took interest in their students, some were performing well, and some wanted to attend high school.[107] Impressions from the attorney general and Mexican consuls seemed to suggest that it was permissible to segregate Mexican children in some locations but unacceptable in others.

White parents and civic organizations in Kansas City aggressively pushed local school officials and succeeded in keeping Mexican children in separate facilities. When White parents drove Mexican youth out of the new Major Hudson Elementary School in 1924 and from Argentine High in 1925, government officials from both nations became involved. White parents nonetheless prevailed. Mexican children were kept out of the new Major Hudson and ordered to return to schools designated for them. Argentine High was somewhat different; after the Alvarado incident, Mexican students were allowed to attend high school in the city.

Cleary maintains the Alvarado case was a partial victory because school segregation would end at the eighth grade and Mexican youth were given access to a high school education—a step forward.[108] He was correct, but we hypothesize that school officials were never concerned about opening Argentine High to Mexican youth. School officials knew their numbers would never change the racial composition of the school because very few made it that far. Cleary recognizes that Mexican attendance at Argentine did not change greatly as a result of the Alvarado case. In fact, he said, until "1939, no more than three Mexican Americans graduated from Argentine High school in any year."[109]

It is difficult to identify the precise reasons why White parents and civic organizations were so aggressive in Kansas City and less confrontational in other parts of the state. Potential explanations highlight compelling issues that Kansas raises with respect to the intersections of race, local conditions, and political power. One explanation why a separate Mexican school was permitted in Kansas City and prohibited in other locations concerns the political power Kansas City possessed, as evidenced in laws that authorized the segregation of Black high school youth only in that city. This law was established in 1905, after White parents demanded segregated high schools following the shooting of a White high school student by a Black man.[110] This incident, twenty years before the establishment of the district's unofficial triracial system, may have reminded officials of the political clout of White residents and the volatility that could arise from unresolved racial tensions. Because Kansas City was the only district in the state permitted to have separate schools for all Black children, the most expedient political option may have been to allow a segregated Mexican school in the city while prohibiting them elsewhere.

The triracial school system allowed school officials to place Mexican children in inferior school facilities. School officials boasted that the Clara Barton Mexican school was built with surplus funds and cost only $7,000. In the same year, Salina spent $65,000 for a modest Black school.[111] Furthermore, the typical school in Kansas City at the time had "a basement, two floors, ten classrooms, an auditorium and stage."[112] It seems to us that Clara Barton sent a powerful message to local residents that Mexicans were third-class citizens and what the district spent on them was all they deserved.

Paradoxically, Mexicans were seen as socially colored but they were not segregated into existing Black schools. The few who made it to the high school in Kansas City after 1925 did not attend Sumner, the Black high school, but rather Argentine High. In other Kansas locations, and on a smaller scale, school districts seemed to function as unofficial triracial systems. The Salina Public Schools, for example, educated White, Black, and Mexican children separately. Given that "Mexican and Colored" children were seen and counted as a single group, it is difficult to explain why school officials did not send Mexican children to the newly constructed Black school. One explanation was that the community passed a school bond specifically to segregate Black children. Matriculating Mexican children in that school may have gone against school bond intentions and weakened the ostensible rationale that Mexican children needed to be Americanized and learn English in separate classrooms. In other words, placing Mexican children in a Black school would reveal that Mexican children were being segregated based on race and not curricular and linguistic rationales. In the end, placing Mexican children in separate classrooms became an acceptable alternative for White parents and school officials.

Finally, other than the Clara Barton Mexican school and the "Mexican annex" at Major Hudson, segregation within White schools became the most common experience for Mexican children in Kansas. Whether it was the separate classroom or the basement floor, Mexican children learned that becoming proficient in English and being "Americanized" did not move them into the educational mainstream. What they experienced in schools was similar to how their parents were treated in their communities. If their parents were forced to live in separate *colonias*, if many businesses refused to serve them, and if they were barred from many public places, why would schools treat them differently? We assert that the segregation of Mexican children in Kansas was not driven by the schools' desire to Americanize them, teach them English, or make them full-fledged citizens. The school was not the great equalizer for Mexican children, and they were never expected to "melt" into the American mainstream.

Chapter 4

Diplomatic Relations to
School Segregation and Jim Crow

The Kansas City public schools sent a powerful message to its residents about where schoolchildren from different racial backgrounds belonged. The school district created a triracial school system that served Black, White, and Mexican children in separate spaces. Whether it was the separate classroom, an annex, the basement floor, or an individual school, Mexican youths learned that becoming proficient in English and becoming "Americans" did little to move them into the educational mainstream. Schools mirrored living conditions in their communities. That is, Mexicans lived in segregated neighborhoods, encountered many businesses that refused to serve them, and lived on the margins of American life.

Mexican consuls were receiving complaints about school segregation and Jim Crow from across the country. These grievances were being forwarded to Mexican ambassadors in Washington, DC, and to the Secretaría de Relaciones Exteriores in Mexico City. As a result, high-ranking American government officials were contacted, they were drawn in, and they became involved. But whether Mexicans were living in the South, the Midwest, the East, or the Southwest, their complaints were similar. Mexican parents were disturbed to learn that their children were largely excluded from White schools, were dismayed to find that White communities despised them, and were upset about how Jim Crow was being directed at them. As these complaints were discussed among Mexican and American government officials, school leaders from across the nation, however, often responded that Mexican children were not segregated based on race. In addition, state governors, town mayors, and local officials almost always challenged the idea that Jim Crow was directed at Mexican communities and maintained that when segregation occurred or service was denied, it was for nonracial purposes, often placing the blame on Mexicans.

We argue in this chapter that written communication between Mexican consuls, Mexican ambassadors, and the Secretaría in Mexico City unveiled that they knew Mexican children were unwanted in White schools, understood Jim Crow laws were unofficially aimed at Mexican communities, and realized Mexicans were not seen as "immigrants," but regarded as a group that was similar to African Americans. Based on archival information accessed from the Archivo in Mexico City, we provide both short and extensive vignettes about how Mexican and American government officials discussed, and responded to, school segregation and Jim Crow in the United States. These vignettes will illustrate how high-ranking American officials responded to Mexican ambassadors and consuls, and the conditions Mexicans faced in their schools and communities.

Setting the Context: Unsanctioned Jim Crow

We are mindful that Jim Crow laws in the South provided a legal structure that sanctioned segregation and discrimination against African Americans in specific states between 1876 and 1965. African Americans were relegated to separate facilities, barred from White establishments, and they were socially, politically, and economically disenfranchised. By the early twentieth century, Jim Crow laws were toughened, apartheid was institutionalized, and African Americans were experiencing hostile living conditions across the South.[1] Less is known about Mexican encounters with Jim Crow in the United States. Although not legally sanctioned, the segregation and discrimination associated with Jim Crow were also unofficially extended to the Mexican-origin population across the nation. Whether it was a single person, a small group, or larger factions, Mexicans were complaining to Mexican consuls in different regions of the United States that establishments were refusing to serve them. In St. Louis, Missouri, for example, Juan R. Almazán wrote a handwritten letter in 1911 to the Mexican consul to inform him that he was thrown out of a tavern in the city. He described how he had been invited by his coworkers to socialize in the establishment at the end of the day. When Almazán entered the tavern, he was singled out, refused service, and told to leave because he was an Indian. Almazán explained to the consul that while he was "Indio," he was under the impression that as a Mexican citizen he had political rights in the United States.[2] What Almazán experienced in the St. Louis tavern was not atypical. Although unsanctioned, individuals who looked like Almazán were rejected from many establishments across the nation. More specifically, Almazán was thrown out of the tavern because of his indigenous or mestizo appearance. This became the racial marker for Mexicans in the United States and prevented them from melting into mainstream life.

About the same time and in the same region, Mexican Consul Jack Danciger contacted Mexican Ambassador Eliseo Arredondo in 1915 to inform him about a situation he was facing with a hospital administrator in Kansas City, Kansas. Danciger sent Arredondo newspaper clippings to show how the local media was covering the case. A new hospital in the city had been built, and the old structure was converted into an annex. The annex was used to serve patients of color in general and African Americans in particular. Because Mexican patients were not being admitted to the new hospital, Consul Danciger called on Dr. George Pipkin, the hospital superintendent, to discuss the matter. Danciger asked Dr. Pipkin if the hospital was also sending Italian, Austrian, German, and other immigrant patients to the annex. Dr. Pipkin replied that they were not. Danciger then asked why they were sending Mexicans to the annex. The newspaper story indicated that Danciger was raising serious questions about the treatment of Mexicans at the hospital and that the incident had international implications.[3]

The press was not clear what the "international implication" was in this case. Danciger, however, was adamant that Mexicans needed to be treated as Caucasians and insisted that the hospital administrator and the health board "recognize Mexicans as members of the white race." Dr. Pipkin, however, refused to comply and the "international implication" did not seem to be a concern. He did not consider Mexicans to be members of the White race, defended the hospital policy, and explained that Mexicans were being treated by the same staff of physicians, were receiving the same medical care, and that "Mexicans, Chinese, Indian and negro patients" were sent to the annex, "so that they can talk to other patients of their own race or language."[4] It was clear that hospital administrators in this city refused to see Mexicans as Caucasians, or members of the White race, and served them in a "separate but equal" facility with other patients of color.[5]

In 1918, Martin Alvarado contacted Mexican Consul Guillermo Seguin to complain about how he and other Mexicans in Oklahoma City were being denied access to public parks.[6] From there Alvarado's complaint went to Mexican Ambassador Don Ignacio Bonillas and it was forwarded to the Department of State. The Department of State ordered the Oklahoma governor to investigate the case. In his response to the Department of State, the governor reported that his Commissioner of Public Property of Oklahoma City had investigated the complaint and he was informed that "Mexicans have access to these parks the same as other races, and all persons, of course, are expected to demean themselves properly while in the parks." He also noted that they were unable to find any "instances wherein Mexican have been expelled from these park grounds, and [they] assume that if any were that such expulsion was the result of misconduct on their part." He communicated that "all citizens and races must necessarily stand on the same footing, and their conduct while in public places would determine their removal or non-removal." Thus, the Oklahoma governor challenged the complaint and asserted that if Mexicans were banned from public parks in the city it was because of their own doing.[7]

In Texas, Mexican Consul Guillermo Seguin received a complaint from Manuel E. Campos and Antonio Meraz. They claimed they and other Mexicans were being denied admission to a Houston theater.[8] The Department of State ordered the mayor of Houston, A. E. Amerman, to look into the case. The mayor instantly responded and reported that his Board of Censors found that "no discrimination against any Mexican citizen . . ." had taken place. Amerman claimed that "Mexicans, along with Americans, have been refused admittance to the theaters" because they were "not clean in his clothing or his person." The mayor continued to explain that the "picture houses, especially the higher class ones, do not encourage the admission of persons to the theatres who are not cleanly, and this refusal is not based upon the nationality of the individual." Amerman also explained to the Department of State that his Board was looking into the conduct of a ticket seller who was admitting "Spaniards" but not "Mexicans." The mayor concluded that Houston theaters had no rules that refused "Mexican citizens entering, except in so far as the individual is not cleanly in his person or his clothing," that no problems existed, and he considered the case to be closed.[9]

Jim Crow practices were targeting Mexicans throughout Texas. In one community, Mexican Consul Gabriel Botello drew attention to a case where an ice cream parlor was serving Mexicans but ordered them to eat on the sidewalk. They were not permitted to eat in the building.[10] To the extent that Mexicans were being treated as second-class citizens in Texas, a group of fifty Mexicans in the town of Victoria came together and signed a petition. The petition was essentially challenging Jim Crow. The group of petitioners named a number of businesses—the Fritz and Fletcher confectionaries, the Princess and Electra theaters, and the Jackson café—that would not serve them. In this petition the group told the Mexican consul that they deserved better and, as "gente civilizada," they wanted the consul to know the social conditions they faced in the community.[11]

A similar complaint took place in Loving, New Mexico. In 1918, Mexican Consul Andres Garcia found that Mexicans were being rejected from several establishments in the community. Garcia contacted New Mexico Governor Washington Ellsworth Lindsey to inform him that a group of Mexicans had signed a petition to protest their treatment in Loving. A number of restaurants had "put up signs prohibiting the entrance of Mexicans." He added that drug stores and barbershops had followed their lead. Consul Garcia explained to the governor that the treatment of Mexicans in Loving conflicted with the war effort, particularly, the recruitment Mexican workers to solve the labor shortage in America.[12]

Mexicans were not only barred from public establishments across the nation, some were being forced out of their communities. In 1923, a race-charged conflict occurred in Johnstown, Pennsylvania, in which an African American and three policemen lost their lives. As a response, the mayor of Johnstown, Joseph Gauffiel, called on "all negros and Mexicans who have not been residents of the city for at least seven years, to leave at once." Mexican Ambassador Don Manuel Tellez contacted the Department of State to protest the expulsion of Mexicans in the city. The Department of State acknowledged that "many Mexican citizens have already left the city, that others are preparing to do so while still others are in jail." Because the Mexican community had a history of working at the Cambria plant of the Bethlehem Steel Corporation, Tellez believed the mayor did not have the authority to expel them from the city.[13] What Mexicans were experiencing in Johnstown was compelling. It was compelling because the town had a rich immigrant history, a place where Germans had deep roots in the community and where Southern and Eastern Europeans later came and settled. While Southern and Eastern Europeans faced discrimination on their arrival, they ultimately melted into the local mainstream.[14] Mexicans in Johnstown, however, had a different experience. They were not dispersed throughout the community. Most settled in Rosedale, the Black quarter. To the extent that Mexicans lived in Rosedale, the mayor did not seem to see them as immigrants but considered them to be a group similar to that of Blacks. It was not surprising that after the disturbance, the mayor called on "all negroes and Mexicans" to leave the town.

We acknowledge that African Americans were living in hostile environments in the South. They were legally subjugated and lynching became prevalent in that part of the country.[15] No other group experienced these conditions in America. The events in Johnstown, Pennsylvania, which called on both Mexicans and African Americans to leave town, remind us that historians have recently documented the brutality Mexicans experienced in the United States. Specifically, William Carrigan and Clive Webb found that between 1848 and 1928, mobs lynched at least 597 Mexicans. The causes of mob violence against Mexicans were related to race, the legacy of Anglo American expansion, economic competition, and diplomatic tensions between Mexico and the United States. Carrigan and Clive found that Mexican resistance against Anglo mobs included armed self-defense, public protest, the establishment of mutual defense organizations, and appeals to the Mexican government for protection. Carrigan and Clive sought to broaden the scholarly discourse of violence in general and lynching in particular by moving beyond the Black/White paradigm. That is, they wanted to place the experience of Mexicans into the history of lynching because, they note, it expands our understanding of how Mexicans sought to protect themselves in the United States.[16]

Between 1904 and 1924, Mexican consuls were receiving complaints from numerous towns in Mississippi. In some cases, Mexicans were being held against their will on plantations; they were not allowed to leave until their work was completed. Others were contesting police brutality, racial tension, and public intimidation. In one case, the Department of State responded to Mexican Ambassador Don Manuel de Aziroz to acknowledge "the killing of Ramon Ramos and the alleged ill treatment of other Mexican citizens near Ruleville, Mississippi."[17] Violence against Mexicans was not only taking place near Ruleville; complaints were also coming from the towns of Pascagoula, Vicksburg, and Mayersville.[18] Moreover, Mississippi Governor James Vardaman wrote to the Mexican consul to acknowledge that complaints from "about the maltreatment of citizens of Mexico" were coming from Mexicans in Bolivar, Coahoma, and Washington counties. The governor, however, quickly asserted that Mexicans were not being mistreated in those counties and that they were pleased with their conditions in their communities.[19]

In 1911, Mexican Ambassador Don Gilberto Crespo y Martinez contacted Philander Knox, the secretary of State, to inform him that Mexicans were facing hostile living conditions in Kansas. Among other things, Secretary Knox ordered Kansas Governor W. R. Stubbs to investigate the shooting of Gregorio Sogobia in Wichita, the attack on and robbery of Mr. Trinidad and Francisco Zavala, and the assault on Pablo Ramos in Macksville. Stubbs promptly responded to Knox and informed him that there was "no foundation whatsoever for any reports of this character that may have reached" the Mexican ambassador. Stubbs told Knox that there were about 4,000 Mexicans in Kansas, that most worked on the railroads, and that they generally lived in "moveable camps under conditions that do not encourage the most desirable habits of living." Stubbs continued to explain that he did not know "of more than one or two occasions, during the three years I have been Governor, where anything like a just complaint has been made by them against Americans." He refused to believe Mexicans were experiencing hostile living conditions and countered that the problem in Kansas was "between the Mexicans themselves and involves Americans only when the latter are called in, usually as officers of the law, to preserve the peace and adjust their differences." Stubbs conveyed to Knox that not all Mexicans were bad, but that "Gambling seems to be at the bottom of all their troubles. On Sundays, and holidays, and especially about pay-day," he continued, "the more irresponsible of them gather in railroads cars to while away the time in their national card games. This brings trouble in the end and they fight." Paradoxically, in light of this type of "trouble," Stubbs believed there were no problems in his state and that, as a whole, there were "satisfactory relations between the Mexicans and the Kansas people who have to deal with them. They get along very well." The governor concluded that the problem was "among the Mexicans themselves and, as it usually the case, it is brought on by the rougher fellows in the camp."[20]

The mistreatment of Mexicans in Kansas did not end in 1911. Soon after, in 1915, a complaint was sent to the Mexican consul by a group of Mexicans living in a *colonia* on the outskirts of Herington, Kansas. The group chose a fellow resident, Juan F. Velasquez, to assist them with the letter. In the petition, they pledged "that what we say in this instrument is truth and nothing but the truth." Mexicans were protesting how police officers were entering the *colonia*, searching for individuals without warrants, and were busting into their homes late at night. As they described other offenses committed against them, they made clear to the Mexican consul that the "only crime with which we are charged is that of being Mexicans."[21]

In this particular case, Mexican Consul Jack Danciger became involved. Danciger wrote a letter to Arthur Capper, governor of Kansas at the time, to explain how Mexicans were being "persecuted and ostracized" in Herington. He demanded intervention, asked the governor to "take extreme measures," and pointed out that Mexicans were just "attempting to live in said town." He asked that something be done "to prevent unjust and unlawful discrimination against Mexican citizens of your community." Danciger asked the governor what actions he was planning to take to "mitigate this outrageous conduct on the part of the citizens of Kansas."[22]

Whether it was in Missouri, Mississippi, Pennsylvania, Oklahoma, Texas, or Kansas, Mexicans were facing Jim Crow and were experiencing hostile living environments. More profound was how high-ranking American government officials generally discounted their complaints. In most cases, state governors and local officials in high positions reported that Mexicans were being treated fairly. The testimonies of Mexicans to Mexican consuls were generally discounted by American government officials. Americans in power chose to believe that, if there was any issue, the blame lay with the Mexicans themselves, and not with White society.

Historians and legal scholars have cited how Mexicans were barred from public accommodations across the Southwest.[23] They did not necessarily use the term *Jim Crow*, because these laws specifically applied to African Americans. However, "Jim Crow"–type signs targeted at Mexicans were posted on many establishments. They read: "We Serve Whites Only," "No Spanish or Mexicans," and "No Mexicans Allowed." As pervasive as these signs were, they have rarely been photographed on actual buildings.[24] With this in mind, we draw attention to how Mexicans experienced Jim Crow in Marked Tree, Arkansas. The incident not only had photographic evidence of discrimination and exclusion but an investigation of the case revealed the practice of Jim Crow was targeted against Mexicans. This incident paralleled and diverged from the experiences of African Americans. That is, both Mexicans and African Americans were relied on to provide low-cost labor, were not recognized as equal to the White population, faced discrimination, were segregated, and were kept on the margins of American life. In spite of these parallels, there were important differences. Although the discrimination and Jim Crow faced by the Mexicans was similar to that of the African American population, it was not sanctioned by law. Jim Crow laws in Arkansas mandated the separation of African Americans from Whites in multiple aspects of life, from schools to buses, restaurants, to public accommodations, and other places. While these laws called for the separation of "Negros" from Whites, there was no mention of Mexicans.[25] Moreover, Mexican laborers were recruited to work in Marked Tree, and they were Mexican citizens. This provided both affordances and constraints to Mexican workers. As a constraint, there were certain protections or advantages not available to them because they were not American citizens. However, as an affordance, their Mexican citizenship provided them access to the Mexican government, and they received some protection in the United States due to the contractual nature of their relationship that had the support of Mexican government officials. This resource was not available to African Americans.

During and after World War II, planters in Arkansas and across the South faced a shortage of cheap agricultural labor. The war had reduced the available workforce, and the economic boom in the postwar years drew many African Americans to northern and western cities. Southern planters found some relief through the implementation of the Bracero program—an agreement between the United States and Mexico to provide legal temporary Mexican labor to businesses in the United States. Thousands of braceros worked in America between 1942 and 1964. While Mexicans were dispersed throughout the United States, about 300,000 worked in the Arkansas fields between 1948 and 1964.[26]

In the town of Marked Tree, "No Mexicans" signs became familiar sights, they were photographed, and they were used as evidence by Mexican consuls to challenge discrimination. In the late 1940s and early 1950s, business establishments in the community refused to serve Mexican workers in restaurants, cafés, theaters, drug stores, and barbershops. Although the Mexican government's ability to protect Mexican citizens in the United States varied across the nation, the situation in Marked Tree illustrates a circumstance where it actively tried to protect braceros. Bracero contracts guaranteed a minimum wage, had a clause that ensured they would be paid at least equal to those of other groups working in the fields, and, more importantly, provided protection against discrimination. But as braceros encountered the Jim Crow South, they found themselves subject to segregation similar to that encountered by African Americans.[27] Indeed, the Mexican consul noted under the "Goldcrest Beer 51" café-cantina photograph that the establishment "sirve a los negros y tambien a los Mexicanos" (see figure 4.6).[28] In English, the establishment served Blacks and Mexicans. These photographs show how business establishments placed both professionally made and homemade signs that read "No Mexicans" (see figures 4.1–4.6).[29] Some businesses

Figure 4.1. *"Riverside Pool Café."* Arkansas. Courtesy of Archivo Histórico Genaro Estrada. Acervo Histórico Diplomático. Secretaría de Relaciones Exteriores. Mexico City.

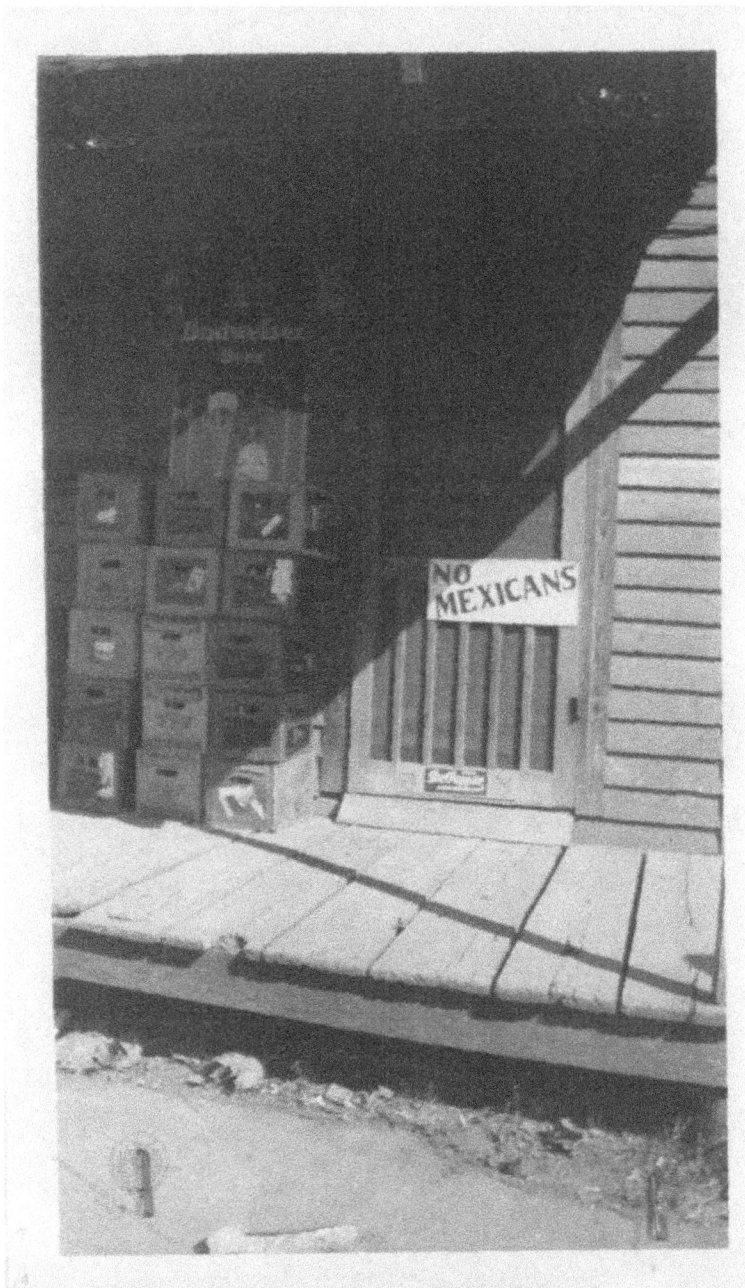

Figure 4.2. "*Ted Hendrix Grocery*." Arkansas. Courtesy of Archivo Histórico Genaro Estrada. Acervo Histórico Diplomático. Secretaría de Relaciones Exteriores. Mexico City.

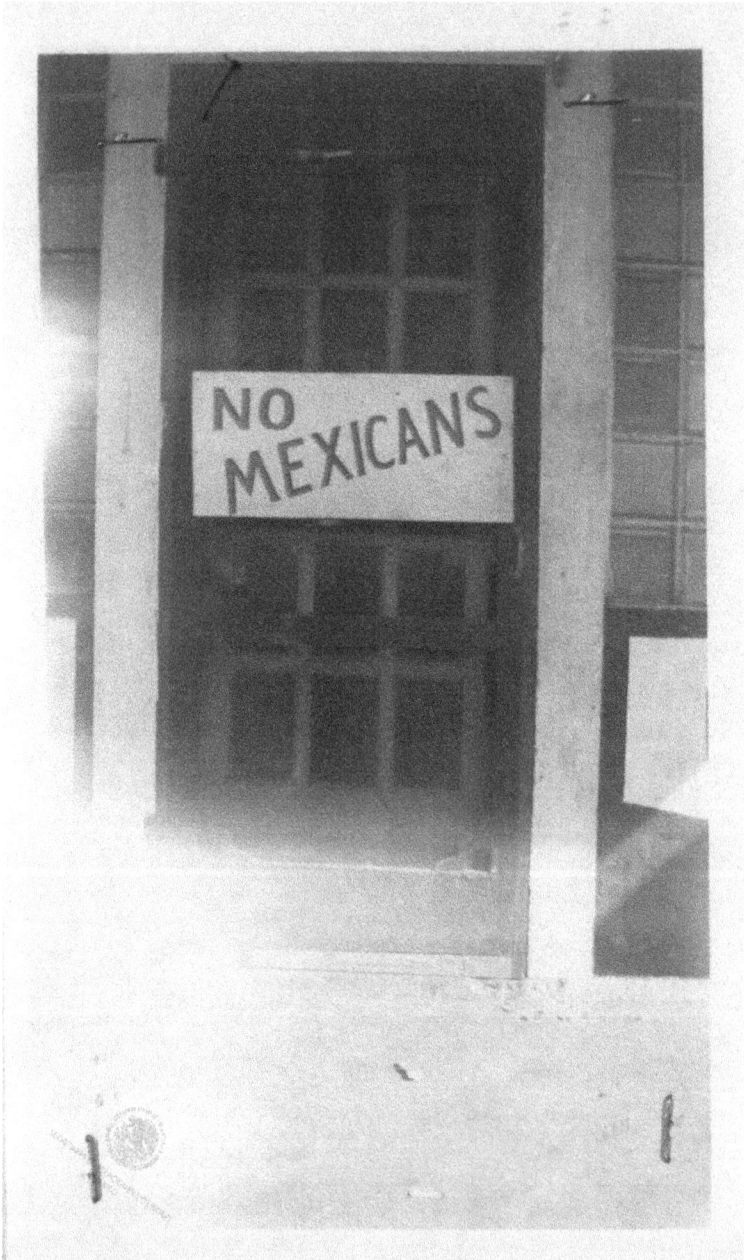

Figure 4.3. "*Come In Cafe.*" Arkansas. Courtesy of Archivo Histórico Genaro Estrada. Acervo Histórico Diplomático. Secretaría de Relaciones Exteriores. Mexico City.

Figure 4.4. *"Cracker Box Cafe."* Arkansas. Courtesy of Archivo Histórico Genaro Estrada. Acervo Histórico Diplomático. Secretaría de Relaciones Exteriores. Mexico City.

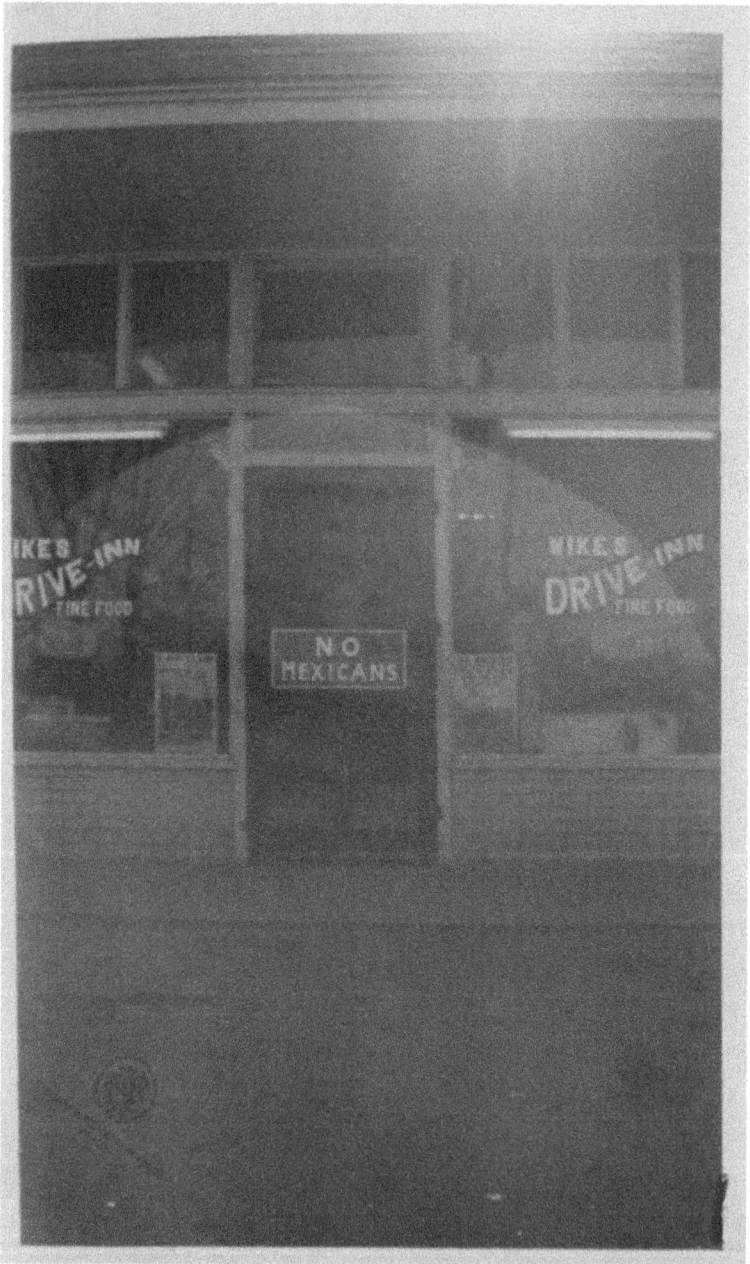

Figure 4.5. "*Wike's Drive Inn*." Arkansas. Courtesy of Archivo Histórico Genaro Estrada. Acervo Histórico Diplomático. Secretaría de Relaciones Exteriores. Mexico City.

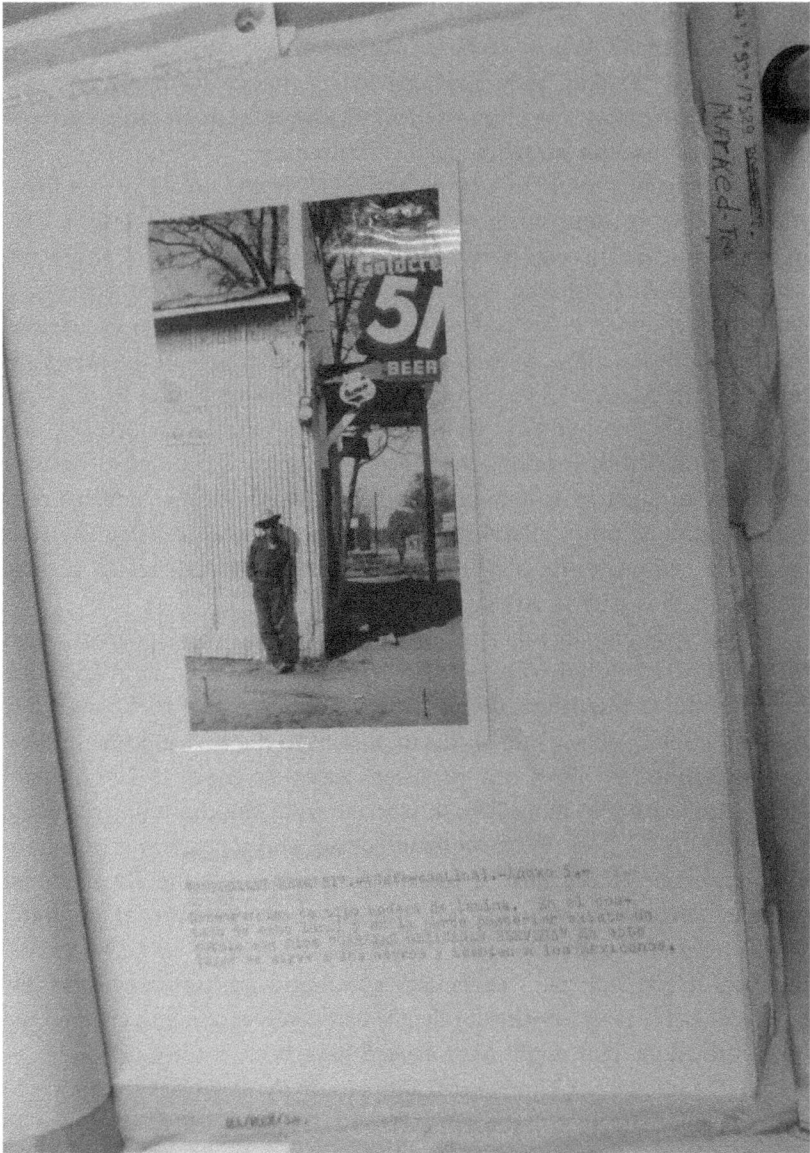

Figure 4.6. "*Goldcrest 51 Beer*." Arkansas. Courtesy of Archivo Histórico Genaro Estrada. Acervo Histórico Diplomático. Secretaría de Relaciones Exteriores. Mexico City.

did not have signs but "owners or operators stated that they did not serve Mexicans."[30] When Mexican workers encountered these signs or were refused services, they appealed for assistance from the Mexican consul. The Mexican consul pressed American officials to intervene, and an investigation was launched in the community.

Investigators found that many businesses would not serve Mexicans. Among other reasons, business owners stated that it was because they were unhygienic. Investigators tested this rationale by taking a bracero who "was dressed in clean work clothes, and sent him to several places with instructions to order coffee." As the Mexican went from business to business to order coffee, he was not served.[31] The results of the investigation gave the Mexican consul reason to use a unique tool at its disposal. Unlike other communities where Mexican families were settling and making America their home, the bracero program was different because they were brought in as temporary workers. This gave the Mexican government unique power. Because the Mexican consul knew that Mexican labor was central to the Marked Tree economy, it threatened to remove braceros in this part of Arkansas.

The economic significance of this threat becomes apparent when the response of the town is seen. Town leaders passed an ordinance that explicitly stated that it was illegal to discriminate against Mexicans. They highlighted that Mexican labor was important to the area and that if racial discrimination and Jim Crow persisted, access to Mexican labor would end.[32] Threatening to pull Mexican workers from the community became a strategy on the part of the Mexican consul, and it sparked action from local government officials. A federal employee with the Employment Services Division, responsible for administering the Bracero program, sent a telegram to the Mexican consul stating that he had checked all the cafés in the Marked Tree vicinity and found no Jim Crow signs. He reported that local government officials had taken action and claimed the "discriminations that might have existed have been corrected."[33]

In addition, the Chamber of Commerce in the town was so concerned with the labor shortage that it sent a letter noting that the quickest way to eliminate discrimination was to purchase the two businesses in the town that refused to serve Mexicans and form a committee to operate those businesses.[34] The promises made by local officials, however, appeared to be hollow and any progress a facade. That is, the "No Mexican" signs that were temporarily removed were displayed again. In a joint investigation between the Mexican consul and the Employment Security Division, they found that conditions had not changed for Mexicans. As a result, the Mexican consul pushed to have Marked Tree ineligible to have Mexican braceros in the area. The Mexican consul contacted the regional director of the US Department of Labor to inform him that the joint investigation "found racial discrimination against Mexican citizens."[35] In a Western Union Telegram, the Mexican consul explained to the regional director that discrimination against Mexicans persisted and that in spite of pledges made to treat Mexicans fairly, "we found discrimination practices widely spread." The Mexican consul issued instructions to immediately cancel work contracts in the Marked Tree area.[36] In Marked Tree, only one farmer was blacklisted, and shortly after this incident, the Mexican government gave up the power to blacklist as part of the Bracero program.[37] In other words, the Mexican government pulled back and Jim Crow continued.

This incident documents how Mexican workers were treated in the South, how "No Mexican" signs were pervasive, and how Jim Crow also targeted Mexicans. Despite the pressure local businesses faced from high-ranking American and Mexican officials and local leaders, they would not capitulate. That is, they continued to refuse to serve Mexicans in stores, theaters, restaurants, and cafés. Even though their labor was central to the town's cotton economy, treating Mexicans as White was unacceptable to business owners in the community. As Warren noted, White farmers preference for Mexican workers "collided with Arkansas society's anti-Mexican norms, despite Mexican consulate's intervention."[38]

Extending Jim Crow: Separate School Facilities

It seems to us that state governors, town mayors, and local officials almost always challenged the idea that Jim Crow was directed at Mexicans. They generally claimed that when Mexicans were denied service in public establishments it was done for nonracial purposes. Mexican consuls, however, saw why Mexicans were rejected. They knew Mexicans were being barred from public establishments because they were not White. We shift our attention to public schools. We will see how Mexican communities confronted some of the same issues in public schools. Within this context, we provide multiple narratives about how American and Mexican government officials discussed the segregation of Mexican children, the rejection of Mexican children in some schools, and how school officials justified separate facilities. We write this chapter with the understanding that language and culture were used by school leaders as pretexts to segregate Mexican children because they were not allowed to segregate them by law.

What becomes compelling in most of these cases we examine is that while American officials were asked to investigate, the investigations were led by White officials, they found only what they wanted to believe, and they did not include the voices or experiences of the Mexicans themselves. Similarly, the attempt to pass a law to segregate Mexican children in California schools failed not only because of the political work of the Mexican community, but also because White cultural organizations became involved. In addition, Mexicans filed complaints about school segregation and Mexican consuls generally responded.

In Texas, Mexican consuls in 1911 were receiving complaints about how Mexican children were being denied admission to White public schools. In the towns of Seguin (Guadalupe County), San Angelo (Green County), and Pearsall (Frio County), Mexican children were rejected in White schools.[39] In Vanderbilt, Texas, Mexican Vice Consul Mauro Castro reported to Mexican Ambassador Manuel Tellez in 1920 that several Mexican children—Ursina Amaya, F. Morales, Pedro Treviño, and Crespin Amaya—were being denied admission to White schools and were being instructed to attend a school that had previously served "la raza de color."[40] In this case, the complaint asserted that Mexican children were being sent to schools that were physically inferior and that such schools had been previously occupied by African American children.

In 1922, Mexican Consul L. Garza Leal became involved in a school segregation dispute in New Braunfels, Texas. Leal was investigating a complaint about how the school district was sending all Mexican children to a special school, a school that was serving non-English-speaking Mexican children. The correspondence between Mexican Consul Garza Leal and the New Braunfels school board president, G. F. Oheim, revealed a strong tension between the board president and the Mexican consul. Leal contacted Oheim to find out if English-speaking Mexican children were allowed to enroll in "regular American" schools in the district or if they were also required to attend the "special school."[41] Oheim replied that it was his pleasure to let Leal know that every one of their schools in the district were "regular American schools." Oheim also informed Leal that Mexican children were "not segregated on account of race or nativity, and that they, if qualified, may enter high school the same as other children."[42]

Oheim, however, did not respond to Leal's question about whether English-speaking Mexican children were allowed to attend regular schools in the school district. As a response, Leal wrote a letter to the *San Antonio Daily Express* to describe how school officials in the school district were sending all Mexican children to a separate school and were "denying them the privilege of entering the high school of your city other than the segregated school for Mexicans." Oheim contacted Leal to inform him he had read the article in the *San Antonio Daily Express* and explained that "Mexican children entering the elementary grades of our public schools are instructed separately and by special teachers in a building erected to make it possible to give them this advantage. They are segregated," he continued, "not on account of their race, but for pedagogical and administrative reasons; not knowing any English and learning this language slowly and with difficulty, these children cannot keep up with others and require special instruction."[43]

Consul Leal knew all Mexican children were being sent to the segregated Mexican school. With this in mind, Leal asked the New Braunfels Mayor, D. G. Blumber, to intervene. Blumber refused to arbitrate, explained he was "not in a position to inform [him] on that subject,"[44] and claimed the issue was out of his control.

The segregation of Mexican American children was increasing in Texas. It was so widespread that Mexican consuls were receiving complaints from different parts of the state. One consul in Texas, Enrique Ruiz, wrote a personal note to the Mexican Ambassador. He informed him how his office was overwhelmed with school segregation complaints. Despite the pressure his office was facing in his region, Ruiz expressed his commitment to challenge segregation, he refused to surrender, promised to push forward, and assured the ambassador that his office was going to respond to all incoming complaints.[45]

Like Texas, Mexican consuls in California were also receiving complaints about the segregation of Mexican children. In a Western Union Telegram in 1919, Mexican Ambassador Ignacio Bonillas wrote to California Governor William Stephens to inform him that he had received notice from Mexican Consuls R. P. De Negri and J. Garza Zertuche that Mexican children were being segregated in public schools in southern California. The message went on to explain that Mexican children were barred from White schools and were being sent to Black schools in the towns of El Centro and Santa Paula.[46]

The Department of State ordered California to investigate the complaint. The governor, as a response, directed the California State Superintendent of Public Instruction, Will C. Wood, to conduct an investigation.

Within weeks, Wood responded and informed the governor that he had "made an investigation of the matters contained in communication from R. P. De Negri, Consul General of Mexico, and J. Garza Zertuche, Consul for Mexico, which was addressed to you on June 7, 1919." Wood also reported that he had received written communication from a number of county superintendents about the segregation of Mexican children in their schools. Wood briefly reported on Ventura, Imperial, Los Angeles, Orange, San Bernardino, and San Diego counties. In Santa Paula (Ventura County), Wood found that Mexican children were segregated in the first two grades. He explained that Mexican children were not segregated because of nationality but because they were non-English-speaking and unable to function in English speaking environments. He asserted that the segregation of Mexican children was an "advantage, since they need special attention." At the Briggs School District (Ventura County), Wood found that there were two school buildings; in one (Rancho Lemoneria) "all the children are Mexican" and the other had few Mexicans but it was mostly White. On this point, Wood was informed that "no segregation [was] ordered by the school board." They maintained that segregation was "natural" because "Mexicans live in a settlement by themselves" and attended schools near the *colonia*. At Saticoy (Ventura County), Wood found that the district also had two buildings; one enrolled Mexican and American children but it was mostly White. In the other "only Mexicans are enrolled. Segregation at Saticoy," noted Wood, "is based on the fact that the Mexican children have not sufficient knowledge of English to do the work that American children can do."[47]

In Imperial County, Wood reported that Mr. A. P. Shibley, the county superintendent, described how "eight years ago the board of trustees of the El Centro School District opened a school in the east side of the city. This served mainly the colored and Mexican population." Wood was informed that Black teachers were hired in the school district, that they were "graduates from our own California State Normal Schools," and that they were serving Mexican children. He was told that Mexican children who had lived on the west side of the track "attended the black school." Wood was informed that Mexican children attended the black school because they had "chosen their places of residence and by so doing have determined where they shall attend school." Wood explained that school boards knew they did not have the legal power to segregate Mexicans, but they were segregated "because it was better for the Mexican children to have a teacher who could give all of his time to them." Thus, he was told that segregation was done for instructional purposes.[48]

In Los Angeles County, County Superintendent Mark Keppel reported to Wood that communities wanted to "to put the Mexicans by themselves." The superintendent explained that he had tried to stop segregation and ordered the school board to obey the law. However, he asserted Mexican children were segregated in order to place them with instructors who could focus on them. He believed school segregation was carried out in his county to give Mexican children an "advantage and not for the disadvantage of the children who are seemingly segregated."[49]

In Orange County, superintendent R. P. Michell reported that Mexican children were not excluded from public schools and that they were not taught by Black teachers. However, he explained how "separate rooms for these children" were created because they "do not know our language when they come to us and do not advance as rapidly as the white children." Superintendent Michell also reported that the Santa Ana school board is "erecting two school buildings for Mexican children. The Mexican children will attend these schools until they are able to do regular grade work." More compelling was how superintendent Michell explained how the "city attorney here ruled that children could be placed in rooms or buildings according to their ability to learn."[50]

In San Bernardino County, County Superintendent Grace C. Stanley informed Wood that no segregation had been tried in her county. She knew that the segregation of Mexican children was against the law. However, she described how school boards were "placing schools in the neighborhoods where the Mexican children lived, the boundary lines established by the boards place the Mexicans by themselves." Stanley's point was that school boards knew they did not have the authority to segregate Mexican children but they drew school boundaries to make sure Mexican and White children attended different schools.[51]

J. F. West, the Superintendent of Schools in San Diego, reported that "there are no segregated schools for Mexican children in San Diego County, with the possible exception of National City, where they established a school in the Mexican quarter." The superintendent explained that "inasmuch as there are no white children living in that community, no discrimination exists. In case these Mexican children desire to attend the other schools, the Board grants them permission, so everything is peaceful."[52]

State Superintendent Wood concluded that based on his "investigation I am clearly of the opinion that there has been no segregation of Mexican children in California on the grounds of nationality or race. Where segregation has been ordered, and this is true in only a few instances, the segregation has been based upon the fact that the children segregated had no knowledge of the English language, and for that reason could not carry the same work as the children of American parentage." Wood explained that "such segregation based upon such grounds is not only perfectly legal but eminently desirable from the standpoint of the non-English speaking children."[53] Thus, in 1919, Wood was convinced by county school superintendents that Mexican children were not segregated based on race, but because of language deficiencies, their assumed inability to keep pace with White children, their need for special teachers, and their residential segregation in *colonias*. We found state superintendent Wood's report to the governor to be incomplete. The report was based on his observations and the written communication with several county superintendents. Nowhere in the report were the opinions or voices of Mexican parents in those communities.

Mexican consuls, however, knew school officials in California were segregating Mexican children based on race. They recognized how school leaders were using language, pedagogy, academic "unpreparedness," and location of schools as pretexts to keep Mexican children segregated. As school segregation increased in California, Mexican consuls recognized that Mexican children were being treated differently than children from other immigrant groups. On this point, when Mexican Consul Guillermo Seguin was informed by the California governor and state superintendent that Mexican children were being segregated in the early grades, he wanted to ask the following question: "si esta segregacion de niños de los grados inferiores ocurre unicamente con los de nacionalidad mexicana o incluye a otras nacionalidades tales como las de Italianos, Portugueses, Griegos, etc."[54] In English, Seguin wanted to ask the governor and state superintendent whether segregation in the early grades was exclusive to Mexicans or if it also included Italian, Portuguese, and Greek children. The spirit of Seguin's proposed question was that Mexican children were not being treated like other immigrant groups. Mexican Consul Ramon DeNegri, moreover, went further. He expressed to the secretaría and the Mexican ambassador that "El Mexicano, en vista de que sus condiciones economicas son muy parecidas a las del negro, es clasificado como este y recibe el mismo tratamiento."[55] In English, DeNegri claimed that because the economic conditions of Mexicans were similar to that of Blacks, they were classified as such and receive the same treatment.

Since 1919, school authorities in California used various strategies to keep Mexican and White children in separate classrooms or separate schools. More compelling was how the state superintendent was able to convince the governor that Mexican children needed to be segregated because they were not proficient in English and because they were unable to academically keep pace with White children. What was being argued by high-ranking education officers and government officials in 1919 continued into the 1920s and beyond. San Miguel and Valencia maintained that a template for the future of Mexican American children was established by the early 1930s: "Forced and widespread school segregation and inferior schooling."[56]

Drawing on this idea, we turn to Mission, Texas. In Mission, a school segregation lawsuit was brewing but the case did not go to court. This incident reveals how Mexican voices bring a different type of challenge that the Mexican consul was often not able to bring, revealing the reasoning of the school board for segregation as a sham. The complaint was about how the Mission School Board of Education decided to construct a junior high near the Mexican *colonia* and how Mexican children were being denied admission to the district's White junior high school. Mission is located near the US-Mexican border. The case was complicated because both Mexican citizens and Mexican American children were involved. In fact, Mexican Consul Lauro Izaguirre reported to the Secretaría that Mission had about 952 Mexican origin school-age children in the community and, of that number, 20 percent were Mexican citizens.[57] Because Mexican consuls could only assist Mexican nationals, they were careful in their intervention. In this case, the Mexican consul monitored the complaint, and a decision was made for Mexicans with US citizenship to lead the charge against segregation. As the Mexican and Mexican American community prepared to challenge the Mission Independent School District, they gathered demographic information, acquired a blueprint of the city that illustrated the location of the schools in question, and collected relevant information about where all children in the district were attending school.[58]

Calling themselves Los Padres de South Mission, a group of Mexican American parents met, organized, wrote a letter, and presented their case at a school board meeting. Los Padres expressed to the board that they were displeased with the board's decision to build a "vocational" junior high school near the *colonia*, asked why their children were being rejected at the Morgan Junior High, and were dismayed that their children did not have access to a rigorous curriculum. Los Padres accused school board members of "racial segregation," asserted it was illegal, that it violated their rights, and that the decision to build the vocational junior school near the *colonia* as a "matter of convenience" was deceitful, discriminatory, and unjust.[59]

Los Padres exhibited a graph that showed that a number of White children who lived in the south side of Mission were "allowed and permitted to attend the Morgan Junior-Hi school." They argued that these children were "being allowed to do so for no apparent reason other than they are not of Mexican or Spanish descent." Los Padres also politicized race. They politicized it in a way they thought would strengthen their argument. They maintained school board members were not recognizing their children as "Caucasian" or members of the "white race." They proclaimed their children were White, wanted them to attend the Morgan Junior High School, and refused to comply with a board policy that was forcing their children to attend the segregated "Mexican Junior High." From their perspective, school board members were segregating their children "on account of race, color, sanitary, health or economic conditions." If the junior high was built as a matter of convenience, they wanted to know why they were not sending White children who lived on the south side to the school so they could be "with children of Mexican or Spanish extraction." In addition, Los Padres expressed how they wanted their children to be exposed to a more rigorous curriculum so they could prepare for high school and college.[60]

As American citizens, Los Padres maintained they were property owners in Mission, that they paid taxes, and stressed again that their children were "descendants of the Caucasian or white race." What school board officials were doing in the school district, they said, was an "open violation of the fourteenth Amendment to the Constitution of the United States, and section 1 of Article 7, Section 7 of Article 7, and Section 19 of Article 1 of the Constitution of the State of Texas, and of Articles VII and IX and Article IX as Amended, of the Treaty of Guadalupe Hidalgo made and entered into by and between the United States of American and the Republic of Mexico, under date of February 2nd 1848" (*sic*).[61]

Los Padres not only raised legal issues, they also presented moral, patriotic, and social concerns. That is, they wanted their children to not only attend good schools, they wanted them in school environments that allowed them to become good "American citizens." They discussed the importance of integration, wanted their children "to intermingle with other children attending the same public free schools," and believed that such environments would foster "lifelong, true and sincere friends in the most democratic of all institutions." That is, they believed such values and friendships were only attainable though "OUR PUBLIC FREE SCHOOLS." Los Padres, in short, protested segregation, claimed it was unjust, and that "no good can come of such separation since it will only retard or practically make it impossible for our children to learn the English language, to Americanize and raise themselves to the standard of true, useful American citizens."[62]

Within ten days, the Mission School Board responded to Los Padres de South Mission. The Board immediately countered that "no segregation of children exists in the Mission Public Schools." They told Los Padres that some students of the "Anglo-Saxon race are now and have been attending the South Mission Junior High school for full time since school started last September." They challenged that strict segregation existed and pointed out how Ernestine Sanchez, Ramon Gonzalez, Mary Flores, Joe Longoria, and Lucile Longoria were attending the Wilson Elementary School. Wilson was the district's White elementary school. They also claimed that a number of Mexican children "are now and have been attending the Morgan Junior High Schools since last September." The problem, the School Board maintained, was that they did "not have the room in the Morgan Junior High School to accommodate all children of Junior High School age that live in the Mission Independent School District. Every room in the Morgan Junior High School is now in use at the present time." The school board challenged racial segregation and claimed "boys of both races have played together on our athletic teams all this year, have attended the same social functions and sat down together at the same table when banquets were held," and reiterated that the prevocational school was constructed to relieve overcrowding at the Morgan Junior High School.[63]

School board members also argued that they had worked hard to maintain a first-class school district and pointed out that ten years earlier they had received an award for the "Americanization of children of Spanish descent in the Roosevelt school by the Secretary of Labor." In their challenge that the vocational junior high was only going to offer manual training, they claimed the school would have courses in modern business, general science, and nature study. The school board concluded that it had done everything within the law and urged the Mexican American community to "cooperate with us in the education of all the children of the people in our community."[64]

In retrospect, school board members straddled a fine line between legal and illegal segregation. That is, they allowed a very small number of Mexican American children to attend White schools and sent a few White students to the vocational junior high school in south Mission. Although Los Padres and the school board did not discuss Mission High in great detail, the school was predominantly White. However, some Mexican youth were attending the high school and a small number were graduating.[65] In the end, the school board refused to respond to the claim that Mexican children were White, they challenged the idea that their schools were segregated, and they manipulated the racial composition of schools in ways that allowed them to maintain segregation.

The Bliss Bill

Mexican ambassadors and Mexican consuls knew school boards from across the nation were segregating Mexican children based on race. Nevertheless, almost all school leaders were arguing that Mexican children were being segregated for educational purposes. There was one attempt, however, where government officials moved from these pedagogical rationales and tried to legally segregate Mexican children on the basis of race. Irving Hendrick noted that on "January 23, 1927 the California Attorney General offered the opinion that Mexicans were Indians, thereby permitting school districts to segregate them."[66] It was the California attorney general—Ulysses S. Webb—who prompted others to try to pass a law that would permit school officials to legally segregate Mexican children. The school code at that time read that the "governing body of the school district shall have the power to establish separate schools for Indian children and the children of Chinese, Japanese or Mongolian parentage."[67] On January 19, 1931, Assemblyman George R. Bliss introduced Assembly Bill 433. The bill would amend section 3.3 of the school code to give school districts the power to "establish separate schools for Indian children, whether born within the United States or not."[68] The amended language to give school leaders the legal authority to segregate Indians who were "born within the United States or not" was key. Without mentioning Mexicans, they wanted to legally segregate them because of their indigenous roots.

As we examine the politics of the "Bliss Bill," we want to add to the narrative by highlighting additional points. In contrast to White officials who wanted to maintain school segregation in the previous section, we highlight the involvement of White cultural groups and others who opposed the bill. After the bill was introduced, a number of activist groups became involved. These groups and organizations pushed state politicians to vote against the bill. Lillian Hill, chief of the Bureau of Attendance and Migratory Schools, was one of them. She became an articulate observer and one of the more forceful critics of the bill. She understood the consequences of the bill, what it meant for Mexican children, and communicated with powerful politicians in the state to vote against the bill. Hill corresponded with California Senator Herbert W. Slater. She informed Slater that the bill was nothing more than a veiled attempt to empower school boards of education to "segregate Mexican children and set up separate schools for them." Hill explained that Mexican children were already segregated in the state and were attending "Mexican schools. . . . [that were] . . . extremely inferior." She also made clear that the bill targeted Mexican children because of their indigenous heritage. She told him it was "un-American and unjust."[69]

Hill also explained to the senator that the bill was not only about segregating Mexican children; it was also a strategy for some Americans to keep Mexicans apart "from normal life in the community." As head of the Bureau of Attendance and Migratory Schools, Hill described how some Americans wanted Mexican children out of schools and sought to work "these Mexican children . . . like slaves in the agricultural fields." She described how some American communities were already refusing "to give Mexican children any type of education—allowing them to work in the fields during the entire day." Others were allowing these children to attend school part of the day. Hill told Slater that Mexicans did not want to be segregated. As a case in point, she referred to the San Diego case (i.e., *Alvarez v. Lemon Grove*) that had already been tried and how it failed. She explained to the senator that the "judge decided against the school board and ruled that these children should return to the Central School." Hill noted how a school board member had publicly pronounced that if they failed to segregate Mexican children, they would "slip a bill thru this legislature which will fix it so we can segregate these greasers." In the final analysis, Hill understood the consequences of segregation and how it was encouraging the "superiority among the American children and a most devastating feeling of inferiority among our adopted children." She told the senator that the bill was a "dangerous piece of legislation."[70]

A number of cultural organizations also challenged the bill. Nellie Foster, the executive secretary of the Inter-Racial Council of San Diego, wrote a letter to Mr. Aceves, the editor of the *Hispano-Americano*, to inform him that a number of groups and organizations were pushing politicians to vote against the bill. They had garnered support from social workers, the Women's Civil Center, and the International House at the University of California at Berkeley, led by Allen C. Blaisdell. Blaisdell, in fact, asked permission to deliver a presentation about the "segregation of Mexican children in this country at the California Conference of Social Work."[71]

Although he did not become involved with the Bliss Bill, Mexican Consul Enrique Ferreira reported to the secretaría that it would have a devastating effect on Mexican children because most were mestizos. In Spanish, Ferreira believed ". . . a la segregacion de todos los niños de origen indio y con el que resultaria afecados muchos de los mexicanos residents en este Estado de California." In English, because the proposed law targeted Mexican children with indigenous roots, it would have a serious impact in the state. Ferreira was optimistic, however, because opposition to the bill was coming from American cultural organizations.[72]

Mexican consuls in California knew the bill aimed to legally segregate Mexican children because of racial differences.[73] The editor of the *Independent Daily News*, a liberal newspaper in southern California, wrote that the bill "to segregate school children of Mexican birth is so outrageous and preposterous that it would hardly seem necessary to point out the injustice of its provisions." While the bill was directed at Indian children, "its real purpose was to discriminate against a race that has contributed substantially to the civilization and progress of the territory now known as California." The children targeted were of Mexican birth or descent. It was "inconceivable that any Californian should propose a restriction that savors of the 'Jim Crow' prejudices of race-baiting." The *Independent Daily* concluded that Americans needed to bring Mexicans in so they could admire and respect American institutions. What the Bliss Bill was trying to do, it said, was to treat Mexicans "like pariahs or wild animals."[74] In the end, the Bliss Bill failed. It did not go forward. According to the editor of the *Hispano Americano*, Mexican children were not going to be legally segregated in public schools. While editor Aceves knew its newspaper coverage had made a difference, he believed the bill was defeated because of the efforts and pressure that came from American cultural organizations.[75]

Mexican challenges to school segregation and Jim Crow reached the highest levels of government in the United States. Although segregation was intended for African Americans in specific states, Mexican ambassadors and Mexican consuls knew these laws unofficially targeted Mexicans in their schools and communities. That is, no state in the nation sanctioned school segregation and Jim Crow for Mexicans. However, Mexicans were targeted by these laws. These developments gained momentum during the early twentieth century. We will see in the next chapter that Mexican Americans continued to resist school segregation. They challenged school segregation through the courts in specific states.

Chapter 5

Legally White, Socially "Mexican," 1930–1947

We saw in chapter 4 how the segregation of Mexican children in public schools was an extension of unofficial Jim Crow. State superintendents and school boards of education were reporting across the nation that Mexican children were not segregated based on race. They maintained that Mexican children were segregated because of language, pedagogy, and because they were academically unprepared to thrive in mainstream classes. In 1919, California State Superintendent Will Wood seemed to convince the governor that it was "perfectly legal" to segregate Mexican children to meet their educational needs. Mexican ambassadors and Mexican consuls, however, knew Mexican children were segregated based on their mestizo appearances. They knew Mexicans in schools were not treated like Italian, Portuguese, Greek, and other immigrant children. Indeed, we saw how Assembly Bill 433 attempted to legally segregate Mexican children. They wanted to modify the California School Code to establish separate schools for Indian children, whether they were born in the United States or not. Although not specifically stated in the Bill, it sought to segregate indigenous Mexican children. Lillian Hill not only saw how the Bill would legally segregate Mexican children, she explained how it would make it easier for those in power to keep them out of schools and in the agricultural fields. She emphasized how schools were already segregated in the state and how it was fostering a climate of superiority among White students and inferiority among Mexican children.

In Mission, Texas, Mexican Americans were challenging school segregation in 1931. Los Padres de South Mission challenged the location of the new vocational junior high, asked why their children were being rejected at Morgan Junior High, and wanted their children to have access to a curriculum that prepared them for high school and beyond. In addition, they not only claimed they were tax-paying Americans, they also maintained that their children were members of the White race. Their arguments, however, fell on deaf ears. School board members strategized, allowed a very small number of Mexican children to attend White schools, sent a few White students to the vocational school, and they were able to maintain a predominantly segregated school district. We will see in this chapter that Mexican Americans continued to resist school segregation; however, we shift our attention away from correspondence and to the courts.

Since the civil rights era, scholars have produced a proliferation of studies that tried to understand the politics of school segregation, school desegregation, and school integration.[1] Two issues are unequivocally clear from these studies: first, de jure segregation, as shown by state statutes and constitutional provisions requiring racial segregation in schools, reflected the desire of Whites to intentionally separate students based on race; and, second, given the attention the *Brown* decision and its aftermath received, Americans have come to understand school segregation as a Black-White issue.[2]

We have noted that Mexican Americans have a long history of resistance to school segregation in the United States.[3] This history, however, did not receive much media attention, some cases were largely ignored in education literature, and the 1914 *Francisco Maestas et al. v. George Shone et al.* case was actually lost in history.[4] With this in mind, legal scholar Kristi Bowman notes that although plaintiffs brought successful challenges to Latino segregation in public schools before *Brown*, the Court made no mention of those cases, or any reference to Latinos, in its 1954 decision. *Brown* ushered in an era of viewing school desegregation in a Black-White binary.[5]

Even those who are familiar with Mexican Americans' educational and historical experiences in the American Southwest are unclear about the intricacies of their segregation. It is not clear whether Mexican Americans experienced de facto or de jure school segregation.[6] At the most basic level, de facto segregation is a condition that occurs "naturally" by fact (i.e., due to housing patterns). In contrast, de jure segregation is imposed by law. The courts used these two terms after the *Brown v. Board of Education* decision to make distinctions between government-mandated racial segregation (de jure) and segregation attributed to private, market-based developments (de facto). As court battles raged over school segregation in the late 1960s and 1970s, this distinction became important because the courts used it to define the limits of their own authority to intervene to end segregation. De jure segregation resulted from intentional governmental actions over which the courts could exercise their oversight; de facto segregation was outside the reach of the judiciary because the courts viewed it as resulting from the interaction of private actions and government actions that were prima facie not discriminatory.[7]

Unlike the de jure segregation African Americans experienced in the American South before *Brown*, the segregation of Mexican Americans has been framed by scholars as de facto because it was the product of local custom and because state governments in the Southwest never sanctioned it. On this point, legal scholar Ariela Gross explains that "most segregation of Mexican Americans was de facto rather than de jure, set in place by custom and local administration rather than state statute."[8] In a sense, Gross is correct. There were no state statutes in the American Southwest that authorized the segregation of Mexican American children in public schools.

However, the idea that the segregation of Mexican Americans was de facto needs to be challenged. Gilbert Gonzalez, for example, argues that "although there were no laws that mandated the practice of segregation, educators did invoke the state power granted to school administrators to adapt educational programs to the special needs of a linguistically and culturally distinct community."[9] Gonzalez further argues that de jure segregation existed in California as a result of local policies made before the 1946 *Mendez v. Westminster* decision, which found that the segregation resulting from such policies was unconstitutional. If segregation continued to exist in California after the *Mendez* decision, he notes, it "would be de facto; the era of de jure segregation, however, had ended in California."[10]

Gonzalez makes a compelling point, but his valuable analysis also illustrates why the distinction between de facto and de jure segregation for Mexican Americans must be addressed. He notes that even though California did not have a state law that authorized the segregation of Mexican Americans, they were in fact experiencing de jure segregation before 1946. He points out that segregation of Mexican Americans was not the result of private actions but of decisions made by school administrators and boards of education. Deconstructing the tension between de jure and de facto segregation, however, was not the central point of Gonzalez's book, and the distinction between de facto and de jure segregation was also underdefined. His point was that the various aspects of segregated schooling—Americanization, testing, tracking, industrial education, and migrant education—were parts of a single system that was designed to process Mexican children as a source of cheap labor and that such segregation perpetuated the low status of the Mexican community within the larger political economy.[11] Similarly, while Guadalupe San Miguel and Richard Valencia note that there "were no legal statutes that mandated such racial/ethnic isolation" for Mexican Americans in the Southwest, once again the politics of de jure and de facto segregation was not a central theme of the study.[12]

Being clear about de jure and de facto is important because how we understand the nature of segregation affects how we think about and address this history. Most Americans do not realize that Mexican American school segregation was widespread in the American Southwest. In fact, segregation was so common, noted Gonzalez, that "in the mid-1930s one study found that 85 percent of surveyed districts in the Southwest were segregated in one form or another, some through high school, others only through the fifth grade."[13] David Montejano also observed that "90 percent of South Texas schools were segregated."[14] Finally, noted San Miguel and Valencia, by the "beginning of the 1930s, the template for the future of Mexican American education was formed. Forced and widespread school segregation and inferior schooling of Mexican American children became the norm."[15] Labeling this "forced and widespread" pattern in the American Southwest as de facto segregation is troubling, however. It allows for easy dismissal of the impact and intentionality of policy decisions made at the local level, and it can hide the deliberate and racial nature of the segregation Mexican Americans experienced.

In this chapter, we argue that de jure segregation occurs when government action results in the segregation of students based on race—regardless of whether that policy is a law mandating segregation at the state level or a decision by local school officials that facilitates racial segregation. We further argue that de jure segregation occurs whether or not the rationale is explicitly racial. Given the social history of Mexican Americans in the Southwest, we believe it is justified to infer that policies resulting in the segregation of Mexican American students were intended to keep them apart from White children, no matter the pedagogical or other rationale provided, and should retroactively be considered de jure segregation.

To support this argument, we examine the social status of Mexican Americans in the Southwest. Unlike African Americans, who were treated as "colored" by the majority White society and whose legal status also reflected their social status, the experiences of Mexican Americans were extremely complex. They were categorized as "White" by the federal government in the Treaty of Guadalupe Hidalgo in 1848, a label that became a double-edged sword for Mexican Americans for more than a century. On the one hand, Mexican Americans used their White status as a strategy to challenge school segregation.[16] On the other hand, their White status was sometimes used against them in that their claim of racial discrimination was not viable because they were legally White.[17] Legal scholar Richard Delgado argued that categorizing Mexican Americans (i.e., Latinos) as White became a strategy to justify the idea that they could not be subjected to racial discrimination.[18] Or, as Gross noted, "Mexican Whiteness was a cynical trump used by the courts to dismiss discrimination claims."[19]

Although Mexican Americans were categorized as White within the legal system, evidence shows that they were treated as people of color in the American Southwest.[20] As Gross points out, "Mexican Americans suffered many of the same Jim Crow practices as African Americans. Not only were they excluded from many public accommodations, like swimming pools, theatres, and restaurants, but more importantly, from the key institutions of public life."[21] Like the infamous sign that read "Colored Only" in the American South, it was common to see signs in many establishments that read "Mexicans and Dogs Not Allowed" in Texas and across the nation.[22]

Neither the American public (i.e., Anglo Americans) nor the American educational system, we argue, recognized Mexican Americans as "White" because most Mexican Americans were racially mixed (i.e., mestizos). The courts, however, were cautious about making decisions based on race because judicial officials knew the US government categorized Mexican Americans as White. Indeed, the courts struggled with the racial status of Mexican Americans, and questions of race were only sometimes acknowledged, but often negated or left unresolved.[23]

This tension between the legal status and social status of Mexican Americans should inform our understanding of why school officials and school boards of education made decisions to segregate Mexican American children.[24] More than anything else, the segregation of Mexican Americans is best understood as reflecting the discrimination that accompanied their colored social status in American life, as opposed to viewing their segregation as the result of benign pedagogical decisions or the fortuitous conjunction of where they lived and where school boundaries were drawn.

Against this backdrop, we examine three desegregation cases—*Independent School District v. Salvatierra, Alvarez v. Lemon Grove,* and *Mendez v. Westminster*—to make sense of Mexican Americans' legal and social experiences.[25]

The Racialization of Mexican Americans

The racial classification of Mexican Americans was complicated from the very beginning; it was politicized and changed over time. Mexicans were categorized as White in 1848 by the US government in order to grant them US citizenship, but their eligibility for citizenship was challenged in Texas in 1897 in *In re Rodriguez*.[26] The US Census changed their White status to "Mexican race" in 1930 and back to "White" in 1940. In 1954, the Supreme Court decided in *Hernandez v. Texas* that Mexican Americans were a distinct class, separate from Whites, and in 1970, *Cisneros v. Corpus Christi ISD* determined that Mexican Americans were an "identifiable ethnic-minority group."[27] Through these events, the racial classification of Mexican Americans was constructed, challenged, altered, and modified again.

The decision to classify Mexicans as White was made under international pressure after the US-Mexican War in 1848, when decisions were being made about how to incorporate large numbers of Mexicans living in the newly ceded territory. Under the Treaty of Guadalupe Hidalgo, the federal government decided to grant citizenship to Mexicans living in the American Southwest. Bowman explains, "the Treaty of Guadalupe Hidalgo ended the Mexican-American War in 1848 and stipulated that former Mexican citizens were to be given 'all the rights of citizens of the United States.' "[28] Because people of color were ineligible for US citizenship during the mid–nineteenth century, the federal government tinkered with the Mexicans' racial classification and categorized them as White.[29] But, in fact, in the American Southwest, the Mexican population was racially mixed. Most were mestizos, both Spanish and Indigenous Mexican.[30][31] Legal scholar George Martinez argues that Mexicans should not have been counted as White because most of them were mestizos.[32]

Martha Menchaca contends that the racialization of Mexicans was messy; racial politics became contentious.[33] Not all Mexicans became citizens, and they were not all treated as White citizens in the newly ceded territory. After the US-Mexican War, the federal government "began the

process of racializing the Mexican population and ascribing them different legal rights on the basis of race."[34] Menchaca notes that "Mexicans
who were White were given full citizenship, while *mestizos*, Christianized
Indians, and *afromestizos* came under different racial laws."[35]

According to Menchaca, "the U.S. government abandoned its federal
responsibilities to its new citizens" and, within a year of the Treaty of
Guadalupe Hidalgo, "Congress gave legislators of the ceded territories and
states the right to determine the Mexicans' citizenship status."[36] In the end,
this "move had a severe impact on Mexicans because the state legislators
chose not to give most people of color the legal rights enjoyed by White
citizens."[37] Even though Mexican mestizos were technically allowed to keep
their property in the Southwest, they were not viewed as White citizens
and did not enjoy the same privileges as their White peers.

Indeed, argues Neil Foley, Mexicans in central Texas "walked the color
line. Heavily recruited by growers throughout the Southwest, Mexicans
were represented variously as nonwhite 'mongrels' who polluted the Anglo
Saxon racial stock."[38] For "many Anglo Texans, Mexicans were not white
and could not be assimilated into Texas society."[39] In the end, for "many
white Texans, a Mexican American was simply a contradiction in terms,
a hybridization of mutually exclusive races, nationalities, and cultures."[40]

Similarly, George J. Sanchez argues that the "source of most of
the emigration to the United States was clearly mestizo/Indian." People
coming from Mexico to the United States during the early twentieth century were "deemed by anthropologists to be dominated by 'acculturated
Indians'—that is, where Indians spoke Spanish and blended native and
European practices."[41] In California, government officials did not view
Mexican immigrants as White. In fact, Sanchez notes that Immigration
Bureau officials categorized Mexican immigrants coming to Los Angeles
according to "racial complexion"—dark, medium, and light/fair brown.
According to Immigration Bureau officials, most Mexican immigrants
(82.9%) in Los Angeles fell under the "dark" category. They were either
mestizo or Indian.[42]

No one has articulated the racialization of Mexican Americans during
that era better than Laura Gomez.

> Although American attitudes were not homogeneous, a broad
> consensus existed among Euro-Americans that Mexicans were
> non-white precisely because they were racially mixed. For many
> Americans, it was the fact of Mexicans' "mongrel" status that

most strongly signaled their racial inferiority. But the collective naturalization of Mexican citizens under the Treaty of Guada-lupe Hidalgo suggested Mexicans had White status given that, at the time, naturalization was limited to White persons. Thus, Mexicans' collective naturalization in 1848 prompted a *legal* definition of Mexicans as "white."[43]

Similar to Menchaca, Foley, Sanchez, and Gomez, Gross argues that "while a small elite of Mexican-American landholders who could prove that they were 'Spanish' maintained white status, the majority of 'Mexicans' were viewed and treated by Anglos as a separate race."[44]

It is not surprising, then, that the federal government's 1848 decision to classify Mexicans as White was challenged in a Texas court almost five decades later. The little-known 1897 *In re Rodriguez* case gives a glimpse of how Mexican Americans were viewed at the turn of the century, how White Americans rejected them, and how states continued to struggle with their racial classification. In 1896, Ricardo Rodriguez, a thirty-seven-year-old man from Guanajuato, Mexico, who had lived in Texas for ten years, petitioned for US citizenship.

His case was challenged and went to court. At the hearing, the briefs of two attorneys of the court, A. J. Evans and T. J. McMinn, stated that Rodriguez was ineligible for citizenship because "he is not a white person, nor an African, nor of African descent, and is therefore not capable of becoming an American citizen."[45]

The point was made that Rodriguez was not seen as a White person but similar to "copper-colored or red men. He has dark eyes, straight black hair, and high cheek bones."[46] In the hearing, it was declared that

> by scientific classification, the applicant is not a White person. He certainly is not in the sense in which these words are commonly used and understood in the every-day life of our people. Hence, under the rule placing the burden upon the applicant to show his eligibility to citizenship, we are of the opinion that his application ought to be refused.[47]

After hearing the case, District Judge Thomas Maxey concluded that when

> all the foregoing laws, treaties, and constitutional provisions are considered, which either affirmatively confer the rights of

citizenship upon Mexicans, or tacitly recognize in them the right of individual naturalization, the conclusion forces itself upon the mind that citizens of Mexico are eligible to American citizenship, and may be individually naturalized by complying with the provisions of our laws.[48]

Concluded Maxey, "In the judgment of the court, the applicant possesses the requisite qualifications for citizenship, and his application will therefore be granted."[49] Thus, Rodriguez won and was granted US citizenship.

Without a doubt, the constitution of Texas and the Treaty of Guadalupe Hidalgo extended US citizenship to Mexicans. Rodriguez, said legal scholar Steven Wilson, was "embraced within the spirit and intent of our laws upon naturalization." The judge accepted Rodriguez's claim that he was not Indian, Spanish, or African but "pure blooded Mexican."[50] While it is not certain what "a pure blooded Mexican" is, Martinez argues that because Mexicans were allowed to be naturalized, and since federal law stipulated that only Whites could become citizens, then, by default, Mexicans became White with respect to naturalization law. For Martinez, the *Rodriguez* case "clearly reveals how racial categories can be constructed through the political process. Through the give and take of treaty making, Mexicans became 'white.' "[51]

It was one issue for Mexican Americans to be legally White and US citizens and another to understand what their lived experiences were truly like. In other words, if Mexican Americans were legally White and US citizens, why was Jim Crow so pervasive and why did school officials and boards of education establish separate classes or schools for them throughout the United States? One way to make sense of this issue is to recognize that Mexican Americans became White on paper for naturalization purposes—as stipulated by the Treaty of Guadalupe Hidalgo and the federal government—but that status was meaningless because it was not recognized by Anglo Americans in the American Southwest.

One of the most piercing statements about where Mexican Americans stood in American life was made during the 1897 *Rodriguez* case. Floyd McGown, a member of the bar from whom Judge Maxey sought advice regarding the interpretation of the naturalization statute, said that Rodriguez, who was a mestizo, was "not a white person. He certainly is not in the sense in which these words are commonly used and understood in the every-day life of our [white] people."[52] Mexican Americans were legally White but socially "colored" in their schools and communities.

The Nature of Color, School Reform, and Social Efficiency

It is against the background of the racialization of Mexican Americans that we begin to examine their segregation in public schools. The legally White but socially colored status of Mexican Americans can be seen in terms of how their mestizo backgrounds ultimately trumped the law.[53] That is, despite the absence of state statutes that permitted or required the segregation of Mexican Americans, it is clear to us that school officials and boards of education made decisions based on mestizo appearances and the resulting racialization. Indeed, it was the contradiction between the law, on the one hand, and perception and treatment, on the other, that makes the segregation of Mexican Americans so unique and confusing.

This segregation also needs to be understood within the context of larger school reform movements and demographic trends taking place in American public schools during the early twentieth century. This was a period when school districts were growing, becoming centralized, and evolving into large bureaucracies. It was also an era when, across the nation, university presidents and college professors were calling for school reform and training a new generation of school administrators.[54] This new breed of school administrators, which David Tyack calls "administrative progressives," were introducing order, using science to make decisions, and trying to make schools systematic and rational.[55] Stanford University's Ellwood P. Cubberley, in particular, developed organizational models of how school systems needed to function and underscored the importance of educational leadership. In his 1922 textbook on public school administration, Cubberley displayed the correct and incorrect ways to organize and operate schools.[56] In his diagrams, he rationalized the chain of command, favored top-down administration, and paid important attention to the school district superintendent. Superintendents were bestowed a crucial role in American public schools because it was the position from which power was wielded, direction expected, and inspiration drawn.[57] Although Cubberley was successful in making superintendents central figures in American public schools, he did not dismiss the importance of state supervision. On this point, he argued that "state oversight and control may render very valuable service. Often the needs and rights of children can only be properly safeguarded by the intervention of the State itself, and this it should have the power to do when neglect is clearly evident."[58] However, it seems that the call for social efficiency during this era—the sorting of all children and placing them in specific programs to purportedly serve their educational needs—was not seen as an infringement on students' needs and rights but a structure that was deemed necessary and appropriate.

With this in mind, the early twentieth century is characterized as a time when educational professionals were in control of schools, when state supervision was somewhat ambiguous, and when school districts were serving large numbers of children from different backgrounds. It was also a period when schools were absorbing large numbers of immigrant children from Southern and Eastern Europe. Cubberley was nervous about this demographic trend. In fact, he believed that immigrants from "southeastern Europe were 'illiterate, docile, often lacking in initiative, and almost wholly without the Anglo-Saxon conceptions of righteousness, liberty, law, order, public decency, and government.' "[59] Though school officials throughout the nation saw Southern and Eastern European children as inferior, the administrative progressives worked hard to Americanize and assimilate them. Given their views on Southern and Eastern Europeans, it was likely that the new breed of school administrators also saw Mexican American children in the United States as inferior. But unlike the European immigrants, who had the potential to become full-fledged Americans, school authorities doubted the Mexican Americans' ability to blend into the American mainstream.[60] Thus, school officials and boards of education across the nation engaged in unofficial segregation by serving most Mexican American children in separate classes or separate schools. Indeed, these separate school settings not only kept Mexican Americans apart from their White peers, but they also allowed school officials across the nation to serve this population differently.[61]

It is within this context that we examine how public schools were receiving Mexican American children. The professionalization of school administrators brought with it deference toward their opinions, an emphasis on local control, and an attitude that suggested they knew what was best for Mexican American children. Therefore, the segregation of Mexican American children was being accomplished on a massive scale by local school officials and school board members who often purported that segregation would help them assimilate and provide better opportunities to learn English. The 1930s was an era when the segregation of Mexican Americans had become the norm, when their racial classification was politicized, when decisions were being made about how to serve them, and when Mexican American parents were starting to challenge segregated schooling.

Challenging Segregation in Court

Although a number of scholars have documented Mexican American challenges to school segregation in *Independent School District v. Salvatierra, Alvarez v. Lemon Grove,* and *Mendez v. Westminster,* we want to further address how these court cases illustrated the complex interaction between the legal and social construction of race.[62] The courts struggled to reconcile the legal White status assigned to Mexican Americans with the discernible fact that this population, for the most part, was racially mixed (mestizos) and treated as non-White. Our examination of these cases also illustrates why school segregation of Mexican Americans in the United States should retroactively be understood as de jure. We make this claim because school segregation reflected the Mexican American's colored status in the United States rather than the legal White status they purportedly held. Moreover, it is important to understand that the actions of local officials were intentional and driven by the fact that Mexican Americans became a racialized group in the United States.

Independent School District v. Salvatierra: Legitimizing Segregation as Pedagogical Choice

In the 1930 *Independent School District v. Salvatierra* case, Mexican Americans filed a lawsuit as taxpayers to enjoin the Del Rio, Texas, school board from entering into a contract to construct a school that would perpetuate the segregation of Mexican American students in the district. The trial court ruled in the Mexican Americans' favor, and the school district appealed the case. The appellate judge agreed with the trial court that school authorities could not "assign [Mexican American students] to separate schools, and exclude them from schools maintained for children of other white races, merely or solely because they are Mexicans."[63] The appellate court reasoned that Mexican Americans were members of the "other White race," and therefore there were no state laws that sanctioned their segregation. However, the appellate court ultimately reversed the ruling of the trial judge because state law granted school boards in Texas the power to manage, regulate, and construct schools in locations of their choice and to grade, classify, and assign students to schools in a responsible manner.

The opinion cited extensively the testimony of the district superintendent, who outlined the district's pedagogical rationale for segregating Mexican American students. The superintendent testified that many of the students were children of migrant workers who entered classes late in the school year. He said that it was appropriate to segregate these students to prevent disruption of the other classes that would occur with the arrival of new students and to preserve the Mexican American students' senses of self-esteem, which would be eroded if they started the school year behind other students.

The opinion stated that housing and teaching elementary-age children of Spanish or Mexican descent in separate buildings without intent to discriminate based on race was legal. The appellate court did not find that school district officials intended to discriminate against Mexican American students, stating that

> since it is not shown in this case that the school authorities are at this time enforcing unlawful segregation against any particular child or children, or intends to do so, or that the individual complainants are suffering or threatened with injury and damage peculiar to themselves, no right of action is open to them, at least in so far as they complain of the alleged policy of the school authorities in so classifying the scholastics as to effect an unlawful segregation of the children of the Mexican race generally.[64]

The court maintained that school officials in Del Rio were performing their duties as educators and that segregating Mexican American children for educational purposes was nothing more than an administrative act that fell within the discretion of the local school board. Thus, the court's ruling implied that segregating Mexican Americans to teach them English and to Americanize them was a rational policy that made curricular and pedagogical sense.

The superintendent in Del Rio appeared to convince the court that segregation was in the best interest of all students. Segregating Mexican children, he said, gave them "better opportunities because of the fact that their teachers are specialized in the matter of teaching them English and American citizenship."[65] The court agreed that teaching Mexican American children English and Americanizing them in separate settings did not constitute unlawful racial segregation.

The policy, however, was not as equitable as it appeared, and the appellate judge's finding that the racial segregation was not intentional is dubious. District policy required Mexican children to attend separate schools that were on a different school-year schedule, since many were part of the migrant farming community and enrolled late in school. In the superintendent's words: "Yes, I testified a while ago relative to some of the Mexicans going off to the cotton fields and the other places and coming in late and attending only part of the year, and presumably that was one reason why I wished to make separate provisions for them."[66]

However, there were White migrant children in the district facing the same issue. The superintendent treated them differently from their Mexican migrant peers. On this point, the superintendent claimed,

> Yes, there are other children, American English speaking children who come in late, but a very small per cent of them. No, I did not send any of those English-speaking children who came in late over to the school where I sent the Mexican or Spanish speaking children . . . I only sent the Spanish speaking children over there, those who came in late.[67]

The *Salvatierra* decision was contradictory and, in many ways, established a precedent in Texas that had serious implications across the American Southwest. It legitimated the idea that Mexican American children could be segregated for instructional purposes and that the courts were willing to defer to the pedagogical expertise of school administrators in advocating for segregation for linguistic purposes, even if the policies resulted in racial segregation. As Wilson noted, "segregation of Mexican American children on purported linguistic grounds became rooted even more deeply in the Southwest."[68]

Evidence also suggests that while Mexican Americans were officially deemed part of "other White" races in Del Rio, they were seen as a group of color in the community. "Naturally," the court observed, "the population of this section is in many communities and counties largely of Spanish and Mexican descent, who may be designated, for convenience of expression in this opinion, as the Mexican race, as distinguished, for like convenience, from all other white races."[69] Though the court saw "Mexican" and "Anglo Saxon" children as of different races, it was not willing to make a decision based on race. It carefully circumvented the issue of race and allowed the school district to segregate Mexican American children based on their purported educational needs. The *Salvatierra* decision found a way to dismiss race and defer to local educational professionals and their pedagogical expertise when addressing segregation.

Indeed, the superintendent's testimony makes clear that, although the segregation of Mexican American students was ostensibly made to meet the pedagogical needs of the students as English language learners, the inconsistent application of the policy to all students and the lack of any evaluation of the students' language abilities show that the policy was intended to segregate students based on race. By our definition, the policy upheld by the court in *Salvatierra* was a form of intentional, legally sanctioned segregation in Texas.

Alvarez v. Lemon Grove: An Unnoticed Victory

One year after the *Salvatierra* case in Texas, Mexican Americans challenged school segregation in Lemon Grove, California. Taking place in a small community outside of San Diego, the 1931 *Alvarez v. Lemon Grove* case is considered among the first "successful" school desegregation cases in the United States. School officials together with the Lemon Grove school board made a decision to construct a separate school for Mexican American children. When the school was completed, school officials would not allow Mexican American children into the regular school. The Mexican American community did not idly stand by. They boycotted, sought assistance from the Mexican consul, and filed a lawsuit.[70] Similar to the case in Del Rio, Texas, school officials in Lemon Grove maintained that Mexican Americans needed to be segregated in order to address their curricular and pedagogical needs. The Mexican school, they argued, was large enough to serve eighty-five students, had a playground that was fully equipped, would better serve Mexican children because of its location, and would Americanize the students and better serve English language learners.[71]

Judge Claude Chambers in Lemon Grove rejected the idea that Mexican American children needed to be segregated in order to best serve their educational needs. In contrast to the *Salvatierra* decision, Judge Chambers did not defer to the pedagogical expertise of the school officials. In fact, he claimed curricular and pedagogical segregation was counter to how these children needed to learn. He said,

> I understand that you can separate a few children, to improve their education they need special attention; but to separate all the Mexicans in one group can only be done by infringing the laws of the State of California. And I do not blame the Mexican children because a few of them are behind (in school work) for this segregation. On the contrary, this is a fact in their favor. I believe that this separation denies the Mexican

children the presence of the American children, which is so necessary to learn the English Language.[72]

The "court ruled that the school board had no legal basis on which to segregate the children. California law did not authorize or permit the maintenance of separate schools for the instruction of pupils of Mexican parentage, nationality and or descent."[73] California law authorized the segregation of certain races, but Mexican Americans, as a reflection of their presumed White legal status, were not listed among the races that school officials could segregate.[74]

The *Lemon Grove* case is of particular interest because it occurred around the same time as *Salvatierra* yet reached the opposite conclusion. Whereas legal segregation was permitted in *Salvatierra* in order to meet the educational needs of Mexican American children, *Lemon Grove* rejected the discretion of school officials to implement policy at the local level that had the effect of segregating Mexican American children on pedagogical grounds. The *Lemon Grove* case, it seems, not only took seriously that the state did not sanction the legal segregation of Mexican Americans, but it called into question the idea that pedagogical segregation was in the best interest of the students. Judge Chambers viewed Mexican Americans as socially colored in the sense that he acknowledged their Americanization as an important educational outcome. However, a key difference was that for him this status was not fixed, and he did not view Mexican American children as incapable or undeserving of the privileges of an education that would help them overcome their socially colored status.

The *Lemon Grove* decision went largely unnoticed for decades. As Alvarez notes, communities in California "did not use the case as a precedent in desegregating Americanization schools and classes that were created for Mexican and Mexican-American children."[75] Although the case marked a victory for Mexican Americans in Lemon Grove, it had no impact in the state, the Southwest, or the nation.

Mendez v. Westminster:
A New Precedent against Segregation

The politics of school segregation were revisited in California a decade and a half later. Some scholars have argued that the 1946 *Mendez v. Westminster* case was to Mexican Americans what the *Brown v. Board of*

Education decision was for African Americans.[76] *Mendez* was significant because it was filed in the US District Court (meaning that it established precedent in federal court and relied on provisions of the US Constitution that could be used to challenge segregation nationwide), and it found that separate was not equal. The decision also stated that segregation violated Mexican American children's rights under the equal protection clause of the Fourteenth Amendment, and, as Valencia has noted, it helped pave the way for the historic 1954 *Brown* decision.[77]

In this case, five Mexican American parents sued the Westminster school district in Orange County, California, for segregating their children. Although school officials maintained that segregation was not racially motivated and that its purpose was to serve English-language learners, the court found that the segregation of Mexican children "was determined largely by the Latinized or Mexican name of the child" and not according to language proficiency.[78] The district court judge rejected the argument that Mexican American students needed to be segregated for educational purposes. In fact, the case showed evidence that

> Spanish speaking children are retarded in learning English by lack of exposure to its use because of segregation, and that commingling of the entire student body instills and develops a common cultural attitude among the school children which is imperative for the perpetuation of American institutions and ideals.[79]

In other words, similar to the *Lemon Grove* case, segregating Mexican American children for educational purposes was seen as a misguided policy because it prevented social interaction and thwarted the opportunity to develop a common cultural attitude. The segregated schools, court records revealed, suggested that Mexican American children were inferior. Although the school district appealed, the district court's decision was upheld. The appellate court ruled that the school officials did not have authority under California law to segregate Mexican American students and that segregating Mexican American children violated the due process and equal protection clauses of the Fourteenth Amendment.

The *Mendez* decision was historic, some scholars have argued, because it ended de jure segregation for Mexican American children in California.[80] This argument, however, is made even though the terms *de jure* and *de facto* were not being applied to segregation at the time of the decision.

The court knew Mexican Americans were being segregated because of their "Latinized" appearance; however, the decision to ban segregation was based on the idea that there were no state statutes that allowed the segregation of public grade schoolchildren of Mexican or Latin descent.

One has to look beyond the legal reasoning in this case to recognize that Mexican American students were experiencing legal segregation. Indeed, school officials in Westminster were intentionally segregating Mexican American children based on their appearance and names rather than on pedagogical grounds. Their Latin appearance and names, we argue, were code for race. School officials in Westminster did not see Mexican Americans as White citizens but as a racially mixed (i.e., mestizo) group. In fact, the politics of skin color became the lightning rod issue that prompted the Mendez family and other Mexican American parents to challenge the school district. Whereas the Mendez children were refused admission to the Westminster Elementary School because of their "Latinized" appearance, the children of Soledad Vidaurri (the aunt of the Mendez children) were admitted to the school because "of their light complexions and their last name, Vidaurri, which was thought to be French."[81] Indeed, school officials were admitting White children into the elementary school and rejecting Mexican American mestizo youth.

The *Mendez* decision was consistent with *Lemon Grove* (although *Lemon Grove* was never cited), but, like *Lemon Grove*, this case did not pave the way for successful challenges of segregation of Mexican American students as *Brown* did for Black segregation. The fact that California did not have a state law that sanctioned the segregation of Mexican Americans remained a key factor in the *Mendez* decision.[82] Although the intentional actions of school officials to segregate Mexican American students in Westminster were thwarted in this instance, it would take another twenty-five years for the courts to decide a case that would explicitly identify the actions of school officials as intentional, race-based segregation and provide clear legal precedent to challenge the segregation of Mexican American students.

The Emergence of De Jure and De Facto

After the 1946 *Mendez* case and through the late 1960s, the mood of the nation changed. The 1954 *Brown* decision, the civil rights movement, the Vietnam War, and other social movements were rapidly changing the character of American life and having an impact on Mexican American school desegregation cases.[83] Although there were few significant cases addressing segregation of Mexican Americans during this time, it was during this period that the distinction between de facto and de jure segregation became legally relevant to Mexican American segregation. Paradoxically, as these terms entered the legal discourse around segregation, their meanings became increasingly unclear. That lack of clarity, together with the unique racial context of Mexican American segregation, explains much of the confusion concerning whether segregation of Mexican American children was de facto or de jure and forms the foundation for our argument that Mexican Americans historically experienced de jure segregation.

The years following the *Mendez* decision saw the Black struggle to end segregation take center stage. The *Brown* case garnered the segregation spotlight in the legal world. As Goodman notes, *Brown* required two key elements to be proven in a segregation case relying on the equal protection clause of the Constitution: racial classification by law and harm due to the classification.[84] The import of this is that the presumed White legal status of Mexican Americans meant that the segregation they experienced was not due to racial classification by law, as was the segregation of Blacks. In part, for that reason, *Brown* was not an immediate answer to Mexican American segregation since it did not open the way for Mexican Americans to challenge segregation on equal protection grounds.

In post-*Brown* litigation, the distinction between de facto and de jure segregation began to develop. The political context surrounding these cases is enmeshed with the civil rights movement, and the laws and legal doctrines of the era are marked with both progress and resistance. The Civil Rights Act of 1964 as interpreted in court cases is important in understanding the distinction between de facto and de jure segregation.

The Supreme Court in *Swann v. Charlotte-Mecklenberg Board of Education* noted that Congress did not want section IV of the Civil Rights Act of 1964, which was concerned with the implementation of desegregation after *Brown*, to grant courts any power to order desegregation absent a showing of discriminatory action by state authorities, including school boards.[85] Thus, through the Civil Rights Act of 1964, Congress created a distinction between segregation that occurred as a result of the discriminatory intent of government officials and segregation that occurred absent such intent. In the eyes of Congress, only racially motivated segregation could be remedied.

The Supreme Court took note of this in addressing the parameters of de jure segregation in *Keyes v. School District No. 1.*[86] In *Keyes*, the Supreme Court addressed segregation in Denver. As with most states in the West, Colorado did not have a statute or constitutional provision requiring segregation. Those statutes requiring segregation were key in showing discriminatory intent in previous cases. The Denver school district was sued after a newly elected school board rescinded actions taken to desegregate the schools adopted by the previous board. The Supreme Court was divided on how to address this decision since there were no statutes or constitutional provisions requiring segregated schooling. This division on the Supreme Court contributed to the confusion concerning the distinction between de facto and de jure segregation.

The majority opinion in Keyes never directly addresses the issue of de facto versus de jure segregation. However, the majority opinion dicta[87] interprets the discussion of the Civil Rights Act of 1964 in *Swann* as making segregative intent by state actors the key to defining de jure segregation.[88] Tying intent to de jure segregation does little to resolve the indeterminacy surrounding the meaning of de jure segregation. Although some clarity comes from their indication that intent to segregate is key to the distinction between de facto and de jure segregation, the Supreme Court left undetermined the important issue of how one proves discriminatory intent. In the following years, lower courts were divided on this question. Some determined that the plaintiffs had to prove the subjective intent of the school board to segregate. Of course, the easiest way to prove intent is if the policy that produces the segregation reflects the intent to segregate by creating racial classifications. Other courts chose an objective standard, where one could infer a school board's intent to segregate if segregation would be a foreseeable result of a school board's actions.[89] One can argue that adopting an objective standard where intent to segregate could be inferred by demonstrating the existence of segregated schools would effectively eliminate the difference between de facto and de jure segregation.

Adding to the confusion was the determination by certain members of the Supreme Court that the distinction between de facto and de jure segregation should be abandoned. In the *Keyes* case, Justices William O. Douglas and Lewis F. Powell, in separate concurrences, both advocated abandoning the distinction between de facto and de jure segregation. Justice Douglas saw no meaningful distinction between the terms, arguing that school segregation resulting from neighborhood segregation and school segregation required by law are both the products of state actions or policies.[90] Justice Powell examined the evolution of the Court's doctrine concerning segregation and concluded that the distinction had outlived its usefulness.[91] Ultimately, though the Supreme Court does say that intent to segregate on the part of the school board is required for de jure segregation, the way the Court avoided saying how parties could prove that intent to discriminate left the distinction muddled for Mexican Americans attempting to challenge segregation.

Also adding to the confusion is the fact that the distinction between de facto and de jure segregation had no particular relevance at the time when the *Mendez* case (or *Salvatierra* and *Lemon Grove*) was decided. Given the important status that *Mendez* has rightly been afforded in the history of desegregation for Mexican Americans, trying to argue persuasively that *Mendez* ended de jure segregation requires the application of a term to a moment in history that precedes the birth of the term. We argue, then, that all of the instances of school segregation in the cases we have thus far discussed were de jure segregation in that the colored social status of Mexican Americans drove local policies that resulted in their segregation. By illustrating the social context in which these cases were decided, we believe that the inference that school officials were acting with discriminatory intent can be validly made from these local school actions that resulted in segregation of Mexican American students.

Discussion

It is our intent here to clarify the politics of de facto and de jure segregation as it applied to Mexican Americans between 1930 and 1947 and how their legal White category played out in their schools and communities. We argued that even though there were no state statutes that sanctioned their segregation, Mexican Americans historically experienced de jure segregation in the United States because school officials took actions that resulted in the intentional segregation of students. It is important to recognize this discrimination as de jure because it connects their experiences in segregated schools to the larger context of how they were racialized and seen as a racially mixed group (mestizos). The segregation of Mexican American students is best seen in this context as reflecting their colored social status and the attendant discrimination as opposed to being the result of benign pedagogical decisions or the fortuitous conjunction of where Mexican Americans lived and where school boundaries were drawn.

Understanding the history of desegregation is important for interpreting the continuing struggle surrounding the racialization and segregation of Mexican Americans in the United States. Segregation for Mexican

Americans is an unfinished matter: "Latino students [Mexican Americans in general] are significantly more segregated than African Americans and segregation has been rapidly growing in states where they have the largest enrollments."[92] When segregation is currently rationalized in American public schools, it is done within the context of demographic shifts, open enrollment, the return to neighborhood schools, charter schools, rezoning school boundaries, curricular differentiation, and other reforms of separation that seem to be natural or inevitable. As Eduardo Bonilla-Silva has explained in his naturalization color-blind frame, many Whites claim that segregation is natural because persons from all racial backgrounds gravitate toward likeness and "that's the way it is."[93]

These arguments frame the current increase in segregation in ways that reflect the thinking behind the de jure/de facto distinction: government action to address segregation is not warranted since segregation is not the result of intentional actions on the part of government officials. The history of Mexican American segregation we present here indicates that this way of thinking about segregation should be abandoned. We should presume that the segregation of Mexican Americans, whether framed by the pedagogical arguments about language and culture acquisition or by arguments surrounding school choice and demographic shifts in the twenty-first century, reflects their social status, which is that of a stigmatized and racialized group. We should not easily accept that the increasing segregation of Mexican Americans is any more "natural" today than it was in the past.

Understanding the history of Mexican American school segregation can also be informative to the courts, which continue to cling to the idea of intentionality when examining segregation. When considering a recent case where school districts were trying to implement plans for voluntary racial integration, the plurality opinion stated that school officials could only consider race in the assignment of students to schools if they have the compelling interest of "remedying past *intentional* discrimination."[94] The history of Mexican American segregation we present here shows that even though the intention to segregate may not be evident in state laws or explicit in policies by school boards that mandate segregation, the many policies that result in segregation do intentionally reflect the social status of Mexican Americans.

When confronted with segregation, the courts and policy makers should not ask whether the segregation is the result of intentional actions. Instead, they should consider the segregation to be a reflection of the social status of Mexican Americans. This means that segregation of Mexican American students is not acceptable unless one also accepts that the social status of Mexican Americans is deserved. As a result, policy makers and the courts should not dismiss segregation as natural or as the result of private choices but, rather, should consider the social status and mestizo heritage of Mexican Americans and address school segregation as part of these larger issues.

Epilogue

If the Mexican origin population generally lived in neighborhoods separate from Whites, if some faced hostile living conditions, and if many experienced Jim Crow–like environments—places that refused to serve them in theaters, stores, parks, restaurants, barbershops, and other public places—why would their children be treated differently in American public schools? This question compelled us to assert that the experiences of Mexicans, Mexican Americans, and Hispanos/as were similar to those of African Americans in the United States in important ways. We add to the existing literature that mostly focuses on the Southwest by exploring other regions of the nation and by drawing from archival sources that have rarely been used by education historians. As we reflect in the opening of our book, professor Max Sylvius Handman maintained in 1928 that America faced an uncertain future because it did not have a "social technique for handling partly colored races."[1] Handman appeared to be pleased that America had "a place for the Negro and a place for the white man," but seemed concerned that there were no techniques to control Mexicans, a partly colored race. Given Handman's unease, we are confident that he was calling for the legal segregation of Mexicans, the kind African Americans were experiencing under the 1896 *Plessy v. Ferguson* decision. But as we saw, there were unofficial social techniques that were used to control and disenfranchise Mexicans. They were used to keep Mexican and White children in separate educational facilities, and Jim Crow–like conditions were extended to Mexican American communities.

We need to understand Handman's position during his time, space, and location. As Ibram X. Kendi notes, racist policies and ideas were produced during particular historical moments. They changed over time to meet social, political, and economic needs. Within the context of our study, Kendi makes a powerful point about the legalization and ban of Jim Crow. He observes how Jim Crow was "overt" for African Americans before the 1960s, and how these laws became outlawed with the Civil Rights Act of 1964. As Jim Crow became illegal, Kendi claims they went "covert." His point was that even though racist policies were not necessarily initiated after 1964, racist intentions became covert.[2] As we look back and examine how Mexican immigrants, Mexican Americans, and Hispanos were treated in their schools and communities, Jim Crow and school segregation were never sanctioned for them in the United States. The quest to segregate them in public schools and disenfranchise them in their communities seemed to function in a "covert" manner Kendi appeared to depict. Also, as Kendi notes the continual changes in the rationales for the segregation of and discrimination against African Americans, our work shows how officials used whatever justifications for the segregation of and discrimination against Mexicans and Mexican Americans, whether they argued that segregation was for the benefit of students learning English or blamed problems on the Mexicans themselves.

In *An American Dilemma*, Gunner Myrdal was correct that Mexicans were kept in a status similar to African Americans, that segregation for Mexicans was just as prevalent, and that Mexicans were not allowed to assimilate into the American mainstream as other European immigrant groups were allowed to do.[3] Whether they were recent immigrants, long-time residents with American citizenship, or those with deep roots in southern Colorado and northern New Mexico, we found that Mexicans were forced to live in segregated neighborhoods, Jim Crow laws crafted for African Americans were unofficially aimed at them, their children were placed in separate classes or separate schools, they were not expected to melt into the American mainstream, and they were seen as a "mongrel" race.[4] But unlike the experiences of African Americans, the segregation of the Mexican-origin population was different because it evolved in ways where laws did not have to be ratified in order to foster their separation. This was central. And this is what made the experiences of Mexicans in their schools and communities so complicated. Their experiences were riddled with legal contradictions, their race was elusive, and they were treated like no other group in the United States. That is, Mexicans were legally White, observable as mestizos, were blocked from the American mainstream, and were treated similar to Blacks.

When Mexicans filed complaints to Mexican consuls about school segregation and Jim Crow, their grievances reached the highest levels of the American and Mexican governments. In one form or another, their complaints were almost always about racial discrimination. As we saw, Juan Almazán became the quintessential Mexican who confronted Jim Crow in 1911. He was ejected from a tavern in St. Louis because he was seen as an "Indio." His mestizo features became the racial marker that got him ejected from that establishment. In 1915, Mexicans in Kansas City were refused treatment in a new hospital. Mexican Consul Jack Danciger was unable to convince the hospital administrator that Mexicans were White. Instead, Mexicans were treated in the hospital annex with other folk of color. They were served in a hospital facility that was considered to be separate but equal. These instances that took place in St. Louis and Kansas City were not isolated cases; they were the rule across much of the United States. We saw how Mexican consuls were receiving complaints from Texas, Kansas, Oklahoma, Arkansas, and New Mexico about how restaurants, barbershops, theatres, drug stores, parks, and other public places were refusing to serve Mexicans. We also saw in 1923 how after a racially charged incident took place in Johnstown, Pennsylvania, the mayor ordered "all negroes and Mexicans" to leave the town. And by the late 1940s and early 1950s, we got a glimpse of how business owners in Marked Tree, Arkansas, refused to serve Mexican braceros. Despite American and Mexican intervention, merchants in the community refused to remove "No Mexican" signs from their business establishments. Mexican braceros were seen and treated similar to Blacks in this southern town. However, in large part, even when the consul acted on their behalf to request that these instances be investigated, the investigations were completed by White officials who, by and large, did not show evidence that they sought out or listened to the experiences of the Mexicans and Mexican-Americans in their communities. Instead they chose to believe that the segregation and discrimination were justified or nonexistent.

How Mexicans were regarded in their communities was a reflection of how they were served in American public schools. Despite region, we found that the mestizo heritage of the Mexican became a racial identifier, but their legal categorization as White was elusive, confusing and used to serve different goals. What we mean here is that in addition to the rationales school officials used to segregate Mexican children—language, pedagogy, and the claim Mexican children could not keep up with White children in mainstream classes—educational leaders "raced" Mexicans in ways that would allow them to maintain segregation. In other words, their race became a moving target over time. We cannot forget the 1914

Maestas case in Alamosa, Colorado. This was an intriguing example of how race was argued by plaintiffs and defendants. This lawsuit was unique because a novel strategy was used at the time to challenge the segregation of Mexican (Hispano/a) children. Mexican Americans rejected their legal White status, claimed they were racially distinct as Mexicans, and used the Colorado State Constitution to challenge segregation because it was illegal for schools to distinguish and classify children in public schools according to color or race.[5] Defendants, however, argued that Mexicans were Caucasians and that they were no different from other White children in the school district.[6] The judge ruled in favor of *Maestas*. The decision, however, was not based on race. It ruled that the school district could not force all Mexican children to the Mexican school, that English-speaking Mexican American children had the right to attend schools near their homes. A case that went unrecognized for over a century, the *Denver Catholic Register* pointed out that it "was the first time in the history of America that a court fight was made over an attempt to segregate Mexicans in school."[7] At this point and time, the *Maestas* case may be the first Mexican American–led school desegregation case in the United States.

One year later—in 1915 and situated in the Deep South—the Mexican's racial background was treated very differently by school officials. Unlike the defendants in the *Maestas* case, who claimed Mexican children were Caucasians and that they were no different from other White children in the school district, a school board member in Cheneyville, Louisiana, claimed Mexican children were "racially mixed," that they had "negro blood," and threw them out of the White school. The Cheneyville incident was also lost in history and absent from public records. That is, available school board minutes provide no record of discussion of the incident by school trustees and the incident was not reported in the local newspaper. And while the US Department of State ordered the Louisiana governor to investigate the incident and that order was passed on to the state superintendent of instruction, there is no record of an investigation. Had this case not been stored in the Archivo Histórico in Mexico City, this story could not have been told.

The Cheneyville case is compelling because it allows us to start a conversation about the racialization of Mexicans and their experiences in public schools in the Deep South. Mexican children were thrown out of a White school by a local school trustee because he perceived them as racially mixed. We documented how school officials in the parish responded to their removal, what the Mexican consulate in New Orleans found and reported, and how the Mexican ambassador and the US Department of State secretary responded, respectively, to the incident. We are clear to point out that this story is incomplete. We do not know if this case was ever resolved. That is, we were unable to uncover or infer whether the Mexican children involved in this case were placed in White schools, Black schools, or whether they were allowed to attend school at all.[8]

Even though this story is incomplete, we know that orders were given by the county superintendent to permit the children to attend school, educators in the parish received instructions to move forward on those orders, and we know what the Mexican consulate in New Orleans found. This information was not inconsequential, as it revealed potential differences in the roles school officials played in the education of Mexican students in the South when compared to cases in the Southwest. While we chiefly wanted to know how school leaders in this Louisiana community responded to the school trustee's actions to keep Mexican children out of a White school, we also wanted to understand how Mexican children were perceived in a place and time where legal segregation was understood in exclusively Black-and-White terms. We believe Mexican children in this Louisiana parish were not seen as Black or White, but we are certain their mestizo appearance is what kept them out of a White school. The school trustee forced the Mexican children out of the school because he saw them as racially mixed and, in order to keep them out of the White school, the Mexican consul reported he believed they had "Sangre de Negros."

In Kansas City, Kansas, the location where Mexican Consul Jack Danciger in 1915 was unable to convince the hospital administrator that Mexicans were White, the public schools in the city responded to Mexicans in a similar way. Unlike Cheneyville, Louisiana, and other communities in the South where a dual system of education existed, we saw how Kansas was different.[9] It was different because it shared features with Northern and Southern states. It was legal to segregate Black children in elementary schools in cities of the first class and in high schools only in Kansas City. The segregation of Mexicans in Kansas was complicated. While not mentioned in state statutes, they were seen as "Gente de Color" in the state.[10] As a result, the Kansas City schools created a triracial school system; a system that educated Black, White, and Mexican children in separate spaces. Because there were no laws in place that allowed for the segregation of Mexican children, we were unable to uncover underlying reasons for the varied responses of the Mexican consul to segregation. It did reveal, however, how they played a significant role in highlighting their treatment. Indeed, the mixed messages from high-ranking Mexican and US government officials added to the complexity of this case. It was difficult to explain why the attorney general would send strong messages to school boards and superintendents that they lacked the authority to construct separate Mexican schools yet fail to challenge the construction of the Clara Barton "Mexican school" in Kansas City. Moreover, why Mexican Consul Miguel Angel Rico acquiesced to the establishment of Clara Barton remains unresolved.

One issue was clear: the triracial school system allowed school officials to place Mexican children in inferior school facilities. Whether they were placed in separate classrooms within White schools, in basement floors, or in a building annex, school officials boasted that the Clara Barton Mexican school was built with surplus funds and cost only $7,000. We saw how in the same year the town of Salina spent $65,000 for a modest Black school.[11] The construction of the Clara Barton School seemed to send a powerful message to local residents that Mexicans were third-class citizens and what the district spent on them was all they deserved.

In addition, when White parents drove Mexican youth out of the new Major Hudson Elementary School in 1924 and from Argentine High in 1925, government officials from both nations became involved. White parents nonetheless prevailed. Mexican children were kept out of the new Major Hudson and ordered to return to schools designated for them. Argentine High was somewhat different; after the Alvarado incident, Mexican students were allowed to attend high school in the city. Cleary maintains the Alvarado case was a partial victory because school segregation would end at the eighth grade and Mexican youth were given access to a high school education—a step forward.[12] He was correct, but we hypothesized that school officials were never concerned about opening Argentine High to Mexican youth. School officials knew their numbers would never change the racial composition of the school because very few made it that far.

By 1931, the politics of race for Mexicans took an interesting turn in California. As we saw, Professor Glen Hoover in 1929 noted that there was an understanding among US government officials that Mexicans, classified as White, were in reality "Indian."[13] Within this context, there was an attempt to legally segregate Mexican children because of their indigenous roots. To be clear, politicians wanted to modify, or amend, the California School Code to establish separate schools for Indian children, "whether they were born in the United States or not."[14] Although not specifically stated in the Bliss Bill, they wanted to segregate Mexican mestizo children. We pointed out how Lillian Hill—the chief of the Bureau of Attendance and Migratory Schools in the state—saw how politicians not only wanted to legally segregate Mexican children but she saw the larger implications of the bill. From Hill's perspective, it was a way for some Americans to keep Mexican children out of schools and in the agricultural fields. Finally, she saw how school segregation fostered a sense of superiority among White students and inferiority among Mexican children. Although the bill did not pass, the segregation of Mexican children continued. We consider this obscure bill to be significant in educational history because it was a moment in time in California when politicians deliberately wanted to legally segregate Mexican children because of their mestizo heritage, and it illustrates some of the roles of cultural and civic organizations played in bringing the experiences of Mexicans to the forefront to battle segregation and discrimination.

As we examined the records at the Archivo Histórico, we saw how Mexican consuls, Mexican ambassadors, and the secretaría in Mexico City came to terms with the idea that Mexicans were unwanted in American schools and society. High-ranking American government officials were contacted, they were drawn in, and they became involved. State officials, however, contested, scoffed, or paid no heed to charges that Mexican children were being segregated. In California, the state superintendent in 1919 reported to the governor that Mexican children were not segregated based on race. While he did not deny that Mexican children were segregated, he maintained segregation was necessary because of linguistic differences, pedagogical needs, academic unpreparedness, and the location of schools. More alarming was how the state superintendent told the governor that segregation was necessary, that it was in the best interest of Mexican children, and that it was legal. In the same year, Mexican Consul Ramon DeNegri saw the segregation and treatment of Mexicans in California quite differently. He claimed that "El Mexicano, en vista de que sus condiciones economicas son muy parecidas a las del negro, es clasificado como este y recibe el mismo tratamiento."[15] Even though the state superintendent told the California governor that Mexicans were not segregated based on race, De Negri knew better and reported that Mexicans were treated similarly to African Americans. The disregard of the experiences of Mexicans by White officials in their investigations and responses illustrates the important actions that Mexicans and Mexican Americans took to make their experiences and stories known. This is illustrated well when in 1931, the group—Los Padres de South Mission in Texas—was challenging the school board about a decision they made to build a junior high school near the Mexican *colonia* and how their children were being denied admission to a White junior high school. As a strategy to integrate the schools, Los Padres claimed their children were racially White, that segregation was a violation of the Fourteenth Amendment, and that they were violating the Constitution of Texas and the Treaty of Guadalupe Hidalgo that was ratified between the United States and Mexico in 1848.[16] While Los Padres insisted their children were White and that they had the "legal" right to attend White schools in the school district, school board members ignored their argument and did not respond to the idea that Mexicans were White. The school board challenged the idea that Mexicans were segregated based on race, claimed they had sent a few Mexican children to White schools, had sent a few White students to the "Mexican" junior high near the *colonia*, and challenged the notion that their schools were racially segregated. The school board was strategic. At the time, they were able to keep selected schools in the school district predominantly White and, at the same time, were able to maintain racial segregation. Even though the school board took strategic actions to maintain segregation, the experiences of Mexicans were made known and were now swept under the rug in reports and investigations by White officials.

We also tried to clarify the politics of de facto and de jure segregation as it applied to Mexican Americans between 1930 and 1947, and how these concepts played out in the courts. We maintained that even though there were no state statutes that sanctioned their segregation, Mexican Americans historically experienced de jure segregation in the United States because school officials took actions that resulted in the intentional segregation of students. It was important to recognize this discrimination as de jure because it connected their experiences in segregated schools to the larger context of how they were racialized and seen as mestizos. The segregation of Mexican American students is best seen in this context as reflecting their colored social status and the attendant discrimination, as opposed to being the result of benign pedagogical decisions or the fortuitous conjunction of where Mexican Americans lived and where school boundaries were drawn.

These arguments frame the current state of segregation in ways that reflect the thinking behind the de jure/de facto distinction: government action to address segregation is not warranted since segregation is not the result of intentional actions on the part of government officials. The history of Mexican American segregation we present in this book indicates that this way of thinking about segregation should be abandoned. We should presume that the segregation of Mexican Americans—whether framed by the pedagogical arguments about language and culture acquisition or by current arguments surrounding school choice and demographic shifts in the twenty-first century—is more about their social status and that of a stigmatized and racialized group. Indeed, we should not easily accept that the increasing segregation of Mexican Americans is any more "natural" today than it was in the past.

Understanding the history of Mexican American school segregation can also be informative to the courts, which continue to cling to the idea of intentionality when examining segregation. When considering a recent case where school districts were trying to implement plans for voluntary racial integration, the plurality opinion stated that school officials could only consider race in the assignment of students to schools if they have the compelling interest of "remedying past *intentional* discrimination."[17] The history of Mexican American segregation we present here shows that even though the intention to segregate may not be evident in state laws or explicit in policies by school boards that mandate segregation, the many policies that result in segregation do intentionally reflect the social status of Mexican Americans.

Though no state statutes explicitly authorized the segregation of Mexican American students, these cases and other accounts and vignettes we provide in this book, illustrate how local school officials made decisions with the intention of achieving the same effect. And when evaluating these actions, it is important to recognize that they should in fact be defined as de jure segregation. Legally, Mexican American students may have been classified as White, but those students experienced segregation because local officials considered them to be *not* White. Schools didn't segregate them to better serve their educational needs or to pursue a societal demand to Americanize them. Rather, they chose to segregate Mexicans because of their social status, discriminating against them on the basis of color and race.

How we understand this history will inform how we see the continuing racialization and segregation of Mexican American students in the United States. Quite simply, this remains an unfinished matter. As Orfield, Kucsera, and Siegel-Hawley note, "Latino students, who were ignored under most older desegregation plans, have become steadily more isolated from Whites over the past four decades and are now the most segregated group of students in the country."[18] To frame the current situation this way is to adopt the de facto view of segregation, which suggests that government remedies are not warranted because government officials did not act intentionally to segregate students. We maintain that, and as these desegregation cases demonstrate, this reasoning is flimsy and should be abandoned or at least reconsidered. The segregation of Mexican origin students isn't any more "natural" today than it was in past decades. Still, though, we recognize that it will not be easy to persuade the courts to recognize that current patterns of school segregation are the result of intentional actions by state and local officials.[19] In the 2007 case *Parents Involved in Community Schools v. Seattle School Dist. No. 1*, the US Supreme Court halted a voluntary integration plan that sought to bring together students of different races. According to the Court's plurality opinion, school officials could only consider race in the assignment of students to schools if they have the compelling interest of remedying past *intentional* discrimination.

If educators and school officials hope to address the growing isolation of Mexican origin students, they will have to be fully aware of these competing narratives about de facto and de jure segregation, and they will have to be willing to challenge the perspective that currently prevails in the courts. When confronted with the realities of school segregation, educators should reflect on the ways in which existing enrollment patterns are shaped by past beliefs and decisions about Mexican Americans. The segregation we experience today isn't natural, and it doesn't result from the mere accumulation of private choices. Rather, it is the outgrowth of long-standing discrimination against Mexican Americans on the basis of their mestizo heritage.

Notes

Introduction

1. Max Sylvius Handman, "Economic Reasons for the Coming of the Mexican Immigrant," *American Journal of Sociology* 35, no. 4 (1930): 601–3. Handman noted that he had presented this paper at the American Sociological Society in Chicago on December 1928, in the Rural Sociology section of the conference.

2. Handman, "Economic Reasons," 606–9. Handman noted that the "native worker demands wages of two Mexicans, but he only does the work of one and a half Mexicans."

3. Handman, "Economic Reasons," 611, 609.

4. Handman, "Economic Reasons," 611.

5. Handman, "Economic Reasons," 611. Handman did not describe what he meant by "how the other half lives." This term was the title from Jacob Riis's book, *How the Other Half Lives: Studies among the Tenements of New York* (New York: Charles Scribner's Sons, 1890). This was an early publication with photographs that documented squalid living conditions in New York City slums in the 1880s. It served as the basis for books that exposed slum conditions to New York City's upper and middle classes.

6. Handman, "Economic Reasons," 609–10.

7. *Plessy v. Ferguson*, 163 U.S. 537 (1896).

8. University of Michigan, Faculty History Project, Memorial of Max Sylvius Handman, LSA Minutes, https://www.lib.umich.edu/faculty-history/faculty/max-sylvius-handman/memorial.

9. Handman, "Economic Reasons," 610, 611.

10. Archivo Histórico Genaro Estrada, Acervo Histórico Diplomático, Secretaría de Relaciones Exteriores (hereafter cited as Archivo Histórico Genaro Estrada). File 635(I).8/59. Letter from Secretary of State Robert Lancing to Mexican Ambassador Don Ygnacio Bonillas about Mexicans in Oklahoma not being permitted in public parks. June 19, 1918; Julie M. Weise, *Corazon De Dixie: Mexicanos in the U.S. South since 1910* (Chapel Hill: University of North Carolina

Press, 2015), 6; see also Nicholas Villanueva, Jr., *The Lynching of Mexicans in the Texas Borderlands* (Albuquerque: University of New Mexico Press, 2017), 153.

11. Margarita Aragon. "The Difference that 'One Drop' Makes: Mexican and African Americans, Mixedness and Racial Categorization in the Early 20th Century." *Subjectivity* 7, no. 1 (2014): 3. Sociologist Margarita Aragon noted that Max Handman was anxious over the neither Black nor White classification of the Mexican, how he was unable to articulate the kind of "trouble" Mexicans would bring to the US because of their racial backgrounds, and drew in "Homi Bhabha's influential conceptualisation of hybridity as a disruptive, disorienting and thus transgressive force." Bhabha explained that there was a paranoid threat of "hybridity" in the United States. In simple terms, this idea complicated the Black-White paradigm.

12. Gunner Myrdal, *An American Dilemma: The Negro Problem and Modern Democracy* (New York: Harper & Brothers, 1944). In this book, Myrdal expresses the belief that there was a vicious cycle in which Whites oppressed African Americans and then pointed to the African Americans' poor performance as reason for the oppression. Myrdal believed that the way out was to either cure White racism or improve the circumstances of African Americans, which would disprove Whites' preconceived notions of their inferiority. Myrdal called this process the "principle of cumulation." To the extent that Myrdal commented on Mexicans, we believe some of his ideas about the "Negro problem" are applicable to Mexican immigrants, Mexican Americans, and Hispanos in the United States.

13. The values Myrdal discussed in his book may have come from William Tyler Page, *The American's Creed*, http://www.ushistory.org/documents/creed.htm; *The American Creed*, as a statement, was printed in the Congressional Record of April 13, 1918; see also http://www.usflag.org/american.creed.html.

14. Walter A. Jackson, *Gunner Myrdal and America's Conscience: Social Engineering & Racial Liberalism, 1938–1987* (Chapel Hill: University of North Carolina Press, 1990), xi.

15. Myrdal, *American Dilemma*, 53.

16. Myrdal, *American Dilemma*, 620.

17. Myrdal, *American Dilemma*, 928.

18. Guadalupe San Miguel, *"Let All of Them Take Heed": Mexican Americans and the Campaign for Educational Equality in Texas, 1910–1981* (Austin: University of Texas Press, 1987); Gilbert Gonzalez, *Chicano Education in the Era of Segregation* (Philadelphia: Balch Institute Press, 1990); Ruben Donato, *Mexicans and Hispanos in Colorado Schools and Communities, 1920–1960* (Albany: State University of New York Press, 2007); we acknowledge that Francisco Balderrama and Robert Alvarez Jr. used Mexican consul records in their work. See Francisco Balderrama, *In Defense of La Raza: The Los Angeles Mexican Consulate and the Mexican Community, 1929 to 1936* (Tucson: University of Arizona Press, 1982):

55–72; Robert Alvarez Jr., "The Lemon Grove Incident," *San Diego Historical Society Quarterly* 32, no. 2 (Spring 1986). In addition, Julie Weise also used consul records to discuss the politics of Jim Crow in Arkansas during the early 1950s; see Weise, *Corazon De Dixie.*

19. Laura E. Gomez, *Manifest Destinies: The Making of the Mexican American Race* (New York: New York University Press, 2007): 83; Steven H. Wilson, Brown over "Other White": Mexican Americans' Legal Arguments and Litigation Strategy in School Desegregation Lawsuits. *Law and History Review* 21, no. 1 (2003): 145–94; see also "Mexicans Portrayed as 'Mongrel Race' Then and Now," interview with professor Gerardo Cadava: https://www.youtube.com/watch?v=W9xA2jA8bdo.

20. Joel Perlmann, *Italians Then, Mexicans Now: Immigrant Origins and Second-Generation Progress, 1890–2000* (New York: Russell Sage Foundation, 2005).

21. David B. Tyack, *The One Best System: A History of American Urban Education* (Cambridge: Harvard University Press, 1974), 132.

22. Tyack, *One Best System*. See sections "The Politics of Pluralism: Nineteenth Century Patterns," 78–109, and "Americanization: Match and Mismatch," 229–55.

23. Tyack, *One Best System*, 247.

24. Oscar Handlin, *The Uprooted: The Epic Story of the Great Migrations that Made the American People* (Boston: Little Brown, 1951); David B. Tyack, ed., *Turning Points in American Educational History* (Waltham, MA: Blaisdell Publishing, 1967), see chapter 8, "Becoming an American: The Education of the Immigrant," 228–63; Colin Greer, *The Great School Legend: A Revisionist Interpretation of American Public Education* (New York, Basic Books, 1972).

25. http://www.irwincollier.com/interdisciplinary-moment-max-sylvius-handman-chicago-sociology-ph-d-1917/. We acknowledge that it was unclear what Max Handman's social class was. He must have been an upper-middle-class Romanian immigrant in order to enter college when he arrived in the United States.

26. Handman, "Economic Reasons," 609–10.

27. https://en.wikipedia.org/wiki/Ambassador_of_Mexico_to_the_United_States.

28. Balderrama, *Defense of La Raza*, ix.

29. Lareen Laglagaron, *Protection through Integration: The Mexican Government's Efforts to Aid Migrants in the United States* (Migration Policy Institute, National Center on Immigrant Integration Policy, 2010), 6.

30. The term *Mexican nationals* is used here to identify those who were not US citizens. The term *Mexican Americans* and *Hispanos* are used to indicate those who had US citizenship.

31. Gilbert G. Gonzalez, *Mexican Consuls and Labor Organizing: Imperial Politics in the American Southwest* (Austin: University of Texas Press, 1999), 2.

32. Gonzalez, *Mexican Consuls*, 2, 5–7.

33. Balderrama, *Defense of La Raza*, ix.

34. Balderrama, *Defense of La Raza*.

35. Archivo Histórico Genaro Estrada. File 592/21/46. "Atropellos a los mexicanos en el estado de Cal. Excluyendo de las escuelas a niños." Letter from Mexican consul in San Francisco, California, to Mexican Ambassador in Washington, DC. June 27, 1919.

36. Archivo Histórico Genaro Estrada. File IV-320-34, Informes sobre la segregacion de ninos mexicanos en las escuelas americanas de Carpenteria, California, 1931; File 11-14-300, Exclucion de ninos Mexicanos en las escuelas de Texas, 1911.

37. Archivo Histórico Genaro Estrada File 635(1).18/59, Letter from Mexican Ambassador Don Ygnacio Bonillas to Luis Rincon. Se le niega el pasa a restaurants y teatros por ser mex. Meryville, Tennessee, August 7, 1918.

38. Gomez, *Manifest Destinies*.

39. University of California, Berkeley, the Bancroft Library, Manuscripts Division, MANC, MSS. 84/38, Taylor, Paul Schuster Papers, Ctn. 13, File 13:43, "Restriction of Mexican Immigration at Issue," *The Coalitionist* 1, no. 6 (December 1929): 3. The original article cited in the *Coalitionist* can be accessed at Glenn E. Hoover, "Our Mexican Immigrants," *Foreign Affairs* 8, no. 1 (October 1929), https://doi.org/10.2307/20028746.

40. Archivo Histórico Genaro Estrada. File 378.4/17, Copia. Letter written to Mexican Consul, October 18, 1911, Mexicans in Garden City complained that the White community banned them from restaurants, barbershops, and other public places.

41. Archivo Histórico Genaro Estrada File 13-14-20, Copia. Letter from Jose Gonzalez to Mexican Consul. November 12, 1920.

42. Archivo Histórico Genaro Estrada, File 13-14-20, Letter (translated to Spanish) from Jerome Hanl, chief of police to Mexican Consul M. N. Morales. December 8, 1920.

43. Archivo Histórico Genaro Estrada, File 13-14-20, Letter from Chief of Police Jerome Hanl in Salina to Mexican Consul M. N. Morales, in Kansas, City, Missouri. December 8, 1920.

44. Rubén Donato, Gonzalo Guzmán, and Hanson, S. Jarrod. "Francisco Maestas et al. v. George H. Shone et al.: Mexican American Resistance to School Segregation in the Hispano Homeland, 1912–1914." *Journal of Latinos and Education* 16, no. 1 (2017): 3–17, see also https://www.tandfonline.com; Rubén Donato, and Jarrod S. Hanson. "Porque tenían sangre de 'NEGROS,': The Exclusion of Mexican Children from a Louisiana School, 1915–1916." *Association of Mexican American Educators Journal*, Open Issue 11, no. 1 (2017): 125–45; Rubén Donato and Jarrod S. Hanson. " 'In These Towns, Mexicans Are Classified as Negroes': The Politics of Unofficial Segregation in the Kansas Public Schools, 1915–1935," *American Educational Research Journal* 54, supplement 1 (2017): 53s–74s, https://doi.org/10.3102/0002831216669781; Rubén Donato and Jarrod S. Hanson. "Legally

White, Socially "Mexican": Mexican Americans and the Politics of De Jure and De Facto Segregation in the American Southwest." *Harvard Educational Review* 82, no. 2 (2012): 202–25. Reprinted with permission.

Chapter 1

1. Francisco Maestas, suing on his own behalf and in behalf of all others in similar situations, Plaintiff, v. Geo. H. Shone, C. L. Lahrmann, Joseph H. Darling as the Board of Education of School District No. 3 Conejos County; and Geo. O. Thompson, as superintendent of School District No. 3, Conejos County. Defendants. Petition by Raymond Sullivan, Attorney for Plaintiffs. Alamosa County. Combined Court. Alamosa, CO 81101. District Civil Roll # 1.

2. Adolpho Romo v. William E. Laird, et al., No. 21617, Maricopa County Superior Court (1925); Independent School District v. Salvatierra, 33 S.W. 2d 790 (Tex.Civ.App.–San Antonio 1930); Alvarez v. Lemon Grove, Civil Action No. 66625 (Superior Court San Diego County, California, 1931). See also Laura K. Munoz, "Romo v. Laird: Mexican American Segregation and the Politics of Belonging in Arizona," *Western Legal History* 26, nos. 1 and 2 (2013).

3. Richard Nostrand, *The Hispano Homeland* (Norman: University of Oklahoma Press, 1992). In this essay, various sources refer to Mexican Americans in Alamosa as "Mexican," "Spanish," and "Spanish Americans." We use the term *Mexican American* with the understanding that Nostrand is correct, that the Mexican American population is different from that of other states in the Southwest. When sources use terms other than *Mexican American*, we respect the language that the sources used by using their terminology.

4. Independent School District v. Salvatierra, 795.

5. Robert R. Alvarez, Jr., "The Lemon Grove Incident: The Nation's First Successful Desegregation Court Case," *Journal of San Diego History* 32, no. 3 (1986): 10–11, http://www.sandiegohistory.org/journal/86spring/lemongrove.htm.

6. Mexican Americans in Alamosa did not have Mexican consul support because they were US citizens. Hispanos, or Spanish Americans, had deep roots in the region. Thirteenth Census of the United States: 1910-Population. Department of Commerce and Labor—Bureau of the Census. Colorado, Conejos County. Alamosa. Precinct 12. The 1910 census notes that Francisco (Frank) had roots to New Mexico, not Mexico. Maestas was also categorized as White in the census.

7. Carlos Kevin Blanton, "The Citizenship Sacrifice: Mexican Americans, The Saunders-Leonard Report, and the Politics of Immigration, 1951–52," *Western Historical Quarterly* 43, no. 3 (Autumn 2009): 299–320.

8. "Alamosa Mexicans Win School Court Fight," *Denver Catholic Register*, March 26, 1914. The *Register* noted that it "was the first time in the history of America that a court fight was made over an attempt to segregate Mexicans in

school." The editor of the *Denver Catholic Register* understood that the Maestas lawsuit was unique. In another story, the *Register* noted that "never before has a question of school segregation arisen here. In some sections of the country court fights have been waged over colored, Chinese and Japanese children but never before have the Mexicans been mixed up in such a contest." "Alamosa School Fight Unique in Court Annals of this State," *Denver Catholic Register*, December 4, 1913.

9. According to historian Danielle Olden, "It was not until the late 1960s that Mexican American civil rights attorneys began to abandon the 'other white' argument. After years of winning school desegregation cases on the basis of their other whiteness . . . Mexican American civil rights attorneys turned to a new argument that emphasized their racial distinctiveness," Danielle R. Olden, "Shifting the Lens: Using Critical Race Theory and Latino Critical Theory to Re-Examine the History of School Desegregation," *Qualitative Inquiry* 21, no. 3 (2015): 235. Also see Richard Valencia, *Chicano Students and Courts: The Mexican American Legal Struggle for Educational Equality* (New York: New York University Press, 2008), 67.

10. J. R. C. Ruybal, interview by Luther Bean, Nancy Denious, and Elinor Kingery, sound recording, Colorado Historical Society, Denver, Colorado, November 20, 1962, item ID: 33317710, call number OH 83. Also see *Alamosa Independent Journal*, February 9, 1912. Luther Bean was one of the first faculty members at Adams State College, Alamosa, Colorado. http://www.museumtrail.org/luther-bean-museum.html.

11. Alamosa Clerk and County Recorder, Records Conejos Co., Warranty Deed Record, Book 72, p. 278. The Alamosa School District purchased the property from Samuel. B. Scholz on August 7, 1909. The property was used to build the Mexican School.

12. "Mexican Kiddies Prove They Are Able to Speak English," *Denver Catholic Register*, January 15, 1914. School enrollments at the Mexican School was provided by School District Superintendent George Thompson at the trial. He also noted that the school had the capacity to serve 200 students. It is important to note that the name of the school evolved, but most official and unofficial records made clear that the school was intended to serve Mexican American children. For example, a photograph of the school in the *Alamosa Manual and Course of Study* in 1911 was captioned as the "Spanish School." The "Spanish School" was featured in the manual and was photographed. It read that "teachers in this school must be persons who can use the Spanish language," *Manual and Course of Study for the Public Schools of Alamosa. Used by Order of, and Approved by, The Board of Education*, May 1, 1911: 59. In 1912, a map company illustrating the town of Alamosa listed the school as the "Mexican Public School" in its index. Sanborn Map Company (11 Broadway, New York), October 1912. It read that Alamosa had a population of 4,000 and was situated in Conejos County. Moreover, the Colorado Educational Directory in 1913–1914 listed the school as "Mexican Preparatory."

Finally, some members of the community referred to it as the Willis School and others simply called it the "Mexican School."

13. "Southern Colorado: Items of Interest Gathered from Exchanges," *Creede (Co.) Candle*, December 11, 1909.

14. *Alamosa Independent Journal*, February 9, 1912.

15. Gerald McKevitt, *Brokers of Culture: Italian Jesuits in the American West, 1848–1919* (Stanford, CA: Stanford University Press, 2007), 257.

16. "Mexicans in Alamosa Say the School Board Discriminates," *Rocky Mountain News*, September 10, 1913.

17. "More Discrimination by School Board," *Denver Catholic Register*, September 11, 1913.

18. "State Board Cannot Stop Segregation of Mexicans," *Denver Times*, September 13, 1913, p. 3. It was puzzling that the story in the *Rocky Mountain News* (September 10) noted that Colorado State Superintendent of Instruction Mary C. C. Bradford was going to seek advice (or an opinion) from Colorado Attorney General Fred Farrar in order to respond to the Mexican American complaint about the school segregation of their children in Alamosa. Apparently, Attorney General Farrar must have informed State Superintendent Bradford that the State Board of Education could not intervene. We searched for correspondence between State Superintendent of Instruction Mary C. C. Bradford and Colorado Attorney General Fred Farrar and found no record of such correspondence. However, in the Biennial Report of the Attorney General in 1913–1914, Attorney General Farrar responded to a query about the segregation of Mexican American children in the Durango School District, specifically citing the Mexican American segregation controversy in Alamosa in his response. The Durango School District Superintendent, Florence Salabar, wanted to know "whether or not it is legal to separate the Mexican children in the public schools, particularly in the first, second and third grades, for the other children." The attorney general responded that school districts in the state had much discretion to operate their schools. However, he noted that as "a matter of law, if the children are excluded by reason of their race, there is no question that such exclusion is illegal." However, he claimed that "if the test is one of language, then it is perfectly proper for it is an exercise of the right of school officials to prescribe the course of study for the best interest of the school." Opinion, see *Biennial Report of the Attorney General of the State of Colorado, 1913–1914* (Denver, CO: Smith-Brooks Printing, State Printers, 1914), 124–25.

19. "State Board Cannot Stop Segregation of Mexicans," *Alamosa Independent Journal*, September 19, 1913. In addition to the *Alamosa Independent Journal* story, a newspaper from Pine Bluffs, Wyoming, wrote a short blurb about the incident in its Colorado events section. In brief, it reported that Mexican American parents in Alamosa had complained to the "state superintendent of public instruction that

the school board of Alamosa has shown class distinction in building a separate school house for the Mexican children." "Colorado News: Gathered from All Parts of the State," *Pine Bluffs (Wy.) Post*, no date.

20. "Trinidad Faces Race War over Mexican Pupils: School Strike against Foreigners Lands in Court," *Denver Post*, November 21, 1913.

21. "School Battle in Alamosa to Enter Courts," *Denver Catholic Register*, November 20, 1913.

22. "Trinidad Faces Race War." We interpreted the "strike" as parents refusing to send their children to the Mexican School. Other newspapers in the area did not seem to cover this story.

23. "School Battle."

24. Ruybal interview.

25. Ruybal interview. Ruybal's interview coincided with what was described in the *1911 Manual and Course of Study for the Public Schools of Alamosa*, and the sentence we noted, "teachers in this school must be persons who can use the Spanish language."

26. Ruybal interview. The press confirmed Ruybal's point that the Spanish American Union met with the board. It was noted that "the Spanish Americans of this city petitioned the school board for the admittance of their children to the nearest school to their homes. The petition cites that the laws of the U.S. or state of Colorado, do not justify a segregation of the scholars attending the public schools, and the practice in vogue in the city is therefore arbitrary. The school board will undoubtedly act upon the petition before the school opens next month." *Alamosa Independent Journal*, August 8, 1913. A week later the press noted that "a large delegation of Mexican residents in this city will meet with the school directors on Monday night, when the proposition of the segregation of the American and Spanish American scholars will be considered, and an endeavor made to have the former school board ruling annulled." *Alamosa Independent Journal*, August 15, 1913.

27. Ruybal interview.

28. "Alamosa Mexicans Plan to Battle for Rights," *Denver Catholic Register*, October 23, 1914. This article confirmed Ruybal's point that he was raising money to fund the lawsuit in the area.

29. Ruybal interview. In addition to Ruybal's interview, it made sense that Francisco Maestas would be named plaintiff because of where his family lived. There were eighteen homes on Ross Avenue and the Maestas family were the only Mexican Americans. His home was seven blocks from the Mexican School. See F. A. McKinney's San Luis Directory, 1913–1914, p. 97.

30. Maestas et al. v. Shone et al., Petition by Raymond Sullivan, Attorney for Plaintiffs, 1–2.

31. *Maestas*, Sullivan, 2.

32. *Maestas*, Sullivan, 2.

33. *Maestas*, Sullivan, 3.

34. *Maestas*, Sullivan, 3.

35. *Maestas*, Sullivan, 3–4. See also, *The School Laws, Annotated, of the State of Colorado, as Amended to Date, January 1, 1912* (Denver, CO: Smith-Brooks Printing, State Printers), 17.

36. *Maestas*, Sullivan, 2, 4.

37. "Directors Think They Are Right," *Alamosa Independent Journal*, November 28, 1913. This story suggested that the number of Mexican American children who were in school beyond the fourth grade increased over 400 percent. This issue was not clear. What was clear was that Mexican Americans were, for the most part, not making it to the local high school. Based on the *Sierra Blanca Journal* (High School Yearbook), there was one Mexican American (Carlos Sanchez) who graduated in 1913. Other than Carlos Sanchez, there were no Mexican Americans enrolled at Alamosa High School in 1913. In 1917, there were no Mexican Americans enrolled at Alamosa High School. See the *Annual Echo*, 1917. High school yearbooks can be retrieved from the Alamosa High School library.

38. "Directors Think." A story in the *Denver Catholic Register* noted that "some of the Alamosa papers are bitterly fighting the Mexicans." See "Alamosa School Fight Unique in Court Annals of this State," *Denver Catholic Register*, December 4, 1913.

39. *Maestas*, Order, Chas. C. Holbrook, Judge.

40. *Maestas*, Defendants, Answer, John T. Adams, 3.

41. *Maestas*, Defendants, 3.

42. *Maestas*, Defendants, 3.

43. The *Denver Post* reported that Adams was trying to make the case that "Mexicans are not a distinct race, but are Caucasians, and therefore cannot be discriminated against as members of a distinct race by Americans." The story was short. It did not challenge Adams's argument about the racial background of Mexican American children, but it did ask its readers if they thought Mexicans were "Caucasians." How the headline of the story was framed seemed to question the idea that Americans would believe Mexicans were Caucasians and think they were indistinguishable from White children. See "Mexican Children Demand Schooling with Americans. Conejos Parents Suit Brought by Parents against Education Board. Are They Caucasians? Authorities Say Discrimination Is Made because They Speak No English," *Denver Post*, January 14, 1914; Also see David G. Garcia in *Strategies of Segregation: Race, Residence, and the Struggle for Educational Equality* (Berkeley: University of California Press, 2018), 43. In Oxnard, California, Garcia notes that from 1916 to 1930 the School Board president and board clerk purchased property in specific neighborhoods that prohibited ownership by "'persons not of the Caucasian race.'" Covenants specified that property could

not be "sold, conveyed, leased or rented to any person of the Negro, Japanese or Chinese race, or to any Mexican, Indian, or East-Indian." While Mexicans were legally White in the US, it was clear that they were not seen as Caucasians.

44. Miguel Maestas was allowed to stay out of school by his father because it was part of the Mexican American parent protest in Alamosa to boycott the segregated Mexican School.

45. *Maestas*, Defendants, 4.

46. *Maestas*, Defendants, 7.

47. *Maestas*, Defendants, 9.

48. *Maestas*, Defendants, 5.

49. *Maestas*, Defendants, 6.

50. *Maestas*, Defendants, 8–9.

51. *Maestas*, Defendants, 10.

52. "School Board Trial," *Alamosa Independent Journal*, January 9, 1914.

53. "Happenings Epitomized," *Alamosa Independent Journal*, January 9, 1914.

54. "Mexican Kiddies."

55. "Mexican Kiddies."

56. "Mexican Kiddies."

57. "Mexican Kiddies."

58. "Mexican Kiddies."

59. "Mexican Kiddies."

60. We acknowledge that sources in the Maestas case conflicted, as some claimed Mexican American children were segregated up to the fourth grade. Others said it was the fifth grade.

61. *Maestas*, Holbrook ruling. This story also has the entire ruling in "Mexican Patrons of Public Schools Win Court Decision," *Hooper-Mosca (Co.) Tribune*, March 21, 1914.

62. *Maestas*, Holbrook ruling.

63. *Maestas*, Holbrook ruling.

64. *Maestas*, Holbrook ruling.

65. See Holbrook's ruling in "Mexican Patrons."

66. "Alamosa Must Give Mexicans Free Schooling: Court Grants Mandamus Prohibiting Segregation of Spanish Speaking Children," *Rocky Mountain News*, March 22, 1914, 6.

67. "Alamosa Schools Ordered to Admit Mexican Children: Bar Lifted by Court Order of Judge Holbrook, in Suit for Boy. 'Pupils Should Be Taken Out of Spanish Classes When They Speak English,'" *Denver Post*, March 23, 1914.

68. "Alamosa Mexicans Win."

69. "Mexican Patrons of Public Schools Win Court Decision," *Alamosa Courier*, March 21, 1914.

70. "'Must Admit Mexicans,' to Have Free Schooling Same as American Children. Judge of District Court Grants Mandamus Prohibiting Segregation of the Spanish Speaking-Children," *Akron (Co.) Weekly Pioneer Press*, March 27, 1914.

71. "Los Ninos Mexicanos Victoriosos": La Corte Concede un 'Mandamus' Prohibiendo la Segregacion de los Niños de Habla Español," *La Revista de Taos*, April 17, 1914.

72. *Maestas et al. v. Shone et al.*, Defendants, Motion to Vacate Judgment and Decree and to Dismiss Action, Order, Chas. C. Holbrook. April 17, 1914, Judge. In the motion, Adams argued that Sullivan's amended petition was not sufficient enough to constitute a cause of action, that the court assumed it had jurisdiction over the lawsuit, and that the order had no support to issue a peremptory Mandamus. Adams also argued that the judgment and decree failed to specify which Spanish-speaking children in the district—other than Miguel Maestas—possessed an understanding of English sufficient for admission to other schools.

73. *Maestas*, Defendants, Motion. J. R. C. Ruybal did not mention in his oral interview that the case was appealed to the Colorado State Supreme Court.

74. Order dated April 24, 1914, in the case of *Maestas v. Shone*.

75. "Decision Rendered," *Alamosa Leader*, March 21, 1914.

76. "Mexican Patrons of Public Schools Win Court Decision: Judge Holbrook Finds Against Discrimination in Education," *Hooper-Mosca (Co.) Tribune*, March 21, 1914.

77. Plessy v. Ferguson, 163 U.S. 537 (1896).

78. Colorado Constitution, Section 427, article 9.

79. "Judge Holbrook Dies," *The Alamosa Leader*, August 29, 1914.

80. In addition to the search conducted in the Colorado State Archives, we were assisted by the librarian at the Colorado State Supreme Court Library. We found no record of the Maestas et al. v. Shone et al. (1914) case.

81. K. L. Bowman, "The New Face of School Desegregation," *Duke Law Journal* 50 (2001): 1751–1808. Brown v. Board of Educ., 374 U.S. 483 (1954), 1763. See also Ariela J. Gross, "'The Caucasian Cloak': Mexican Americans and the Politics of Whiteness in the 20th-Century Southwest," *Georgetown Law Journal* 95 (2006). http://heinonline.org/HOL/Page?handle=hein.journals/glj95&div=17&g_sent=1 - 404.

82. Gross, "Caucasian Cloak," 347. See also G. A Martinez, "The Legal Construction of Race: Mexican Americans and Whiteness," *Harvard Latino Law Review* 2 (1997). Clare Sheridan, "Another White Race: Mexican Americans and the Paradox of Whiteness in Jury Selection," *Law and History Review* 21, no. 1 (Spring, 2003): 1. http://www.jstor.org/stable/3595070.

83. S. H. Wilson, "Brown over 'Other White': Mexican Americans' Legal Arguments and Litigation Strategy in School Desegregation Lawsuits," *Law and History Review* 21, no. 1 (2003). Neil Foley, *The White Scourge: Blacks, Mexicans, and Poor Whites in Texas Cotton Culture* (Berkeley: University of California Press, 1997), 61. On this point, Foley noted that in 1920, the population in Mexico was about 14 million. Of that number, 10 percent were White, 30 percent Indian, and 60 percent mixed (mestizo).

84. Martinez, "Legal Construction," 327.

85. Laura E. Gomez, *Manifest Destinies: The Making of the Mexican American Race* (New York: New York University Press, 2007), 83.

86. Gross, "Caucasian Cloak," 341.

87. Thirteenth Census of the United States: 1910-Population. Department of Commerce and Labor-Bureau of the Census, Colorado, Conejos County, Precinct 12, Alamosa, Sheet No. 22 B. The racial classification of Francisco Maestas and his family in the 1910 Census was *W* for White.

88. Maestas et al. v. Shone et al., Petition by Raymond Sullivan, Attorney for Plaintiffs, 2.

89. "Alamosa Mexicans Win."

90. "Alamosa Mexicans Win."

91. "Suit That Alleges Discrimination Won by Alamosa Mexican," *Denver Catholic Register*, March 23, 1916. Also see, The People of the State of Colorado v. Henry H. Hamilton and James H. Williams, Reference #32, Alamosa District Court, Alamosa, Colorado, Term: March 3–15, 1916.

92. As was noted in United States v. Alamosa County, Colorado, 306 F. Supp. 2d 1016 (D. Colo. 2004), "discriminatory practices existed in Alamosa County, particularly during the first half of the twentieth century. These practices created or exacerbated socioeconomic disparities between Hispanic and Anglo residents. Official action and social activism, particularly during the last fifty years, however, have reduced the discriminatory climate in the county. This has improved educational and socioeconomic conditions for Hispanic residents and contributed to increasing diversity within the Hispanic population."

Chapter 2

1. Salvador Lozano, Report to Francisco Villavicencio, Archivo Histórico Genaro Estrada, January 23, 1916, File 494.14/18. "Porque tenían sangre de Negros" translates to "because they had Negro blood."

2. Eliseo Arredondo to Robert Lansing, secretary of State of the United States, Washington, DC, February 21, 1916, Archivo Histórico Genaro Estrada, File 494.14/18.

3. Arredondo to Lansing, February 21, 1916.

4. James D. Anderson, *The Education of Blacks in the South, 1860–1935* (Chapel Hill: University of North Carolina Press, 1988); Plessy v. Ferguson, 163 US 537, 16 S. Ct. 1138, 41 L. Ed. 256 (1896).

5. *The Birth of a Nation*. Directed by D. W. Griffith. United States, 1915.

6. Juan Gómez-Quiñones, *Roots of Chicano Politics, 1600–1940* (Albuquerque: University of New Mexico Press, 1994); Robert E. Quirk, *An Affair of Honor: Woodrow Wilson and the Occupation of Veracruz* (New York: Norton, 1962).

7. Richard Wormser, *D. W. Griffith's the Birth of a Nation (1915)* (2002), http://www.pbs.org/wnet/jimcrow/stories_events_birth.html.

8. Exclucion de Niños en las Escuelas de Texas, 1911, Archivo Histórico Genaro Estrada, File 11-14-300); Exclucion de Niños Mexicanos de las Escuelas Publicas de San Francisco, CA, 1919, Archivo Histórico Genaro Estrada, File 16-29-156.

9. At this time, Louisiana had not passed a compulsory education law that would have required the Perez and Lopez children to attend school (Jones, 1967), and we found no evidence that the voters of Rapides Parish, the local school district or local ward had approved compulsory education for the area as permitted under Louisiana law.

10. After we returned from Mexico City (i.e., the Archivo Histórico Genaro Estrada, Acervo Histórico Diplomático, Secretaría de Relaciones Exteriores), we traveled to Alexandria, Louisiana, and examined school board minutes from the Rapides Parish Schools (school district office) and additional historical sources available at the Rapides Parish Library, the Louisiana History Museum, and the Louisiana State University at Alexandria. In addition, primary and secondary sources, including books, journal articles, newspapers, census records, pamphlets, unpublished papers, online sources, and other material were used in this study.

11. Arnoldo De León, *Tejano West Texas* (College Station: Texas A&M University Press, 2015).

12. De León, *Tejano*, 107.

13. De León, *Tejano*.

14. Julie M. Weise, "Mexican Nationalisms, Southern Racisms: Mexicans and Mexican Americans in the U.S. South, 1908–1939," *American Quarterly* 60, no. 3 (2008).

15. Weise, Mexican Nationalisms.

16. Weise, Mexican Nationalisms.

17. Weise, Mexican Nationalisms, 763.

18. Julie M. Weise, *Corazón de Dixie: Mexicanos in the U.S. South since 1910* (Chapel Hill: University of North Carolina Press, 2015), 35–36.

19. Weise, Mexican Nationalisms.

20. Weise, Mexican Nationalisms.

21. Weise, *Corazón de Dixie*, 55.

22. Weise, *Corazón de Dixie*, 61.

23. Weise, *Corazón de Dixie*, 68.

24. *Lum v. Rice*, 275 U.S. 78 (1927).

25. Weise, *Corazon de Dixie*, 70.

26. Weise, *Corazon de Dixie*, 70.

27. Juan Almazán to Mexican Consulate, Washington, DC, August 3, 1911, Archivo Histórico Genaro Estrada, File 377.7/37.

28. Luis Rincón to Mexican Consulate in Washington, DC, August 5, 1918, Archivo Histórico Genaro Estrada, File 635 (1) 18/59.

29. Mexican Consulate, Seguin, Texas, to Ignacio Bonillas in Washington, DC, June 14, 1918, Archivo Histórico Genaro Estrada, File 635 (1) 8/59.

30. Weise, Mexican Nationalisms.

31. Jimmy Charlene Hammond, "A Brief History of Cheneyville, Louisiana." Unpublished manuscript, 1967, Watson Special Collection, Northwestern State University of Louisiana, 2.

32. Hammond, "A Brief History," 13.

33. United States Bureau of the Census. *Thirteenth Census of the United States Taken in the Year 1910: Statistics for Louisiana* (Washington, DC, 1913); United States Bureau of the Census. *Fourteenth Census of the United States Taken in the Year 1920* (Washington, DC, 1922).

34. Rapides Parish School Board, *Minutes of the Rapides Parish School Board*, vol. 7-29 (Alexandria, LA, 1915).

35. "Obituary for Walter P. Ford," *The Town Talk* [Alexandria, LA], March 9, 1916.

36. George Mason Graham Stafford, *Three Pioneer Rapides Families: A Genealogy* (Baton Rouge, LA: Claitors Pub. Division, 1946); Solomon Northup, *Twelve Years a Slave* (Auburn: Derby and Miller, 1853).

37. W. H. Orr to D. B. Showalter, November 1, 1915, Archivo Histórico Genaro Estrada, File 494.14/18.

38. Orr to Showalter, November 1, 1915.

39. Ivey Cannon to D. B. Showalter, November 1, 1915, Archivo Histórico Genaro Estrada, File 494.14/18).

40. Cannon to Showalter, November 1, 1915.

41. Cannon to Showalter, November 1, 1915.

42. Cannon to Showalter, November 1, 1915.

43. Cannon to Showalter, November 1, 1915.

44. D. B. Showalter to J. H. Johnson, November 1, 1915 (Archivo Histórico Genaro Estrada, File 494.14/18.

45. Showalter to Johnson, November 1, 1915.

46. J. M. Johnson to D. B. Showalter, November 2, 1915, Archivo Histórico Genaro Estrada, File 494.14/18.

47. Weise, *Corazón de Dixie*, 50.

48. Salvador Lozano, Report to Francisco Villavicencio, Archivo Histórico Genaro Estrada, January 23, 1916, File 494.14/18.

49. Lozano to Villavicencio, January 23, 1916.

50. Lozano to Villavicencio, January 23, 1916.

51. Lozano to Villavicencio, January 23, 1916. Given the time and location of this incident, it is plausible that W. P. Ford referenced "black blood" to throw the Mexican children out of the White elementary school because it referenced

the notion of what is popularly referred to as the "one-drop rule," which has been used historically to draw lines of racial classification. The "one-drop rule" was a way of referring to racial classification based on the idea of "hypodescent"—the consequential assignment of children of mixed unions (usually Black and White) to the group with the lower status. In this case, the mestizo features of the Mexican children were probably visible to Ford. Legal scholars have argued that the one-drop rule was uniquely American, complicated, rooted in colonial history, strengthened during antebellum America, and set social and legal boundaries for African Americans during the early twentieth century. For historical and legal interpretations of the "one-drop rule," see Daniel J. Sharfstein, "Crossing the Color Line: Racial Migration and the One-Drop Rule, 1600–1860," *Minnesota Law Review* 91, no. 592 (2007), http://scholarship.law.vanderbilt.edu/faculty-publications/386; Christine B. Hickman, "The Devil and the One Drop Rule: Racial Categories, African Americans, and the U.S. Census," *Michigan Law Review* 95, no. 1161 (1997). Available at https://repository.law.umich.edu/mlr/vol95/iss5/2; Kenneth A. Davis, "Racial Designation in Louisiana: One Drop of Black Blood Makes a Negro," *Hastings Constitutional Law Quarterly* 3, no. 199 (1976): 207. Available at *https://repository.uchastings.edu/hastings_constitutional_law_quaterly/vol3/iss1/7*; Murray, Pauli. *States' Laws on Race and Color* (Athens: University of Georgia Press, 1951). We also want to note that Louisiana has an interesting and complicated relationship with the one-drop rule and the classification of mixed-race individuals. See Raymond T. Diamond and Robert J. Cottrol, "Codifying Caste: Louisiana's Racial Classification Scheme and the Fourteenth Amendment," *Loyola Law Review* 29 (1983): 255. However, given this historical moment and the setting of Cheneyville, it is a plausible inference that Ford was utilizing the arguments based on hypodescent to race the children in a way that permitted their exclusion.

52. Lozano to Villavicencio, January 23, 1916.

53. Lozano to Villavicencio, January 23, 1916.

54. Lozano to Villavicencio, January 23, 1916.

55. Lozano to Villavicencio, January 23, 1916.

56. Lozano to Villavicencio, January 23, 1916.

57. Lozano to Villavicencio, January 23, 1916.

58. Lozano to Villavicencio, January 23, 1916.

59. Francisco R. Villavicencio to Eliseo Arredondo, February 2, 1916, Archivo Histórico Genaro Estrada, File 494.14/18.

60. Third Assistant Secretary of State to Eliseo Arredondo, February 29, 1916, Archivo Histórico Genaro Estrada, File 494.14/18.

61. Third Assistant Secretary, 1916.

62. Third Assistant Secretary, 1916.

63. Second Assistant Secretary of State to Eliseo Arredondo, March 16, 1916, Archivo Histórico Genaro Estrada, File 494.14/18.

64. Second Assistant Secretary, 1916.

65. Sue Eakin, *Rapides Parish: An Illustrated History* (Northridge, CA: Windsor Publications, 1987).

66. Eakin, *Rapides Parish*, 47.

67. Gómez-Quiñones, *Roots*.

68. Francisco E. Balderrama, *In Defense of La Raza: The Los Angeles Mexican Consulate and the Mexican American Community, 1929–1936* (Tucson: University of Arizona Press, 1982); Gilbert G. Gonzalez, *Mexican Consuls and Labor Organizing: Imperial Politics in the American Southwest* (Austin: University of Texas, 1999).

Chapter 3

1. It is important to note that the available Alamosa School District Board Minutes begin in the 1940s. Earlier School Board Minutes in the District were not available.

2. Minutes of the Board of Education, April 24, 1930, City of Hutchinson (Kansas).

3. Minutes, April 24, 1930.

4. Rubén Donato, *Mexicans and Hispanos in Colorado Schools and Communities, 1920–1960* (Albany: State University of New York Press, 2007); Gilbert G. Gonzalez, *Chicano Education in the Era of Segregation* (Philadelphia: Balch Institute Press, 1990); Laura K. Muñoz, "Romo v. Laird: Mexican American Segregation and the Politics of Belonging in Arizona," *Western Legal History* 26, nos. 1 and 2 (2013); Guadalupe San Miguel, *"Let All of Them Take Heed": Mexican Americans and the Campaign for Educational Equality in Texas, 1910–1981* (Austin: University of Texas Press, 1987).

5. Larry G. Rutter, "Mexican Americans in Kansas: A Survey and Social Mobility Study, 1900–1970" (unpublished master's thesis, Kansas State University, 1972).

6. J. Neale Carman and Associates, *Foreign Language Units of Kansas, Vol. II: Account of Settlement and Settlements in Kansas* (Lawrence: The University Press of Kansas, 1974).

7. "A 'Jim Crow' School in Kansas," *Springfield Republican*, February 24, 1905, http://genealogytrails.com/kan/wyandotte/newspaperitems.html.

8. Judith F. Laird, "Argentine, Kansas: The Evolution of a Mexican-American Community, 1905–1940" (unpublished PhD diss., University of Kansas, 1975).

9. J. Morgan Kousser, "Before Plessy, Before Brown: The Development of the Law of Racial Integration in Louisiana and Kansas," in *Toward a Usable Past: Liberty Under State Constitutions*, ed. Paul Finkelman and Stephen E. Gottlieb (Athens: University of Georgia Press, 1991).

10. Chester I. Long, F. Dumont Smith, and Hugh P. Farrelly, *Revised Statutes of Kansas (Annotated) 1923* (Topeka: Kansas State Printing Plant, 1923): §72-1724.

11. Long et al., *Revised Statutes*, §72-1724.

12. Long et al., *Revised Statutes*, §72-1809.

13. Board of Education v. Tinnon, 26 Kan. 1 (1881).

14. Kristi L. Bowman, "The New Face of School Desegregation," *Duke Law Journal* 50 (2001): 1763.

15. Laura E. Gomez, *Manifest Destinies: The Making of the Mexican American Race* (New York: New York University Press, 2007).

16. George A Martinez, "The Legal Construction of Race: Mexican Americans and Whiteness," *Harvard Latino Law Review* 2 (1997): 327.

17. Rubén Donato and Jarrod Hanson, "Legally White, Socially 'Mexican': The Politics of De Jure and De Facto School Segregation in the American Southwest," *Harvard Educational Review* 82, no. 2 (Summer 2012); Ariela J. Gross, " 'The Caucasian Cloak': Mexican Americans and the Politics of Whiteness in the Twentieth-Century Southwest," *Georgetown Law Journal* 95 (2007); Ian Haney López, "Race, Ethnicity, Erasure: The Salience of Race to Latcrit Theory," *California Law Review* 85, no. 5 (1997); Steven H. Wilson, "Brown over 'Other White': Mexican Americans' Legal Arguments and Litigation Strategy in School Desegregation Lawsuits" *Law and History Review* 21, no. 1 (Spring 2003).

18. Robert Oppenheimer, "Acculturation or Assimilation: Mexican Immigrants in Kansas, 1900 to World War II," *The Western Historical Quarterly* 16, no. 4 (October 1985).

19. Petition of 27 Mexican parents in Herington, Kansas, to the Mexican consul, December 31, 1915.

20. Anonymous to Mexican consul, October 18, 1911, Archivo Histórico Genaro Estrada, File 378.4/17.

21. J. F. Vasquez, Letter, January 4, 1916, Archivo Histórico Genaro Estrada, File 479.1/7.

22. Jose Gonzalez to Mexican consul, November 12, 1920, Archivo Histórico Genaro Estrada, File 13-14-20.

23. Jerome Hanl, chief of police, to Mexican Consul M. N. Morales, November 1, 1920, Archivo Histórico Genaro Estrada, File 13-14-20.

24. Hanl to Morales, December 8, 1920.

25. Rutter, "Mexican Americans in Kansas"; see also Domingo Ricart, *Just across the Tracks: Report on a Survey of Five Mexican Communities in the State of Kansas (Emporia, Florence, Newton, Wichita, Hutchinson)* (Lawrence: University of Kansas, 1950).

26. Acting Secretary of State in Washington, DC to Don Manuel C. Tellez, Mexican Charge de'Affairs, n.d., Archivo Histórico Genaro Estrada, File 1451-1.

27. Laird, "Argentine, Kansas."

28. Laird, "Argentine, Kansas"; Robert M. Cleary, "The Education of Mexican-Americans in Kansas City, Kansas, 1916–1951" (unpublished master's thesis, University of Missouri, 2002).

29. Laird, "Argentine, Kansas," 193.

30. Laird, "Argentine, Kansas."

31. Cleary, "Education," 6.

32. "Seek Mexican School: Argentine, Armourdale Districts Wish Separate Rooms for Foreigners," *Kansas City Kansan*, October 11, 1922, 7.

33. "Mexican School Planned: Emerson P.T.A. Committee Named to Make Arrangements for Institution in Argentine," *Kansas City Kansan*, October 16, 1922.

34. "Mexican School Planned."

35. "To Talk Mexican School: Education Board to Take Up Matter of Building for Foreigners Tonight," *Kansas City Kansan*, December 11, 1922, 2.

36. "School Districts of City Are Announced: Table, Showing Where Children of All Districts Will Attend Classes Is Issued," *Kansas City Kansan*, September 5, 1923, 6.

37. "Funds Surplus Pays for Mexican School: Building Erected at Cost of 7,000 but Taxpayers Are Not Burdened," *Kansas City Kansan*, September 23, 1923, 8b.

38. Laird, "Argentine, Kansas"; Loren L. Taylor, *The Consolidated Ethnic History of Wyandotte County* (Kansas City: Kansas Ethnic Council, 2000); see also Loren L. Taylor and R. Marin, *A Short Ethnic History of the Mexican People in Wyandotte County* (Kansas City: Kansas Ethnic Council, 2000).

39. Serda, Daniel. "Finding Latin Roots: Hispanic Heritage in Kansas City." *Kansas Preservation* 33 (2011): 12. https://www.kshs.org/resource/survey/kckhistorichispanicamericanplaces2011.pdf.

40. Cleary, "Education," 66.

41. Laird, "Argentine, Kansas."

42. Mexican Consul Romulo Vargas to Kansas Governor, May 24, 1924, Kansas Historical Society, Gov. Davis, Correspondence File, Educational Matters, Box 214, Folder 4.

43. Governor Jonathan Davis to J. W. Miley, State Superintendent of Public Instruction May 27, 1924, Kansas Historical Society, Gov. Davis, Correspondence File, Educational Matters, Box 214, Folder 4.

44. Jess W. Miley to Governor Jonathan Davis, May 29, 1924, Kansas Historical Society, Gov. Davis, Correspondence File, Educational Matters, Box 214, Folder 4.

45. Miley to Davis, May 29, 1924.

46. Miley to Davis, May 29, 1924.

47. Mexican consul to Governor Jonathan Davis, August 28, 1924, Kansas Historical Society, Gov. Davis, Correspondence File, Educational Matters, Box 214, Folder 4.

48. "Solves Racial Problem: Mexican Children Will Be Enrolled in Old Major Hudson School, Say Authorities," *Kansas City Kansan*, September 17, 1924, 10.

49. "Solves Racial Problem," 10.

50. "Solves Racial Problem," 10.

51. Western Union Telegram from Mexican consul to Governor Jonathan M. Davis, September 19, 1924, Kansas Historical Society, Correspondence File, Educational Matters, Box 214, Folder 4.

52. "School Racial Row Is Over: Judge Orders Six Mexican Boys Involved in the Major Hudson Squabble to Change Enrollment," *Kansas City Kansan*, February 4, 1925, 4.

53. "State Officials into Mexican Pupil Row. Attorney General Gets Affidavit from Pearson Following Consul's Complaint," *The Kansas City Kansan*, October 17, 1925.

54. "State Officials."

55. "State Officials."

56. "State Officials."

57. Cleary, "Education," 115.

58. Mary I. Beverage, *Saturnino Alvarado: Civil Rights Activist, 1883–1955* (Kansas City Public Library, n.d.), https://pendergastkc.org/article/biography/saturnino-alvarado; Mary Sanchez, "KCK School to Salute Pioneering parent," *Kansas City* [Kansas] *Star*, August 31, P2003.

59. The Mexican consul records were accessed from the Archivo Histórico Genaro Estrada. Acervo Histórico Diplomático. Secretaría de Relaciones Exteriores located in Mexico City: Edificio Triangular Ala "B" Basamento. Ricardo Flores Magon No. 2 Col. Guerrerro C.P. 06300. Mexico D.F.

60. Cleary, "Education," 117.

61. Cleary, "Education," 116–17.

62. Cleary, "Education," 117.

63. "Federal Injunction Mexican Possibility: Hayward Declares That U.S. Courts Might Act to Stifle School Row," *The Kansas City Kansan*, October 28, 1925; "Mexican Case Goes to Topeka," *Kansas City Kansan*, October 29, 1925; 1925; "Mexican Crisis to Consul: Attorney Hayward Will Find Out What Bearing Treaty Has on Armourdale School Affair," *Kansas City Kansan*, November 21, 925; "Mexican Parley Delayed: Hayward's Conference With Attorney General Relative to School Rumpus Here Is Postponed," *Kansas City Kansan*, October 16, 1925; "Mexican Row in K. C. Schools Up to State Dept: Trouble Caused by Objection of Parents Is Near International Proportions," *Kansas City Kansan*, October 24, 1925; "Special School Is Unfair, Says Mexican Envoy: J. Garza Zertuche, Consul General, Is in K.C. to Suggest Remedy," *Kansas City Kansan*, November 9, 1925.

64. Cleary, "Education," 122.

65. Cleary, "Education," 124.

66. Cleary, "Education," 124.

67. Laird, "Argentine, Kansas," 195.

68. Laird, "Argentine, Kansas."

69. Laird, "Argentine, Kansas," 196.

70. Serda, Finding Latin Roots, 13.

71. Secretary of Chamber of Commerce in Salina to W. S. Hausner, September 16, 1920, Salina [Kansas] City Schools, School Board Minutes.

72. Secretary to Hausner, September 16, 1920.

73. Letter from Secretary of the Saline County Ministerial Association, October 18, 1920, Salina [Kansas] City Schools, School Board Minutes; Letter Written by Board President Dr. O. D. Walker, January 8, 1921, Salina [Kansas] City Schools, School Board Minutes.

74. Letter by Walker, January 8, 1921.

75. Annual Report of the Salina Public Schools for the Year Ending June 30, 1923 (Salina Public Library, Salina KS).

76. Annual Report of the Salina Public Schools Year Ending June 30, 1928 (Salina Public Library, Salina KS); compare with Susan N. Reitz, "The Historical Development of the Salina, Kansas School System, 1861–1970" (unpublished PhD diss., Kansas State University, 1995).

77. Annual Report of the Salina City Schools, September 5, 1933 (Salina Public Library, Salina, KS).

78. Annual Report of the Salina City Schools for the Year Ending June, 1936 (Salina Public Library, Salina, KS).

79. Carman and Associates, *Foreign Language Units*; Ricart, "Just across the Tracks."

80. Emporia City School Board Minutes (Emporia City Schools, Emporia, KS, n.d.).

81. Peach, School Board President and Nora Wood, Secretary, to Mesars, Sarry Wade, J. C. Brogan, C. J. Stout and Other Petitioners from Central Avenue District (Emporia City Schools, January 8, 1923).

82. Peach and Wood to Sarry Wade et al.

83. Peach and Wood to Sarry Wade et al.

84. Peach and Wood to Sarry Wade et al.

85. Rider Stockdale, Superintendent Horton City Schools, Kansas, to State Attorney General, April 4, 1929, Kansas Historical Society, Attorney General Numerical Files, No. 119, Schools, 1929–1934.

86. Stockdale to State Attorney General, April 4, 1929.

87. Stockdale to State Attorney General, April 4, 1929.

88. State Attorney General to Superintendent Rider Stockdale, April 8, 1929, Kansas Historical Society, Attorney General Numerical Files, No. 119, Schools, 1929–1934.

89. US Census Bureau, Decennial Census, 1910; US Census Bureau, Decennial Census, 1920; US Census Bureau, Decennial Census, 1930; http://www.census.gov/prod/www/decennial.html.

90. Carman and Associates, *Foreign Language Units*, 223.

91. Minutes of the Board of Education, July 30, 1925, City of Hutchinson (Kansas).

92. Minutes of the Board of Education, July 2, 1931, City of Hutchinson (Kansas).

93. "Want School for Mexicans: Residents of South Part of Hutchinson Make Demand on School District," *Hutchinson* [Kansas] *News*, May 6, 1930.

94. "Want School."

95. "Want School."

96. "Want School."

97. J. E. Geyer to Attorney General W. A. Smith, May 23, 1930, Kansas Historical Society, Attorney General-Numerical Files No. 119, Schools (1929–1934).

98. Geyer to Smith, May 23, 1930.

99. Attorney General W. A. Smith to J. E. Geyer, May 26, 1930, Kansas Historical Society. Attorney General-Numerical Files No. 119, Schools (1929–1934).

100. "Can't Segregate Mexican Children: Board of Education Told It Cannot Provide Separate School Facilities," *The Hutchinson* [Kansas] *News*, June 2, 1930.

101. Mauro Garcia, parent of El Comité Patriótico, to Mexican Consul Alfredo Vasquez, September 8, 1930, Archivo Histórico Genaro Estrada, File 3521-1.

102. Alfredo C. Vasquez, consul of Mexico, to C. D. Jennings, Hutchinson School Board President, June 12, 1930, Archivo Histórico Genaro Estrada, File 3521-1.

103. C. D. Jennings to Mexican Consul Alfredo Vasquez, September 12, 1930, Archivo Histórico Genaro Estrada, File 3521-1.

104. Jennings to Vasquez, September 12, 1930.

105. Kathie Hinnen, "Mexican Immigrants to Hutchinson, Kansas, 1905–1940: How a Temporary Haven Became Home" (unpublished master's thesis, Southwest Missouri State University, 1998), 85–86.

106. James D. Anderson, *The Education of Blacks in the South, 1860–1935* (Chapel Hill: University of North Carolina Press, 1988).

107. Alfredo Vasquez, Mexican consul, to Sr. Consul General Mexican in New Orleans, LA, May 22, 1929, Archivo Histórico Genaro Estrada, File IV-264-34.

108. Cleary, "Education."

109. Cleary, "Education," 125.

110. David J. Peavler, "Drawing the Color Line in Kansas City: The Creation of Sumner High School," *Kansas History: A Journal of the Central Plains* 27 (2005).

111. Salina City School Board Minutes, Salina City Schools, Salina Unified School District, Salina, KS (n.d.).

112. Cleary, "Education," 64–65.

Chapter 4

1. Jim Crow Laws, History.com Editors, February 28, 2018, accessed July 16, 2019, https://www.history.com/topics/early-20th-century-us/jim-crow-laws.

2. Juan R. Almazan to Mexican consulate in St. Louis, Missouri. August 7, 1911, File 377.7.37, Archivo Histórico Genaro Estrada, Acervo Histórico Diplomático, Secretaría de Relaciones Exteriores (hereafter cited as Archivo Histórico Genaro Estrada).

3. Jack Danciger to Mexican Ambassador Eliseo Arredondo, December 10, 1915; in this file was the newspaper clip: "Mexican in Negro Hospital, Protest," *Kansas City Post.* December 7, 1915; "Mexican Consul Protests," *Kansas City Journal*, December 7, 1915; "Los Mexicanos Deben Ser Tratados Rectamente," *El Cosmopolita*, December 4, 1915, File 461.5.15, Archivo Histórico Genaro Estrada.

4. Danciger to Mexican Ambassador.

5. Danciger to Mexican Ambassador.

6. Guillermo Seguin to Mexican Ambassador Don Ignacio Bonillas, May 31, 1918; Department of State Secretary Robert Lansing to Mexican Ambassador Don Ygnacio Bonillas, June 19, 1918; Mexican Ambassador Ignacio Bonillas to Mexican consul Guillermo Seguin, June 20, 1918; Acting Secretary of State to Mexican Ambassador Ignacio Bonillas, July 31, 1918; Mexican Consul Guillermo Seguin to Mexican Ambassador Ignacio Bonillas, August 14, 1918, File 635 (1).8.59, Archivo Histórico Genaro Estrada.

7. Department of State to Mexican Consul, July 31, 1918; Mexican Ambassador to Department of State, June 20, 1918; Department of State Lansing to Mexican Ambassador Don Ygnacio Bonillas, June 19, 1918, File 635(1).8.59, Archivo Histórico Genaro Estrada.

8. Consul Guillermo Seguin to Mexican Ambassador Ignacio Bonillas, August 27, 1918, File 592.8.46, Archivo Histórico Genaro Estrada.

9. Consul Seguin to Mexican Consul in San Antonio, August 27, 1918; A. E. Amerman, Houston Mayor, to Mexican Consul in San Antonio, September 20, 1918, File 592.8/46, Archivo Histórico Genaro Estrada.

10. Gabriel Botello to Mexican Ambassador, July 10, 1919, File 592.26.46, Archivo Histórico Genaro Estrada.

11. Petition written to Mexican Consul Gabriel Botello from group of Mexican residents in Victoria, Texas, April 15, 1920, File 653.24.25, Archivo Histórico Genaro Estrada.

12. Vice Consul Andres Garcia to New Mexico Governor Lindsey, August 17, 1918, File 592.8/46, Archivo Histórico Genaro Estrada.

13. Mexican consulate to Mexican Ambassador, September 20, 1923; Acting Secretary of State to Don Manuel Tellez, September 22, 1923; Newspaper clipping "Diplomat Protests Ban on Mexicans" (no date), File: 1451-1, Archivo Histórico Genaro Estrada.

14. "Johnstown's Immigration History," https://www.jaha.org/attractions/heritage-discovery-center/johnstown-history/johnstowns-immigration-history/.

15. Becky Little, "America's First Memorial to Its 4,400 Lynching Victims," accessed April 20, 2018, https://www.history.com/news/lynching-museum-alabama-national-memorial-for-peace-and-justice.

16. William D. Carrigan and Clive Webb, "The Lynching of Persons of Mexican Origin or Descent in the United States, 1848–1928," *Journal of Social History* 37, no. 2 (Winter 2003), 411–38; See also Nicholas Villanueva Jr., *The Lynching of Mexicans in the Texas Borderlands* (Albuquerque: University of New Mexico Press, 2017); Simon Romero, "Lynch Mobs Killed Latinos across the West:. The Fight to Remember the Atrocities Is Just Starting," *New York Times*, March 2, 2019, https://www.nytimes.com/2019/03/02/us/porvenir-massacre-texas-mexicans.html.

17. Department of State to Mexican Consul Don Manuel de Azpiroz, January 25, 1905, File 260(1)13.36, Archivo Histórico Genaro Estrada.

18. A. A. Chaney, Attorney at Law, to Mexican consul, April 6, 1912, Files: 1451-6, Archivo Histórico Genaro Estrada; "Excerpt of Report of Department of Justice Concerning Alleged Persecution of Mexican citizens at Mayerville, Mississippi" (n.d.), Files 1451-8, Archivo Histórico Genaro Estrada.

19. Governor of Mississippi James Kimble Vardaman to Vice Consul of Mexico, Scranton, Mississippi, December 21, 1904, File 394.15.15, Archivo Histórico Genaro Estrada.

20. W. R. Stubbs to Secretary of State Philander Knox, November 16, 1911, File 378.4.17, Archivo Histórico Genaro Estrada.

21. Petition written and signed from twenty-six Mexicans in Herington, Kansas, to the Mexican consul, December 31, 1915, File 479.1/7, Archivo Histórico Genaro Estrada.

22. Jack Danciger, Mexican Consul to Arthur Capper, Governor of Kansas (n.d.), File 479.1/7, Archivo Histórico Genaro Estrada.

23. Steven H. Wilson, "Brown over 'Other White': Mexican Americans' Legal Arguments and Litigation Strategy in School Desegregation Lawsuits," *Law and History Review* 21, no. 1 (Spring 2003); David Montejano, *Anglos and Mexicans in the Making of Texas, 1836–1986* (Austin: University of Texas Press, 1987).

24. Susanne Gamboa, "History of Racism Against Mexican-Americans Clouds Texas Immigration Law," June 3, 2017, https://www.nbcnews.com/news/latino/history-racism-against-mexican-americans-clouds-texas-immigration-law-n766956; Fernanda Echavarria and Marlon Bishop, " 'No Mexicans Allowed': School Segregation in the Southwest," March 11, 2016, https://www.latinousa.org/2016/03/11/no-mexicans-allowed-school-segregation-in-the-southwest/.

25. Walter L. Pope, *A Digest of the Statutes of Arkansas, Embracing All Laws of a General Nature in Force at the Close of the Regular Session of the General Assembly of 1937* (Texarkana, TX, Helms Printing Company, 1937) §11535(c).

26. Julie Weise, *Corazon de Dixie: Mexicanos in the U.S. South Since 1910* (Chapel Hill, University of North Carolina Press, 2015).

27. Ruben Gaxiola to Mexican Ambassador in Washington, DC, November 19, 1949, File TM-26-32, Archivo Histórico Genaro Estrada.

28. See photo "Goldcrest Beer 51." Also see Naomi Warren. "Agents of Humanity: Race and Dignity in Arkansas." In A State by State History of Race and Racism in the United States. Patricia Reid-Merritt (ed.). ABC-CLIO-Greenwood

(2019). Warren notes that in Marked Tree they were "not accepted socially, and Mexicans often felt more comfortable among African Americans," 71.

29. "No Mexican" signs, File TM-26-32, Archivo Histórico Genaro Estrada.

30. "Joint Investigation" (n.d.), File TM-26-32. Archivo Histórico Genaro Estrada.

31. Report from A. Cano, Mexican consul and W. A. Doyle, USES Representative, Joint Investigation Report Alleged Discrimination Marked, Tree, Ark., October 8, 1951, File TM-26-32, Archivo Histórico Genaro Estrada.

32. "An Ordinance Prohibiting Discrimination against Mexican Nationals because of Their Ancestry or Nationality," Ordinance No. 29. October 9, 1952, Jess M. Wike, Mayor, File TM-26-32, Archivo Histórico Genaro Estrada.

33. J. Lee Wright, Sheriff of Poinsett County, Jess M. Wike, Mayor of Marked Tree, and Finley Smith, Chief of Police of Marked Tree, to A. Cano del Castillo, Consul of Mexico, Memphis, Tennessee, August 31, 1951, SRE: File TM-26-32, Archivo Histórico Genaro Estrada.

34. Marked Tree Chamber of Commerce to Mexican Consul A. Cano Del Castillo, October 8, 1952, File TM-26-32, Archivo Histórico Genaro Estrada.

35. Letter from A. Cano del Castillo, Mexican Consul to Denton O. Rushing, Employment Security Division, November 23, 1949, File TM-26-32, Archivo Histórico Genaro Estrada.

36. Western Union Telegram from Mexican Consul Cano de Castillo to Ed McDonald, US Department of Labor, October 6, 1951, Archivo Histórico Genaro Estrada; see also A. Cano del Castillo to Mexican Consul General, November 24, 1951, File TM-26-32, Archivo Histórico Genaro Estrada.

37. Weise, *Corazon*.

38. Warren. "Agents of Humanity: Race and Dignity in Arkansas," 71.

39. "La exclusion de niños Mexicans en las escuelas de Texas," Secretaría de Relación Exteriores, January 6, 1911, File 11-14-300, Archivo Histórico Genaro Estrada.

40. Mexican Consul Mauro Castro to Manuel Tellez, First Secretary of the Mexican Embassy in Washington, DC, November 16, 1920, File: 663.10.10, Archivo Histórico Genaro Estrada.

41. Mexican Consul L. Garza Leal to G. F. Oheim. June 6, 1922, File 631.48.58, Archivo Histórico Genaro Estrada.

42. G. F. Oheim, president of the school board, to L. Garza Leal, Mexican consul, June 12, 1922, File 631.48.58, Archivo Histórico Genaro Estrada.

43. G. G. Oheim to L. Garza Leal, Mexican Consul, June 2, 1922, File 631.48.58, Archivo Histórico Genaro Estrada.

44. Mayor F. G. Blumberg to Garza Leal, Mexican consul, May 27, 1922, File 631.48.58, Archivo Histórico Genaro Estrada.

45. Enrique D. Ruiz to C. Encargado de Negocios de Mexico, ad-Interim, Ref: segregación niños mexicanos de las Escuelas Oficiales de este estado, October 18, 1922, File 631-48.58, Archivo Histórico Genaro Estrada.

46. Western Union Telegram from Mexican Ambassador Ignicio Bonillas to California Governor, June 8, 1919, File 592.21.46, Archivo Histórico Genaro Estrada; the Mexican Ambassador's complaint to the governor became public and was cited in a Southern California newspaper. Newspaper clipping, "Envoy Asks Segregation in Schools Be Stopped," *The Call*, June 7, 1919, File 592.21.46 (83) File: 16-29-156, Archivo Histórico Genaro Estrada.

47. Report from State Superintendent of Instruction Will Wood to California Governor William Stephens, June 26, 1919, File 16-29-156, Archivo Histórico Genaro Estrada.

48. Will Wood to California Governor, File 16-29-156, Archivo Histórico Genaro Estrada.

49. Will Wood to California Governor, File 16-29-156, Archivo Histórico Genaro Estrada.

50. Will Wood to California Governor, File: 16-29-156, Archivo Histórico Genaro Estrada.

51. Will Wood to California Governor, File 16-29-156, Archivo Histórico Genaro Estrada.

52. Will Wood to California Governor, File 16-29-156, Archivo Histórico Genaro Estrada.

53. Will Wood to California Governor, File 16-29-156, Archivo Histórico Genaro Estrada.

54. Guillermo S. Seguin, Mexican Vice Consul to Jose Garza Zertuche, Mexican Consul in Los Angeles, July 10, 1919, File 16.29.156, Archivo Histórico Genaro Estrada.

55. Mexican Consul Ramon DeNegri to S. Diego Fernandez, head of SRE in Mexico City, June 27, 1919, File 592.21.46, Archivo Histórico Genaro Estrada; see also Acting US Secretary of State to Mexican Ambassador Ignacio Bonilla, July 18, 1919, File 592.21.46, Archivo Histórico Genaro Estrada. The Department of State wrote to Mexican Ambassador Don Ygnaico Bonillas to inform him that he had received information that "the State Board of Education of California proposes to exclude gradually Mexican children from the public schools for children of the white race and place them in establishments intended for negroes."

56. Guadalupe San Miguel and Richard Valencia, "From the Treaty of Guadalupe Hidalgo to Hopwood: The Educational Plight and Struggle of Mexican Americans in the Southwest," *Harvard Educational Review* 68, no. 3 (1998): 370.

57. Lauro Izaguirre to Consul in Mexico City, March 28, 1931, File: IV-323-6, Archivo Histórico Genaro Estrada.

58. Letter from Consul Enrique Santibañez to Departamento de Protección, September 11, 1930; letter from Enrique Santibanez to Manuel Gonzales, September 17, 1930, File: IV-323-6; blueprint of the town of Mission and the location of Morgan Junior High and the Vocational Junior High, File IV-264-32, Archivo Histórico Genaro Estrada.

59. Felipe Garcia, Alfredo Garza, and Matias Garza to Mission School Board Members, December 30, 1930, File IV-323-6, Archivo Histórico Genaro Estrada.

60. Felipe et al. to Members, File IV-323-6, Archivo Histórico Genaro Estrada (1175–1182).

61. Felipe et al. to Members, File IV-323-6, Archivo Histórico Genaro Estrada.

62. Felipe et al. to Members, File IV-323-6, Archivo Histórico Genaro Estrada.

63. Mission School Board Members to Felipe Garcia, Alfredo Garza, and Matia Garza, January 7, 1931, File IV-323-6, Archivo Histórico Genaro Estrada.

64. Members to Felipe et al., File IV-323-6, Archivo Histórico Genaro Estrada.

65. Graduating class photos, Mission High School Library, accessed from the Mission High School Library. In 1934, thirty-two graduated from Mission High School. Of those, eight were Mexican American graduates.

66. Irving G. Hendrick. *The Education of Non-Whites in California, 1849–1970* (San Francisco, CA: R & E Research Associates), 1977, 87.

67. Page from the California School Code, 119, File IV-12-14, Archivo Histórico Genaro Estrada. Also available in California. *School Code of the State of California and Acts of the Forty-eighth Regular Session of the Legislature Supplemental Thereto.* Sacramento, California State Printing Office, C. H. Smith, State Printer, 106–7 (1929).

68. Assembly Bill, No. 433, January 19, 1931, Referred to Committee on Education, File IV-320-34, Archivo Histórico Genaro Estrada.

69. Lillian Hill to Senator Herbert Slater, March 17, 1931, File IV-320-34, Archivo Histórico Genaro Estrada.

70. Hill to Slater, File IV-320-34, Archivo Histórico Genaro Estrada; see also Garcia, *Strategies of Segregation* (56). In his study of Oxnard, Garcia notes that after 1934, school board members assigned students in some of its schools according to race, created all-Mexican classes, enforced social separation outside of class, institutionalized a school-within-a-school model of segregation, and they "formalized a racial hierarchy in schools that positioned Mexicans as an inferior group."

71. Nelle Foster to Mr. Aceves, editor of the Hispano-Americano, April 11, 1931, File IV-320-34, Archivo Histórico Genaro Estrada.

72. "Proyecto de Ley 'Bliss' para segregar Niños origen indio escuelas este Estado," Enrique Ferreira to Mexican Ambassador in Washington, DC, and Consul General in San Francisco, CA, May 19, 1931, File IV-320-34, Archivo Histórico Genaro Estrada.

73. El Secretario to Mexican Ambassador, July 28, 1931, File IV-212-14, Archivo Histórico Genaro Estrada.

74. "Bliss Bill Is Un-American: An Injustice to Descent Citizens," *Independent Daily News*, April 11, 1931.

75. "La Niñez Mexicana no Será Excluida de las Escuelas: El Triunfo de la causa de la Justicia y La Razón Debe Principalmente a Sociedades Cultas Amer-

icans," *Hispano Americano*, April 21, 1931, File IV-320-34, Archivo Histórico Genaro Estrada.

Chapter 5

1. Gary Orfield and Susan E. Eaton, *Dismantling Desegregation: The Quiet Reversal of Brown v. Board of Education* (New York: W. W. Norton, 1996).

2. Stacey Lee, *Unraveling the "Model Minority" Stereotype: Listening to Asian American Youth* (New York: Teachers College Press, 2009); Robert L. Linn and Kevin G. Welner, eds., *Race-Conscious Policies for Assigning Students to Schools: Social Science Research and the Supreme Court Cases* (Washington, DC: National Academy of Education, 2007); Gary Orfield, ed., *Latinos: Remaking America* (Berkeley: University of California Press, 2008); Gary Orfield, Mark D. Bachmeier, David R. James, and Tamela Eitle, "Deepening Segregation in American Public Schools: A Special Report from the Harvard Project on School Desegregation," *Equity and Excellence in Education* 30, no. 2 (September 1997).

3. Richard Valencia, *Chicano Students and the Courts: The Mexican American Legal Struggle for Educational Equality* (New York: New York University Press, 2008).

4. Rubén Donato, *The Other Struggle for Equal Schools: Mexican Americans during the Civil Rights Era* (Albany: State University of New York Press, 1997). When we say lost in history, we are referring to the *Francisco Maestas et al. v. George Shone et al.* case.

5. Kristi L. Bowman, "The New Face of School Desegregation," *Duke Law Journal* 50 (April 2001), 1752–53.

6. We note that using the terms de facto and de jure with respect to segregation is anachronistic prior to the 1954 *Brown v. Board of Education* decision, as it was not until the aftermath of *Brown* that the availability of remedies for segregation would depend on the distinction. However, because segregation has come to be understood in these terms, and scholars have described pre-*Brown* segregation in these terms, we use these terms to make the argument (retroactively) that the segregation experienced by Mexican Americans in all of the cases described should be understood as de jure.

7. We realize that there are problems with the framing of de facto segregation. As Highsmith (2009, 13) eloquently argues, the "notion of de facto segregation is a sacred and enduring myth in American society." The problem with de facto segregation is that it "allowed municipal legislators, urban planners, school board members, suburban officials, and federal housing administrators in these communities to deny responsibility for the public policies that upheld racial divisions" (2009, 14). Moreover, supporters of de facto segregation "routinely employed the language of northern innocence to reassign and deflect blame

for the color line." Northern "whites insisted that segregation reflected personal preference unlike in the South, where the state required Jim Crow" (2009, 15).

8. Ariela J. Gross, "Texas Mexicans and the Politics of Whiteness," *Law and History Review* 21, no. 1 (Spring 2003), 358.

9. Gilbert G. Gonzalez, *Chicano Education in the Era of Segregation* (Philadelphia: Balch Institute Press, 1990), 13.

10. Gonzalez, *Chicano Education*, 155.

11. Gonzalez, *Chicano Education*.

12. Guadalupe San Miguel and Richard Valencia, "From the Treaty of Guadalupe Hidalgo to Hopwood: The Educational Plight and Struggle of Mexican Americans in the Southwest," *Harvard Educational Review* 68, no. 3 (1998), 370.

13. Gonzalez, *Chicano Education*, 21–22.

14. David Montejano, *Anglos and Mexicans in the Making of Texas, 1836–1986* (Austin: University of Texas Press, 1987), 160.

15. San Miguel and Valencia, 370.

16. Benjamin Marquez, *LULAC: The Evolution of a Mexican American Political Organization* (Austin: University of Texas Press, 1993); Guadalupe San Miguel, Jr., *"Let all of Them Take Heed": Mexican Americans and the Campaign for Educational Equality in Texas, 1910–1981* (Austin: University of Texas Press, 1987).

17. Ariela J. Gross, " 'The Caucasian Cloak': Mexican Americans and the Politics of Whiteness in the Twentieth-Century Southwest," *Georgetown Law Journal* 95 (2007); Ian Haney López, "Race, Ethnicity, Erasure: The Salience of Race to Latcrit Theory," *California Law Review* 85, no. 5 (1997).

18. Richard Delgado, quoted in Kristi L. Bowman, "The New Face of School Desegregation," *Duke Law Journal* 50 (2001).

19. Gross, "Texas Mexicans," 201.

20. Albert Camarillo, *Chicanos in a Changing Society: From Mexican Pueblos to American Barrios in Santa Barbara and Southern California, 1848–1930* (Cambridge, MA: Harvard University Press, 1979); George A Martinez, "The Legal Construction of Race: Mexican Americans and Whiteness," *Harvard Latino Law Review* 2 (1997); Montejano, *Anglos and Mexicans*.

21. Gross, "Caucasian Cloak," 360. See also Montejano, *Anglos and Mexicans*; Valencia, *"Chicano Students"*; Steven H. Wilson, "Brown over 'Other White': Mexican Americans' Legal Arguments and Litigation Strategy in School Desegregation Lawsuits," *Law and History Review* 21, no. 1 (Spring 2003).

22. Wilson, "Brown over 'Other White,' " 184.

23. For the purpose of this argument, we limited our analysis to *Independent School District v. Salvatierra* (1930), *Alvarez v. Lemon Grove* (1931), *Mendez v. Westminster* (1946), and *Cisneros v. Corpus Christi ISD* (1970).

24. David G. García, " 'A Few of the Brightest, Cleanest Mexican Children': Origins of School Segregation as a Form of Mundane Educational Racism in Oxnard, California, 1900–1940" (2011). García argues that in Oxnard, California,

there was an "unwritten, yet understood 'racial contract'" that "enabled school segregation to be implemented as a form of mundane educational racism. Such commonplace educational practices included accommodating White parents' demands for separate classrooms, while shuffling Mexican students back and forth without consideration" (2011, 3–4). This unwritten but understood racial contract, we believe, was a standard practice across the American Southwest.

25. Independent School District v. Salvatierra, 33 S.W. 2d 790 (Tex.Civ. App.–San Antonio 1930; Alvarez v. Lemon Grove, Civil Action No. 66625 (Superior Court San Diego County, Cal. 1931); Mendez v. Westminster School District, 64 F. Supp 544 (S.D. Cal. 1946) (No. Civ. 4292).

26. In re Rodriguez, 81 Fed. 337 (W.D. Tex. 1897).

27. Hernandez v. Texas. 347 U.S. 475 (1954); Cisneros v. Corpus Christi ISD.

28. Bowman, "The New Face," 1763; see also Gross, "Caucasian Cloak."

29. Gross, "Caucasian Cloak"; Martinez, "Legal Construction"; Clare Sheridan, "'Another White Race': Mexican Americans and the Paradox of Whiteness in Jury Selection," *Law and History Review* 21, no. 1 (2003).

30. Neil Foley, *The White Scourge: Blacks, Mexicans, and Poor Whites in Texas Cotton Culture* (Berkeley: University of California Press, 1997); Wilson, "Brown Over 'Other White.'"

31. On this point, Foley notes that in 1920 the population in Mexico was about 14 million. Of that number, 10 percent were White, 30 percent Indian, and 60 percent mixed (mestizo).

32. Martinez, "Legal Construction."

33. Martha Menchaca, *Recovering History, Constructing Race: The Indian, Black and White Roots of Mexican Americans* (Austin: University of Texas Press, 2001).

34. Menchaca, *Recovering History*, 217.

35. Menchaca, *Recovering History*, 217.

36. Menchaca, *Recovering History*, 217.

37. Menchaca, *Recovering History*, 218.

38. Foley, *The White Scourge*, 13.

39. Foley, *The White Scourge*, 53.

40. Foley, *The White Scourge*, 8.

41. George J. Sanchez, *Becoming Mexican American: Ethnicity, Culture and Identity in Chicano Los Angeles, 1900–1945* (New York: Oxford University Press, 1993), 30.

42. Sanchez, *Becoming Mexican*.

43. Laura E. Gomez, *Manifest Destinies: The Making of the Mexican American Race* (New York: New York University Press, 2007), 83.

44. Menchaca, *Recovering History*; Foley, *The White Scourge*; Sanchez, *Becoming Mexican*; Gomez, *Manifest Destinies*; Gross, "Caucasian Cloak," 341.

45. In re Rodriguez, 337.

46. In re Rodriguez, 337–38.

47. In re Rodriguez, 346.

48. In re Rodriguez, 354.

49. In re Rodriguez, 355.

50. Wilson, "Brown over 'Other White,'" 152–53.

51. Martinez, "Legal Construction," 326–27.

52. In re Rodriguez: 346.

53. Jeanne M. Powers, "Forgotten History: Mexican American School Segregation in Arizona." *Equity and Excellence in Education* 41, no. 4 (October 2008).

54. David Tyack, *The One Best System: A History of American Urban Education* (Cambridge, MA: Harvard University Press, 1974).

55. Tyack, *One Best System*.

56. Ellwood P. Cubberley, *Public School Administration: A Statement of the Fundamental Principles Underlying the Organization and Administration of Public Education* (New York: Houghton Mifflin, 1922).

57. David Tyack and Elisabeth Hansot, *Managers of Virtue: Public School Leadership in America, 1829–1980* (New York: Basic Books, 1982).

58. Cubberley, *Public School Administration*, 23.

59. Tyack, *One Best System*, 132.

60. Gonzalez, *Chicano Education*.

61. This is the central argument in Gonzalez, *Chicano Education*.

62. San Miguel, "*Let all of Them Take Heed*"; Philippa Strum, *Mendez v. Westminster: School Desegregation and Mexican-American Rights* (Lawrence: University Press of Kansas, 2010); Richard Valencia, "The Mexican American Struggle for Equal Educational Opportunity in Mendez v. Westminster: Helping to Pave the Way for Brown v. Board of Education," *Teachers College Record* 107, no. 3 (March 2005).

63. Valencia, *Chicano Students and the Courts*.

64. Independent School District v. Salvatierra, 795.

65. Independent School District v. Salvatierra, 796.

66. Independent School District v. Salvatierra, 792.

67. Independent School District v. Salvatierra, 792–93.

68. Independent School District v. Salvatierra, 793.

69. Wilson, "Brown over 'Other White,'" 157.

70. Archivo Histórico Genaro Estrada, File IV-324-14. Asunto "San Diego, Consulado. Informe sobre separacion de niños mexicanos en la escuela de Lemon Grove, Cal." In this file, see letter sent from Enrique Fereira to the Secretaría in Mexico City. "Segregacion de niños mexicanos esculas de Lemon Grove, Cal." March 16, 1931; letter "POR ACTOS DE AUTORIDADES. Gastos hechos en el caso de la demanda de los niños de Lemon Grove, Cal." Letter from Enrique Ferreira to the Secretaría in Mexico City. March 21, 1931. It is important to note

that the Mexican government was cautious about getting involved in the case. Nevertheless, Mexican Consul Enrique Ferriera carefully monitored the case, communicated with local school district administrators, and reported to the Mexican Ambassador in Washington DC and the Secretaría in Mexico City. After the case was decided, Consul Ferriera acknowledged that a few Mexican businesses and organizations had contributed funds to help pay for the legal fees in the lawsuit.

71. Independent School District v. Salvatierra, 794.

72. Robert R. Alvarez, "The Lemon Grove Incident: The Nation's First Successful Desegregation Court Case." *Journal of San Diego History* 32, no. 3 (Spring 1986).

73. Alvarez, "The Lemon Grove Incident," 11.

74. Archivo Histórico, File IV-324-14. We accessed the Alvarez v. Lemon Grove decision in the Archivo Histórico archives in Mexico City. Judge Claude C. Chambers signed the decision on March 11, 1931. Chambers ruled that California did not "authorize or permit the establishment or maintenance of separate schools for the instruction of pupils of Mexican parentage, nationality, and/or descent," that the school board in Lemon Grove did not have the power to maintain separate schools for the instruction of Mexican pupils, that Robert Alvarez and other Mexican children could not be segregated because of their Mexican parentage, and the Mexican children were to be allowed to attend the regular school in the school district.

75. Alvarez, "The Lemon Grove Incident," 10–11.

76. Alvarez, "The Lemon Grove Incident," 12.

77. Strum, *Mendez v. Westminster.*

78. Valencia, "*Chicano Students and the Courts*"; Valencia, "The Mexican American Struggle."

79. Mendez v. Westminster School District, 550.

80. Mendez v. Westminster School District, 549. Wollenberg argues that *Mendez* "ended nearly a century of de jure school segregation in California" (1976, 135) and "was part of a process which stripped away the formal structure of legalized segregation and exposed the underlying conditions of racism and reaction that divided the American people and plague [*sic*] their consciences" (1976, 135). Gonzalez notes that *Mendez* ended the era of de jure segregation in California (1990). See also Valencia, who notes that "although the *Mendez* case helped to end *de jure* segregation in California, Mexican American students remained highly segregated and, in fact, became more segregated over the decades following the ruling" (2005, 411).

81. Gonzalez, Chicano Education, 150.

82. Gonzalez, *Chicano Education;* Valencia, "The Mexican American Struggle"; Charles Wollenberg, *All Deliberate Speed: Segregation and Exclusion in California Schools, 1855–1975* (Berkeley: University of California Press, 1976).

83. Donato, *The Other Struggle.*

84. Frank I. Goodman, "De Facto School Segregation: A Constitutional and Empirical Analysis." *California Law Review,* 60, no. 2 (March 1972).

85. Swann v. Charlotte-Mecklenburg Bd. of Ed., 402 U.S. 1, 17–18 (1970).

86. Keyes v. School District No. 1, 413 U.S. 189 (1973).

87. The term "dicta" refers to portions of decisions that are not central to the courts' disposition of the case.

88. Swann v. Charlotte-Mecklenburg Bd. of Ed., 402 U.S. 1, 17–18 (1970).

89. For a more complete discussion concerning the indeterminacy surrounding the distinction between de facto and de jure segregation, see Martinez (1993).

90. Keyes v. School District No. 1.

91. Keyes v. School District No. 1. We are sympathetic with Justice Douglas's argument that the distinction be eliminated completely as it is problematic. However, given the persistence of the terms in how we understand segregation, we focus our arguments here on whether Mexican American segregation should be understood as de facto or de jure and leave the argument for elimination of the distinction, and the importance of intent, for another article.

92. Gary Orfield and John T. Yun, *Resegregation in American Schools* (Cambridge, MA: Civil Rights Project, Harvard University, 1999), 21.

93. Eduardo Bonilla-Silva, *Racism without Racists: Color-Blind Racism and Racial Inequality in Contemporary America* (Boulder: Rowman & Littlefield, 2010), 37.

94. Parents Involved in Community Schools v. Seattle School Dist. No. 1, 551 U.S. 701 (2007), citing Milliken v. Bradley, 433 U.S. 267, 280n14 (1977). It should be noted that the concurring opinions also discussed the need for past intentional racial discrimination to be present in order to justify race-based solutions to segregation.

Epilogue

1. Max Sylvious Handman, "Economic Reasons for the Coming of the Mexican Immigrant," *American Journal of Sociology* 35, no. 4 (1930): 601–3.

2. Ibram X. Kendi, *Stamped from the Beginning: The Definitive History of Racist Ideas in America* (New York: Nation Books, 2016), 8–9.

3. Gunner Myrdal, *An American Dilemma: The Negro Problem and Modern Democracy* (New York: Harper and Brothers, 1944).

4. Laura E. Gomez, *Manifest Destinies: The Making of the Mexican American Race* (New York: New York University Press, 2007): 83; Steven H. Wilson, "Brown over "Other White": Mexican Americans' Legal Arguments and Litigation Strategy in School Desegregation Lawsuits," *Law and History Review* 21, no. 1 (2003): 145–94. See also "Mexicans Portrayed as 'Mongrel Race' Then and Now," Interview

with professor Gerardo Cadava, https://www.youtube.com/watch?v=W9xA2jA8 bdo.

5. According to historian Danielle Olden, "It was not until the late 1960s that Mexican American civil rights attorneys began to abandon the 'other white' argument. After years of winning school desegregation cases on the basis of their other whiteness . . . Mexican American civil rights attorneys turned to a new argument that emphasized their racial distinctiveness," Danielle R. Olden, "Shifting the Lens: Using Critical Race Theory and Latino Critical Theory to Re-Examine the History of School Desegregation," *Qualitative Inquiry* 21, no. 3 (2015): 235. Also see Richard Valencia, *Chicano Students and Courts: The Mexican American Legal Struggle for Educational Equality* (New York: New York University Press, 2008), 67.

6. Garcia, *Strategies of Segregation*, 43. We saw in David Garcia's case study in Oxnard, California, that between 1916 and 1930, Mexicans were prohibited from purchasing property in certain neighborhoods because they were "persons not of the Caucasian race." We extrapolate from Garcia's work and have confidence that Mexicans were not seen as Caucasians in the United States.

7. "Alamosa Mexicans Win School Court Fight," *Denver Catholic Register*, March 26, 1914.

8. At this time, Louisiana had not passed a compulsory education law that would have required the Perez and Lopez children to attend school (Jones, 1967), and we found no evidence that the voters of Rapides Parish, the local school district or local ward had approved compulsory education for the area as permitted under Louisiana law.

9. James D. Anderson, *The Education of Blacks in the South, 1860–1935* (Chapel Hill, NC: University of North Carolina Press, 1988).

10. Jose Gonzalez to Mexican Consul, November 12, 1920, File 13-14-20, Archivo Histórico Genaro Estrada, Acervo Histórico Diplomático, Secretaría de Relaciones Exteriores. We saw how in 1920 Mexicans in Lyons informed the Mexican consul that they were not served in public establishments because they were seen as "GENTE DE COLOR."

11. Annual Report of the Salina Schools, n.d.

12. Robert M. Cleary, "The Education of Mexican-Americans in Kansas City, Kansas, 1916–1951" (unpublished master's thesis, University of Missouri, 2002).

13. University of California, Berkeley, the Bancroft Library, Manuscripts Division, MANC, MSS. 84/38, Taylor, Paul, Schuster Papers, Ctn. 13, File 13:43, "Restriction of Mexican Immigration at Issue," *The Coalitionist* 1, no. 6 (December 1929): 3. The original article cited in the *Coalitionist* can be accessed at Glenn E. Hoover, "Our Mexican Immigrants," *Foreign Affairs* 8, no. 1, Oct. 1929, https://www.foreignaffairs.com/articles/mexico/1929-10-01/our-mexican-immigrants, 99.

14. Assembly Bill, No. 433, January 19, 1931, Referred to Committee on Education, File IV-320-34, Archivo Histórico Genaro Estrada.

15. Mexican Consul Ramon DeNegri to S. Diego Fernandez, head of SRE in Mexico City, June 27, 1919, File: 592.21.46 (814), Archivo Histórico Genaro Estrada. See also Acting US Secretary of State to Mexican Ambassador Ygnacio Bonillas, July 19, 1919, File: 592.21.46. The Department of State wrote to Mexican Ambassador Don Ygnaico Bonillas to inform him that he had received information that "the State Board of Education of California proposes to exclude gradually Mexican children from the public schools for children of the white race and place them in establishments intended for negroes."

16. Felipe Garcia, Alfredo Garza and Matias Garza to Mission School Board Members, December 30, 1930, File IV-323-6, Archivo Histórico Genaro Estrada.

17. *Parents Involved in Community Schools v. Seattle School Dist. No. 1*, 551 U.S. 701 (2007), citing *Milliken v. Bradley*, 433 U.S. 267, 280, n. 14 (1977). It should be noted that the concurring opinions also discussed the need for past intentional racial discrimination to be present in order to justify race-based solutions to segregation.

18. Gary Orfield, John Kucsera, and Genevieve Siegal-Hawley, *E. Pluris . . . Separation: Deepening Double Segregation for More Students* (Los Angeles, CA: Civil Rights Project/Proyecto Derechos Civiles, 2012), 76.

19. Richard Rothstein, "The Myth of De Facto Segregation," *Phi Delta Kappan* 100, no. 5 (2019): 35–38.

Bibliography

Books and Articles

Alvarez, Robert R. "The Lemon Grove Incident: The Nation's First Successful Desegregation Court Case." *Journal of San Diego History* 32, no. 3 (Spring 1986): 116–35. http://www.sandiegohistory.org/journal/86spring/lemongrove.htm.

Anderson, James D. *The Education of Blacks in the South, 1860–1935.* Chapel Hill: University of North Carolina Press, 1988.

Aragon, Margarita. "The Difference that 'One Drop' Makes: Mexican and African Americans, Mixedness and Racial Categorization in the early 20th Century." *Subjectivity* 7, no. 1 (2014): 18–36.

Balderrama, Francisco E. *In Defense of La Raza: The Los Angeles Mexican Consulate and the Mexican American Community, 1929–1936.* Tucson: University of Arizona Press, 1982.

Beverage, Mary I. *Saturnino Alvarado: Civil Rights Activist, 1883–1955.* Kansas City Public Library, n.d. https://pendergastkc.org/article/biography/saturnino-alvarado.

Blanton, Carlos Kevin. *The Strange Career of Bilingual Education in Texas, 1836–1981.* College Station: Texas A&M University Press, 2007.

———. "The Citizenship Sacrifice: Mexican Americans, The Saunders-Leonard Report, and the Politics of Immigration, 1951–52." *Western Historical Quarterly* 43, no. 3 (Autumn 2009): 299–320.

Bonilla-Silva, Eduardo. *Racism without Racists: Color-Blind Racism and Racial Inequality in Contemporary America.* Boulder, CO: Rowman & Littlefield, 2010.

Bowman, Kristi L. "The New Face of School Desegregation." *Duke Law Journal* 50 (April 2001): 1751–808.

Camarillo, Albert. *Chicanos in a Changing Society: From Mexican Pueblos to American Barrios in Santa Barbara and Southern California, 1848–1930.* Cambridge, MA: Harvard University Press, 1979.

Carman, J. Neale and Associates. *Foreign Language Units of Kansas, Vol. II: Account of Settlement and Settlements in Kansas.* Lawrence: University Press of Kansas, 1974.

Carrigan, William D., and Clive Webb. "The Lynching of Persons of Mexican Origin or Descent in the United States, 1848–1928." *Journal of Social History* 37, no. 2 (Winter 2003), 411–38.

Carson, Clayborne, David J. Garrow, Gerald Gill, Vincent Harding, and Darlene Clark Hine, eds. *The Eyes on the Prize Civil Rights Reader: Documents, Speeches, and Firsthand Accounts from the Black Freedom Struggle, 1954–1990.* New York: Viking Penguin, 1991.

Carter, Thomas P. *Mexican Americans in School: A History of Educational Neglect.* New York: College Entrance Examination Board, 1970.

Collier, Irwin. "Interdisciplinary Moment: Max Sylvius Handman, Chicago Sociology Ph.D. 1917." *Irwin Collier* (blog). Economics in the Rear-View Mirror. Archival Artifacts from the History of Economics. http://www.irwincollier.com/interdisciplinary-moment-max-sylvius-7handman-chicago-sociology-ph-d-1917/.

Cubberley, Ellwood P. *Public School Administration: A Statement of the Fundamental Principles Underlying the Organization and Administration of Public Education.* New York: Houghton Mifflin, 1922.

Davis, Kenneth A. "Racial Designation in Louisiana: One Drop of Black Blood Makes a Negro," *Hastings Constitutional Law Quarterly* 3 (1976): 199. https://repository.uchastings.edu/hastings_constitutional_law_quaterly/vol3/iss1/7.

De León, Arnoldo. *Tejano West Texas.* College Station: Texas A&M University Press, 2015.

Donato, Rubén. *Mexicans and Hispanos in Colorado Schools and Communities, 1920–1960.* Albany: State University of New York Press, 2007.

———. *The Other Struggle for Equal Schools: Mexican Americans during the Civil Rights Era.* Albany: State University of New York Press, 1997.

Donato, Rubén, and Hanson, Jarrod. "'In These Towns, Mexicans Are Classified as Negroes': The Politics of Unofficial Segregation in the Kansas Public Schools, 1915–1935." *American Educational Research Journal* 54, Supplement 1 (2017): 53s–74s.

———. "Legally White, Socially 'Mexican': The Politics of De Jure and De Facto School Segregation in the American Southwest." *Harvard Educational Review* 82, no. 2 (2012): 202–25.

———. "Porque tenían sangre de 'NEGROS': The Exclusion of Mexican Children from a Louisiana School, 1915–1916." *Association of Mexican American Educators Journal*, Open Issue 11, no. 1 (2017): 125–45.

Donato, Rubén, Gonzalo Guzmán, and Jarrod Hanson. "Francisco Maestas et al. v. George H. Shone et al.: Mexican American Resistance to School Segregation in the Hispano Homeland, 1912–1914." *Journal of Latinos and Education* 16, no. 1 (2017): 3–17.

Eakin, Sue. *Rapides Parish: An Illustrated History.* Northridge, CA: Windsor Publications, 1987.

Foley, Neil. *The White Scourge: Blacks, Mexicans, and Poor Whites in Texas Cotton Culture.* Berkeley: University of California Press, 1997.

García, David G. *Strategies of Segregation: Race, Residence, and the Struggle for Educational Equality.* Berkeley: University of California Press, 2018.

García, David G., and Tara J. Yosso. " 'Strictly in the Capacity of Servant': The Interconnection between Residential and School Segregation in Oxnard, California, 1934–1954." *History of Education Quarterly* 53, no. 1 (2013): 64–89.

García, David, Tara Yosso, Frank Barajas. " 'A Few of the Brightest, Cleanest Mexican Children': School Segregation as a Form of Mundane Racism in Oxnard, California," 1900–1940. *Harvard Educational Review* 82, no. 1 (2012): 1–25.

Gomez, Laura E. *Manifest Destinies: The Making of the Mexican American Race.* New York: New York University Press, 2007.

Gómez-Quiñones, Juan. *Roots of Chicano Politics, 1600–1940.* Albuquerque: University of New Mexico Press, 1994.

Gonzalez, Gilbert G. *Chicano Education in the Era of Segregation.* Philadelphia, PA: Balch Institute Press, 1990.

———. *Mexican Consuls and Labor Organizing: Imperial Politics in the American Southwest.* Austin: University of Texas, 1999.

Goodman, Frank I. "De Facto School Segregation: A Constitutional and Empirical Analysis." *California Law Review* 60, no. 2 (March 1972): 275–437.

Greer, Colin. *The Great School Legend: A Revisionist Interpretation of American Public Education.* New York, Basic Books, 1972.

Griffith, D. W., and Thomas Dixon. *Birth of a Nation.* Los Angeles, CA: Triangle Film Corp., 1915.

Gross, Ariela J. " 'The Caucasian Cloak': Mexican Americans and the Politics of Whiteness in the Twentieth-Century Southwest." *Georgetown Law Journal* 95 (2007): 337–392.

———. "Texas Mexicans and the Politics of Whiteness." *Law and History Review* 21, no. 1 (Spring 2003): 195–205.

Handman, Max Sylvious. "Economic Reasons for the Coming of the Mexican Immigrant," *American Journal of Sociology* 35, no. 4 (1930): 601–11.

Handlin, Oscar. *The Uprooted: The Epic Story of the Great Migrations that Made the American People.* Boston: Little Brown, 1951.

Haney López, Ian F., "Race, Ethnicity, Erasure: The Salience of Race to Latcrit Theory." *California Law Review* 85, no. 5 (1997): 1143–211.

Hendrick, Irving G. *The Education of Non-Whites in California, 1849–1970.* San Francisco, CA: R & E Research, 1977.

Hickman, Christine B. "The Devil and the One Drop Rule: Racial Categories, African Americans, and the U.S. Census," *Michigan Law Review* 95, 1161–265 (1997). https://repository.law.umich.edu/mlr/vol95/iss5/2.

Hoover, Glenn E. "Our Mexican Immigrants." *Foreign Affairs* 8, no. 1 (1929): 99–107. https://doi.org/10.2307/20028746.

Jackson, Walter A. *Gunner Myrdal and America's Conscience: Social Engineering and Racial Liberalism, 1938–1987*. Chapel Hill: University of North Carolina Press, 1990.

Kena, G., L. Musu-Gillette, J. Robinson, X. Wang, A. Rathbun, J. Zhang, S. Wilkinson-Flicker, A. Barmer, and E. Velez. *The Condition of Education 2015* (NCES 2015-144). US Department of Education, National Center for Education Statistics, Washington, DC. Retrieved November 30, 2020 from http://nces.ed.gov/pubsearch.

Kendi, Ibram X. *Stamped from the Beginning: The Definitive History of Racist Ideas in America* New York: Nation Books, 2016.

Kirp, David L. *Just Schools: The Idea of Racial Equality in American Education*. Berkeley: University of California Press, 1982.

Kousser, J. Morgan. "Before Plessy, before Brown: The Development of the Law of Racial Integration in Louisiana and Kansas." In *Toward a Usable Past: Liberty Under State Constitutions*, edited by Paul Finkelman and Stephen E. Gottlieb, 213–70. Athens: University of Georgia Press, 1991.

Kurlaender, Michal, and Jon T. Yun. "Fifty Years after Brown: New Evidence of the Impact of School Racial Composition on Student Outcomes." *International Journal of Educational Policy, Research, and Practice: Reconceptualizing Childhood Studies* 6, no. 1, 2005.

Laglagaron, Lareen. *Protection through Integration: The Mexican Government's Efforts to Aid Migrants in the United States*, Migration Policy Institute, National Center on Immigrant Integration Policy, 2010.

Lee, Stacey. *Unraveling the "Model Minority" Stereotype: Listening to Asian American Youth*. New York: Teachers College Press, 2009.

Linn, Robert L., and Kevin G. Welner, eds. *Race-Conscious Policies for Assigning Students to Schools: Social Science Research and the Supreme Court Cases*. Washington, DC: National Academy of Education, 2007.

List of Ambassadors of Mexico to the United States. https://en.wikipedia.org/wiki/Ambassador_of_Mexico_to_the_United_States.

Long, Chester I., F. Dumont Smith, and Hugh P. Farrelly, *Revised Statutes of Kansas (Annotated) 1923*. Topeka: Kansas State Printing Plant, 1923.

Marquez, Benjamin. *LULAC: The Evolution of a Mexican American Political Organization*. Austin: University of Texas Press, 1993.

Martinez, George A. "Legal Indeterminacy, Judicial Discretion and the Mexican-American Litigation Experience: 1930–1980." *UC Davis Law Review* 27, no. 3 (1993): 555–619.

———. "The Legal Construction of Race: Mexican-Americans and Whiteness." *Harvard Latino Law Review* 2 (1997): 321–48.

McKevitt, Gerald. *Brokers of Culture: Italian Jesuits in the American West, 1848–1919*. Stanford, CA: Stanford University Press, 2007.

Menchaca, Martha. *Recovering History, Constructing Race: The Indian, Black and White Roots of Mexican Americans*. Austin: University of Texas Press, 2001.

"Mexicans Portrayed as 'Mongrel Race' Then and Now." Interview with professor Gerardo Cadava. https://www.youtube.com/watch?v=W9xA2jA8bdo.

Montejano, David. *Anglos and Mexicans in the Making of Texas, 1836–1986*. Austin: University of Texas Press, 1987.

Muñoz, Laura K. "Romo v. Laird: Mexican American Segregation and the Politics of Belonging in Arizona." *Western Legal History* 26, nos. 1 & 2 (2013): 97–132.

Murray, Pauli. *States' Laws on Race and Color*. Athens: University of Georgia Press 1951.

Myrdal, Gunner. *An American Dilemma: The Negro Problem and Modern Democracy*. New York: Harper and Brothers, 1944.

Northup, Solomon. *Twelve Years a Slave*. 1953. Edited by David Wilson. First Avenue Editions, 2014.

Olden, Danielle R. "Shifting the Lens: Using Critical Race Theory and Latino Critical Theory to Re-Examine the History of School Desegregation." *Qualitative Inquiry* 21, no. 3 (2015): 250–61.

Oppenheimer, Robert. "Acculturation or Assimilation: Mexican Immigrants in Kansas, 1900 to World War II." *Western Historical Quarterly* 16, no. 4 (October 1985): 429–48.

Orfield, Gary. *Must We Bus? Segregated Schools and National Policy*. Washington, DC: Brookings Institution, 1978.

———, ed. *Latinos: Remaking America*. Berkeley: University of California Press, 2008.

Orfield, Gary, and John T. Yun. *Resegregation in American Schools*. Cambridge, MA: Civil Rights Project, Harvard University, 1999.

Orfield, Gary, John Kucsera, and Genevieve Siegel-Hawley, *E. Pluribus . . . Separation: Deepening Double Segregation for More Students*. Los Angeles: Civil Rights Project/Proyecto Derechos Civiles, 2012.

Orfield, Gary, Mark D. Bachmeier, David R. James, and Tamela Eitle. "Deepening Segregation in American Public Schools: A Special Report from the Harvard Project on School Desegregation." *Equity and Excellence in Education* 30, no. 2 (September 1997): 5–24.

Orfield, Gary, and Susan E. Eaton. *Dismantling Desegregation: The Quiet Reversal of Brown v. Board of Education*. New York: W. W. Norton, 1996.

Orfield, Gary, Erica Frankenberg, Jongyeon Ee, and John Kuscera. *Brown at 60: Great Progress, a Long Retreat and an Uncertain Future*. Los Angeles: Civil

Right Project/Proyecto Derechos Civiles, 2014. https://civilrightsproject. ucla.edu/research/k-12-education/integration-and-diversity/brown-at-60- great-progress-a-long-retreat-and-an-uncertain-future.

Page, William Tyler. *The American's Creed.* http://www.ushistory.org/documents/ creed.htm.

Peavler, David J. "Drawing the Color Line in Kansas City: The Creation of Sumner High School," *Kansas History: A Journal of the Central Plains* 27 (2005): 188–201.

Perlmann, Joel. *Italians Then, Mexicans Now: Immigrant Origins and Second-Generation Progress, 1890–2000.* New York: Russell Sage Foundation, 2005.

Powers, Jeanne M. "Forgotten History: Mexican American School Segregation in Arizona." *Equity and Excellence in Education* 41, no. 4 (October 2008): 467–81.

Quirk, Robert E. *An Affair of Honor: Woodrow Wilson and the Occupation of Veracruz.* New York: Norton, 1962.

Ricart, Domingo. *Just Across the Tracks: Report on a Survey of Five Mexican Communities in the State of Kansas (Emporia, Florence, Newton, Wichita, Hutchinson).* Lawrence: University of Kansas, 1950.

Riis, Jacob. *How the Other Half Lives: Studies among the Tenements of New York.* New York: Charles Scribner's Sons, 1890.

Rothstein, Richard. "The Myth of De Facto Segregation." *Phi Delta Kappan* 100, no. 5 (2019): 35–38.

Salinas, Guadalupe. "Mexican-Americans and Desegregation of Schools in the Southwest." *Houston Law Review* 8 (1971): 929–51.

Sanchez, George J. *Becoming Mexican American: Ethnicity, Culture and Identity in Chicano Los Angeles, 1900–1945.* New York: Oxford University Press, 1993.

San Miguel, Guadalupe, Jr. *"Let all of Them Take Heed": Mexican Americans and the Campaign for Educational Equality in Texas, 1910–1981.* Austin: University of Texas Press, 1987.

San Miguel, Guadalupe, Jr., and Richard Valencia. "From the Treaty of Guadalupe Hidalgo to Hopwood: The Educational Plight and Struggle of Mexican Americans in the Southwest." *Harvard Educational Review* 68, no. 3 (1998): 353–412.

Serda, Daniel. Finding Latin Roots: Hispanic Heritage in Kansas City. *Kansas Preservation* 33 (2011): 8–15. https://www.kshs.org/resource/survey/kckh-istorichispanicamericanplaces2011.pdf.

Sharfstein, Daniel J., "Crossing the Color Line: Racial Migration and the One-Drop Rule, 1600–1860." *Minnesota Law Review* 91 (2007): 627. https:// scholarship.law.umn.edu/mlr/627.

Sheridan, Clare. "'Another White Race': Mexican Americans and the Paradox of Whiteness in Jury Selection." *Law and History Review* 21, no. 1 (2003): 1–34.

Stafford, George Mason Graham. *Three Pioneer Rapides Families: A Genealogy.* Baton Rouge, LA: Claitors Publishing Division, 1946.

Strum, Philippa. *Mendez v. Westminster: School Desegregation and Mexican-American Rights.* Lawrence: University Press of Kansas, 2010.

Taylor, Loren L. *The Consolidated Ethnic History of Wyandotte County.* Kansas City: Kansas Ethnic Council, 2000.

Taylor, Loren L., and R. Marin. *A Short Ethnic History of the Mexican People in Wyandotte County.* Kansas City: Kansas Ethnic Council, 2000.

Tyack, David, ed. *Turning Points in American Educational History.* Waltham, MA: Blaisdell, 1967.

———. *The One Best System: A History of American Urban Education.* Cambridge, MA: Harvard University Press, 1974.

Tyack, David, and Elisabeth Hansot. *Managers of Virtue: Public School Leadership in America, 1829–1980.* New York: Basic Books, 1982.

Valencia, Richard. *Chicano Students and the Courts: The Mexican American Legal Struggle for Educational Equality.* New York: New York University Press, 2008.

———. "The Mexican American Struggle for Equal Educational Opportunity in Mendez v. Westminster: Helping to Pave the Way for Brown v. Board of Education." *Teachers College Record* 107, no. 3 (March 2005): 389–423.

Villanueva, Nicholas, Jr. *The Lynching of Mexicans in the Texas Borderlands.* Albuquerque: University of New Mexico Press, 2017.

Warren, Naomi. "Agents of Humanity: Race and Dignity in Arkansas." In *A State by State History of Race and Racism in the United States,* edited by Patricia Reid-Merritt, 57–84. Westport, CT: ABC-CLIO/Greenwood, 2019.

Weise, Julie M. *Corazón De Dixie Mexicanos in the U.S. South since 1910.* Chapel Hill: University of North Carolina Press, 2015.

———. "Mexican Nationalisms, Southern Racisms: Mexicans and Mexican Americans in the U.S. South, 1908–1939." *American Quarterly* 60, no. 3 (2008): 749–77.

Wilson, Steven H. "Brown over 'Other White': Mexican Americans' Legal Arguments and Litigation Strategy in School Desegregation Lawsuits." *Law and History Review* 21, no. 1 (Spring 2003): 145–94.

Wollenberg, Charles. *All Deliberate Speed: Segregation and Exclusion in California Schools, 1855–1975.* Berkeley: University of California Press, 1976.

Court Cases

Adolpho Romo v. William E. Laird, et al., No. 21617, Maricopa County Superior Court (1925).

Alvarez v. Lemon Grove, Civil Action No. 66625 (Superior Court San Diego County, Cal. 1931).

Board of Education v. Tinnon, 26 Kan. 1 (1881).

Brown v. Board of Education of Topeka. 374 U.S. 483 (1954).

Cisneros v. Corpus Christi ISD, 324 F. Supp. 599 (S.D. Tex. 1970).

Gong Lum v. Rice. 258 U.S. 78 (1927).

Hernandez v. Texas. 347 U.S. 475 (1954).

In re Rodriguez, 81 Fed. 337 (W.D. Tex. 1897).

Independent School District v. Salvatierra, 33 S.W. 2d 790 (Tex.Civ.App.–San Antonio 1930).

Keyes v. School District No. 1, 413 U.S. 189 (1973).

Mendez v. Westminster School District, 64 F. Supp 544 (S.D. Cal. 1946) (No. Civ. 4292).

Parents Involved in Community Schools v. Seattle School Dist. No. 1, 551 U.S. 701 (2007).

Plessy v. Ferguson. 163 US 537, 16 S. Ct. 1138, 41 L. Ed. 256 (1896).

Swann v. Charlotte-Mecklenburg Board of Education, 402 U.S. 1, 17–18 (1970).

School District and College Records

Annual Report of the Salina City Schools, September 5, 1933. Salina Public Library, Salina KS.

Annual Report of the Salina City Schools for the Year Ending June, 1936. Salina Public Library, Salina KS.

Annual Report of the Salina Public Schools for the Year Ending June 30, 1923. Salina Public Library, Salina KS.

Annual Report of the Salina Public Schools Year Ending June 30, 1928. Salina Public Library, Salina KS.

Emporia City School Board Minutes. Emporia City Schools. Emporia, Kansas (n.d.).

Minutes of the Board of Education, July 30, 1925. City of Hutchinson (Kansas). July 6, 1925 to July 1, 1927.

Minutes of the Board of Education, April 24, 1930. City of Hutchinson (Kansas). July 1, 1929 to July 1, 1932.

Minutes of the Board of Education, July 2, 1931. City of Hutchinson (Kansas). July 1931 to July 1933.

Rapides Parish School Board. *Minutes of the Rapides Parish School Board*. Vol. 7–29, Alexandria, LA, 1915.

Salina City School Board Minutes. Salina City Schools. Salina Unified School District. Salina, KS, n.d.

Newspaper Articles

"A 'Jim Crow' School in Kansas." *Springfield Republican*, February 24, 1905. http://
genealogytrails.com/kan/wyandotte/newspaperitems.html.

Alamosa Independent Journal. February 9, 1912.

"Alamosa Mexicans Plan to Battle for Rights." *Denver Catholic Register*, October
23, 1914.

"Alamosa Mexicans Win School Court Fight: Segregation of Spanish Must Cease."
Denver Catholic Register, March 26, 1914.

"Alamosa Must Give Mexicans Free Schooling: Court Grants Mandamus Prohibiting Segregation of Spanish Speaking Children." *Rocky Mountain News*,
March 22, 1914.

"Alamosa Must Stop Its Segregation of Mexicans." *Denver Catholic Register*, March
26, 1914.

"Alamosa School Fight Unique in Court Annals of this State." *Denver Catholic
Register*, December 4, 1913.

"Alamosa Schools Ordered to Admit Mexican Children: Bar lifted by Court Order
of Judge Holbrook, in Suit for Boy. 'Pupils Should Be Taken Out of Spanish
Classes When They Speak English.'" *Denver Post*, March 23, 1914.

"Bliss Bill Is Un-American: An Injustice to Descent Citizens." *Independent Daily
News*, April 11, 1931.

"Can't Segregate Mexican Children: Board of Education Told it Cannot Provide
Separate School Facilities." *Hutchinson* [Kansas] *News*, June 3, 1930.

"Colorado News: Gathered from All Parts of the State." *Pine Bluffs* [Wyoming]
Post, n.d.

"Decision Rendered." *Alamosa Leader*, March 21, 1914.

"Directors Think They Are Right." *Alamosa Independent Journal*, November 28, 1913.

"Federal Injunction Mexican Possibility: Hayward Declares that U.S. Courts Might
Act to Stifle School Row." *Kansas City Kansan*, October 28, 1925.

"Happenings Epitomized." *Alamosa Independent Journal*, January 9, 1914.

"Judge Holbrook Dies." *Alamosa Leader*, August 29, 1914.

"Los Ninos Mexicanos Victoriosos: La Corte Concede un 'Mandamus' Prohibiendo la Segregacion de los Niños de Habla Español." *La Revista de Taos*,
April 17, 1914.

"Mexican Case Goes to Topeka." *Kansas City Kansan*, October 29, 1925.

"Mexican Children Demand Schooling with Americans. Conejos Parents Suit
Brought by Parents against Education Board. Are They Caucasians? Author-
ities Say Discrimination Is Made because They Speak No English." *Denver
Post*, January 14, 1914.

"Mexican Crisis to Consul: Attorney Hayward Will Find Out What Bearing Treaty
Has on Armourdale School Affair." *Kansas City Kansan*, November 2, 1925.

"Mexican Kiddies Prove They Are Able to Speak English." *Denver Catholic Register*, January 15, 1914.

"Mexican Parley Delayed: Hayward's Conference with Attorney General Relative to School Rumpus Here Is Postponed." *Kansas City Kansan,* October 16, 1925.

"Mexican Patrons of Public Schools Win Court Decision." *Hooper-Mosca* [Colorado] *Tribune*, March 21, 1914.

"Mexican Patrons of Public Schools Win Court Decision: Judge Holbrook Finds against Discrimination in Education." *Hooper-Mosca (Co.) Tribune*, March 21, 1914.

"Mexican Patrons of Public Schools Win Court Decision." *Alamosa Courier*, March 21, 1914.

"Mexican Row in K. C. Schools up to State Dept: Trouble Caused by Objection of Parents Is Near International Proportions." *Kansas City Kansan*, October 24, 1925.

"Mexican School Planned: Emerson P.T.A. Committee Named to Make Arrangements for Institution in Argentine." *Kansas City Kansan*, October 16, 1922.

"Mexicans in Alamosa Say the School Board Discriminates." *Rocky Mountain News*, September 10, 1913.

"More Discrimination by School Board." *Denver Catholic Register*, September 11, 1913.

" 'Must Admit Mexicans,' to Have Free Schooling Same as American Children. Judge of District Court Grants Mandamus Prohibiting Segregation of the Spanish Speaking-Children." *Akron (Co.) Weekly Pioneer Press*, March 27, 1914.

"Obituary for Walter P. Ford." *Alexandria* [Louisiana] *Daily Town Talk*, March 9, 1916.

Romero, Simon. "Lynch Mobs Killed Latinos Across the West: The Fight to Remember the Atrocities Is Just Starting." *New York Times*, March 2, 2019, https://www.nytimes.com/2019/03/02/us/porvenir-massacre-texas-mexicans.html.

Sanchez, Mary. "KCK School to Salute Pioneering Parent." *Kansas City* [Kansas] *Star*, August 31, 2003.

"School Battle in Alamosa to Enter Courts." *Denver Catholic Register*, November 20, 1913.

"School Board Trial." *Alamosa Independent Journal*, January 9, 1914.

"School Districts of City Are Announced: Table, Showing Where Children of All Districts Will Attend Classes Is Issued." *Kansas City Kansan*, September 5, 1923, 6.

"School Racial Row Is Over: Judge Orders Six Mexican Boys Involved in the Major Hudson Squabble to Change Enrollment." *Kansas City Kansan*, February 4, 1925, 4.

"Seek Mexican School: Argentine, Armourdale Districts Wish Separate Rooms for Foreigners." *Kansas City Kansan*, October 11, 1922, 7.

"Solves Racial Problem: Mexican Children Will Be Enrolled in Old Major Hudson School, Say Authorities." *Kansas City Kansan*, September 17, 1924.

"Southern Colorado: Items of Interest Gathered from Exchanges." *Creede* [Colorado] *Candle*, December 11, 1909.

"Special School Is Unfair, Says Mexican Envoy: J. Garza Zertuche, Consul General, Is in K.C. to Suggest Remedy." *Kansas City Kansan*, November 9, 1925.

"State Board Cannot Stop Segregation of Mexicans." *Alamosa Independent Journal*, September 19, 1913.

"State Officials into Mexican Pupil Row. Attorney General Gets Affidavit from Pearson Following Consul's Complaint." *Kansas City Kansan*, October 17, 1925.

"Suit That Alleges Discrimination Won by Alamosa Mexican." *Denver Catholic Register*, March 23, 1916.

"To Talk Mexican School: Education Board to Take Up Matter of Building for Foreigners Tonight." *Kansas City Kansan*, December 11, 1922.

"Trinidad Faces Race War over Mexican Pupils: School Strike against Foreigners Lands in Court." *Denver Post*, November 21, 1913.

"Want School for Mexicans: Residents of South Part of Hutchinson Make Demand on School District." *Hutchinson* [Kansas] *News*, May 6, 1930.

Unpublished Theses

Cleary, Robert M. "The Education of Mexican-Americans in Kansas City, Kansas, 1916–1951." Unpublished master's thesis, University of Missouri, 2002.

Franco, Hector. "The Mexican People in the State of Kansas." Unpublished master's thesis, University of Wichita, 1950.

Highsmith, Andrew R. "Demolition Means Progress: Race, Class and the Destruction of the American Dream in Flint, Michigan." PhD diss., University of Michigan, 2009. http://hdl.handle.net/2027.42/62230.

Hinnen, Kathie. "Mexican Immigrants to Hutchinson, Kansas, 1905–1940: How a Temporary Haven Became Home." Unpublished master's thesis, Southwest Missouri State University, 1998.

Jones, Wallace. L., Jr. "A History of Compulsory School Attendance and Visiting Teacher Services in Louisiana." PhD Diss., Louisiana State University Historical Dissertations and Theses, 1967. http://digitalcommons.lsu.edu/gradschool_disstheses/1340.

Laird, Judith F. "Argentine, Kansas: The Evolution of a Mexican-American Community, 1905–1940." Unpublished PhD diss., University of Kansas, 1975.

Leis, Ward W. "The Status of Education for Mexican Children in Four Border States." Master's thesis, University of Southern California Dissertations and Theses, 1931. http://digitallibrary.usc.edu/cdm/ref/collection/p15799coll30/id/11630.

Reitz, Susan N. "The Historical Development of the Salina, Kansas School System, 1861–1970." Unpublished PhD diss., Kansas State University, 1995.

Rutter, Larry G. "Mexican Americans in Kansas: A Survey and Social Mobility Study, 1900–1970." Unpublished master's thesis, Kansas State University, 1972.

Archival Materials, Speeches, and Reports

Archivo Histórico Genaro Estrada. Acervo Histórico Diplomático. Secretaría de Relaciones Exteriores. Mexico City, Mexico.

Alamosa Clerk and County Recorder. Records Conejos Co. Warranty Deed Record, Book 72.

Biennial Report of the Attorney General of the State of Colorado, 1913–1914. Denver, CO: Smith-Brooks Printing, 1914.

Hammond, Jimmie Charlene. "A Brief History of Cheneyville, Louisiana." Unpublished manuscript, 1967. MS, Watson Special Collection, Northwestern State University of Louisiana.

Kansas Historical Society. Attorney General Numerical Files, no. 119, Schools (1929–1934).

Kansas Historical Society. Gov. Davis. Correspondence File. Educational Matters. Box 214, Folder 4.

Letter from State Attorney General to Superintendent Rider Stockdale, April 8, 1929. Kansas Historical Society. Attorney General Numerical Files, no. 119, Schools (1929–1934).

Peach, and Nora Wood. Letter from Peach, School Board President and Nora Wood, Secretary to Mesars, Sarry Wade, J. C. Brogan, C. J. Stout, and Other Petitioners from Central Avenue District, Emporia City Schools, January 8, 1923.

Ruybal, J. R. C. Interview by Luther Bean, Nancy Denious, and Elinor Kingery, sound recording, Colorado Historical Society, Denver, Co., November 20, 1962, item ID: 33317710, call number OH 83.

Taylor, Paul. University of California, Berkeley, Bancroft Library, Manuscripts Division, MANC, MSS. 84/38, Taylor, Paul Schuster Papers, Ctn. 13, File 13:43, "Restriction of Mexican Immigration at Issue." *The Coalitionist*, 1, no. 6 (December 1929).

University of Michigan, Faculty History Project, Memorial of Max Sylvius Handman, LSA Minutes, https://www.lib.umich.edu/faculty-history/faculty/max-sylvius-handman/memorial.

US Department of Commerce, Bureau of the Census. *Fourteenth Census of the United States Taken in the Year 1920*. Washington, DC: Government Printing Office, 1922.

US Department of Commerce, Bureau of the Census. *Sixteenth Decennial Census of the United States: Instructions to Enumerators. Population and Agriculture* 1940. Washington, DC, 1940.

US Department of Commerce, Bureau of the Census. *Thirteenth Census of the United States Taken in the Year 1910*. Washington, DC: Government Printing Office, 1913.

Index

Page numbers in *italics* indicate illustrations.